# The Injustice of Punishment

*The Injustice of Punishment* emphasizes that we can never make sense of moral responsibility while also acknowledging that punishment is sometimes unavoidable. Recognizing both the injustice and the necessity of punishment is painful but also beneficial. It motivates us to find effective means of minimizing both the use and severity of punishment, and encourages deeper inquiry into the causes of destructive behavior and how to change those causes in order to reduce the need for punishment. There is an emerging alternative to the comfortable but destructive system of moral responsibility and just deserts. That alternative is not the creation of philosophers but of sociologists, criminologists, psychologists, and workplace engineers; it was developed, tested, and employed in factories, prisons, hospitals, and other settings; and it is writ large in the practices of cultures that minimize belief in individual moral responsibility. The alternative marks a promising path to less punishment, less coercive control, deeper common commitment, and more genuine freedom.

**Bruce N. Waller** is professor of philosophy at Youngstown State University. He is the author or editor of fourteen books, including *Against Moral Responsibility* (2011) and *The Stubborn System of Moral Responsibility* (2015), as well as numerous journal articles.

# Routledge Research in Applied Ethics

# The Injustice of Punishment

Bruce N. Waller

Routledge
Taylor & Francis Group

NEW YORK AND LONDON

First published 2018
by Routledge
711 Third Avenue, New York, NY 10017

and by Routledge
2 Park Square, Milton Park, Abingdon, Oxon OX14 4RN

*Routledge is an imprint of the Taylor & Francis Group, an informa business*

Library of Congress Cataloging-in-Publication Data
Names: Waller, Bruce N., 1946– author.
Title: The injustice of punishment / by Bruce N. Waller.
Description: 1 [edition]. | New York : Routledge, 2017. | Series: Routledge research in applied ethics ; 8 | Includes bibliographical references and index.
Identifiers: LCCN 2017033614 | ISBN 9781138506398 (hardback : alk. paper)
Subjects: LCSH: Punishment—Moral and ethical aspects. | Criminal justice, Administration of—Moral and ethical aspects. | Social justice.
Classification: LCC HV8665 .W355 2017 | DDC 174/.3—dc23
LC record available at https://lccn.loc.gov/2017033614

ISBN: 978-1-138-50639-8 (hbk)
ISBN: 978-1-315-14691-1 (ebk)

Typeset in Sabon
by Apex CoVantage, LLC

MIX
Paper from
responsible sources
FSC
www.fsc.org   FSC® C013056

Printed and bound in Great Britain by
TJ International Ltd, Padstow, Cornwall

# Contents

# Preface

Belief in moral responsibility is obsolete, and cannot be justified in light of our contemporary understanding of human animals and their behavior (Waller 2011). It is held in place not by convincing arguments, but by its central place in a larger system of thought (Waller 2015a). This book does not argue for those claims: I have already put together the best arguments I can manage for both, and philosophers abler than I have developed powerful arguments against belief in moral responsibility. Instead, this book is an attempt to answer two basic challenges to the rejection of moral responsibility. First, if you reject moral responsibility and just deserts, what do you do about punishment? This was the challenge from Dan Dennett (2012) in response to *Against Moral Responsibility* (Waller 2011). I tried to offer an answer at that time, but was by no means satisfied with it; and Dennett's challenge has troubled my sleep, as well as my waking philosophical moments, for years since. Often after an argument, typically a few hours later, people think with regret of "what I should have said". For some of us, it takes a little longer. In my case, it needed about five years. I like this answer better, but whether Dennett—or anyone else—will find it satisfactory is another matter. In any case, I am deeply indebted to Dennett, not only for pushing me to think much harder about this question, but also for his remarkable work on the question of free will, and for providing the model of how productive philosophical work must incorporate developments in many areas of scientific research. The second challenging question also came from Dennett's review: if you want to reject the moral responsibility system, what would you put in its place? Whatever flaws the moral responsibility system may have, it will not be abandoned until we have something better.

The answer to both those challenging questions will ultimately merge: the best way of dealing with the problem of punishment is by placing the problem in the larger context of a new systemic alternative to the moral responsibility system. In that system, punishment will be minimized but not eliminated, and it will still be unjust; but the benefits of facing honestly the inevitable injustice of punishment—and rejecting destructive schemes to portray punishment as *justly deserved*—will be substantial. The basic project, then, is the proposal of a radically different alternative to the moral responsibility system: a system that can replace the moral responsibility system and move moral responsibility to the museum of obsolete philosophical systems. That is not to suggest that the moral responsibility system has been a failure; to the contrary, it has been quite valuable. Unfortunately, it has long overstayed its usefulness, and now blocks the path to a better system.

Inventing a new system to replace the moral responsibility system sounds like a very ambitious—or incredibly arrogant—undertaking. So it would be, if this were the proposal of a newly invented system. It is not. Rather, it is the presentation of a system that has been developing for years. The basic elements are already there, and they fit together to form a new system that has proved its practical worth and harmonious structure. In some respects it has been tested and tried in the philosophical arena; in more important ways it has been tested and has proved its worth in factories, prisons, and hospitals. It has been developed and studied and tested by criminologists, sociologists, psychologists, biologists, and workplace engineers. This radically new system is better suited for our contemporary scientific understanding of human behavior, and it is the work of many hands.

My hands were not among them. I am merely reporting how those various elements coalesced to form a remarkable system that—for lack of a common name—we might refer to as the no-blame system model. It brings together the *no-blame* approach (and makes it *universal*, rather than drawing a line beyond which blame is allowed), the *system* (as opposed to the individualistic) model, and the *commitment* (rather than control) approach to management. The no-blame system approach does not eliminate punishment; however, it offers a different perspective on punishment and reduces the need for (and use of) punishment. It provides better protection for individual rights: protection that—philosophical orthodoxy notwithstanding—the moral responsibility system erodes rather than strengthens. In contrast to the moral responsibility system, it encourages rather than blocks deeper inquiry. Finally, it enhances the natural free will that is of great value for many animals, including humans.

# Acknowledgments

Daniel Dennett's philosophical work combines rigorous analysis with careful study of relevant scientific research, and is written in an accessible and engaging and often humorous style. There is no one's work I have criticized more extensively, and there is no one's work I admire more. Notwithstanding our deep disagreement on the question of moral responsibility, Dennett's work has deepened and broadened my understanding of many questions, including the issue of moral responsibility and particularly the question of free will. It was Dennett's generous yet critical review of *Against Moral Responsibility* that pushed me to think harder about his basic and powerful objections to my position, and this book is largely the result of trying to answer those objections.

Robert Kane, John Lemos, and Saul Smilansky are among the many philosophers who deeply oppose my rejection of moral responsibility; and their writings and especially the enormously helpful and pleasant conversations I have enjoyed with them have been especially important in making me aware of weaknesses in my own position as well as giving me a broader appreciation of the issues involved. My conversations with these fierce opponents have been most enjoyable, congenial, and productive, and have often demonstrated that those with whom you deeply disagree can be important sources of insight and friendship.

The Justice Without Retribution Network—directed by Gregg Caruso, Farah Focquaert, Derk Pereboom, and Elizabeth Shaw—has been a tremendously valuable resource, and the conferences arranged by the network are especially productive. My many conversations with Gregg, Farah, Derk, and Elizabeth have been both delightful and profoundly productive, and the Network has also put me in touch with a number of people—especially Michael Corrado, Adrian Raine, and John Callender—whose work I particularly admire and from which I have learned much.

I have been most fortunate to spend my career in the Department of Philosophy and Religious Studies at Youngstown State University, with colleagues who have provided friendship as well as remarkable insights from their wide variety of studies. I am grateful to all of them, and particularly for many conversations with Tom Shipka, Chris Bache, Mustansir Mir, Deborah

Mower, and Gabriel Palmer-Fernandez; and especially to my long-time colleague and friend, Brendan Minogue, who has been for many years—and countless gin and tonics—my toughest critic and most frequent companion for philosophical discussion. There are many others at YSU—faculty, students, and administrators—who have been sources of insight as well as very pleasant company for many years; one who stands out is my weekly luncheon companion for many years, Homer Warren, who has broadened and deepened my understanding of a wide range of topics. Our invaluable department secretary for most of the years when this book was written, Mary Dillingham, made my life (while suffering through my years as department chair) much easier and more enjoyable, and her remarkable efficiency freed up many hours for research and writing. Thanks also to Gerald Massey for his insights as well as his generous encouragement.

My greatest debt, always, is to my family, my special and constant source of joy and pride: my son Russell, his wife, Robyn, and their amazing children Nathanael and Josephine; my son Adam and his companion, Josh; my wonderful and warm and patient wife, Mary; and our sprightly and affectionate poodle, Maggie.

# 1 Beyond the Moral Responsibility System

"What do you do about punishment?" For those of us who *reject* moral responsibility and just deserts, that is a common question. Although it is posed as a question, it is really a challenge: your rejection of moral responsibility fails, because you have no way of dealing with the problem of punishment, and punishment is unavoidable. Saul Smilansky (2011) argues that the problem of punishment drives those who deny moral responsibility into a *reductio ad absurdum* of their whole project. Daniel Dennett (2012) was generous and insightful in his review of *Against Moral Responsibility* (Waller 2011), but he argued that the case against moral responsibility ultimately runs aground on the basic problem of punishment. This book is an attempt to answer that tough challenge: if we deny moral responsibility and just deserts, how do we deal with the problem of *punishment*?

The problem of punishment is a difficult challenge. If we try to answer it from *within* the basic assumptions of the moral responsibility system, the challenge is impossible. But that adds another level of difficulty to the basic challenge: in order to develop a plausible answer, one must answer from the perspective of a different system altogether. A plausible answer will require some account of a *system* that can compete with—and even supplant—the moral responsibility system. Fortunately, no heavy construction work is required, for most of it has already been done—not by philosophers, but by sociologists, criminologists, workplace safety specialists, psychologists, and workplace engineers. This book describes that new construction, and indicates how that challenging question—what do you do about punishment?—is answered within that emerging system.

That is not to suggest that the answer offered will win easy acceptance. This book makes a claim that many will regard as outrageous: *all* punishment is *unjust*; no one ever under any circumstances justly deserves punishment. Supporting that claim requires swimming against a very strong current, and there is a potential confusion that could make the task even more difficult. *No one* ever justly deserves punishment; that does *not* imply that no one ever acts in ways that are morally wrong. To the contrary, many people have rotten characters, and many people consistently act in ways that are morally egregious, and all of us at least occasionally perform morally bad acts. The claim is not that no one is morally bad, or that no one ever commits morally bad acts; rather, the claim is that no one *ever* justly deserves punishment, no matter how vile his or her character and behavior.

One other qualification. The claim in this book is that all punishment is unjust; it is *not* the claim that we can or even should eliminate all punishment. Daniel Dennett (2008, 258) asserts that "a world without punishment is not a world any of us would want to live in." I disagree: I would love to live in a world without punishment. However, such a world is unlikely to exist in the foreseeable future, and perhaps never. So the argument of this book is *not* an argument for the elimination of all punishment; rather, the argument is that all punishment is *unjust*, and we are better off recognizing that injustice rather than celebrating punishment as some form of "just deserts" or "righteous retribution." Punishment may indeed be necessary in the world in which we live; but it is a necessary wrong, an unavoidable element of injustice in a world that is *not* just.

For most people—whether folk or philosophers—it seems obvious that at least some times in some circumstances (when all the procedures and safeguards are scrupulously followed) punishment is *just* and *justly deserved*. Of course, many of those same people acknowledge that in our society, the administration of punishment is grossly *un*just: the innocent are wrongly punished, punishment is too harsh and too extensive, various forms of prejudice distort punitive procedures, and punitive measures are not applied in a fair and just manner. Still—they would insist—there are some cases when punishment is justly deserved. Why do we commonly believe that punishment is just? A belief that deeply entrenched is not a simple solitary belief. If I believe that I left my book on the dining room table, I may simply be mistaken. If I believe that there are no physical chairs, tables, or books—there are only minds and ideas—that is not the same sort of belief at all. I believe there is no "Loch Ness monster"—some massive sea creature long believed extinct—dwelling deep in the depths of Loch Ness; but I could be wrong. But there is no way I *simply* could be mistaken about the existence of Medusa, a woman with aggressive snakes growing out of her scalp who causes everyone who looks upon her face to turn to stone: such a creature would destroy practically everything we believe concerning biology, not to mention other branches of science. In like manner, belief in the *justice* of punishment is locked in place by a *system* of beliefs, including deep commitment to striking back against painful experiences, a profound but largely nonconscious belief in a just world, belief in human uniqueness, deep belief in individual moral responsibility, and belief that "just deserts" are an essential element of human dignity. The belief that punishment is *justly deserved* is at the center of an interlocking system, and challenging that belief first requires challenging some of the key elements that hold that central belief firmly in place.

## The Basic Problem of Punishment

What do we do about punishment? For many people—especially those currently living in the United States or the United Kingdom—that is not a troubling question. There may be some qualms about the massive incarceration rate in the United States, or about the brutal conditions in many prisons (especially the notorious Supermax prisons where inmates suffer solitary confinement for extended periods), or about the alarming number of mistaken convictions. Perhaps there should be some *reforms* in our criminal punishment system (though many favor an even harsher punishment regime); but few people find punishment itself to be problematic.

Though it may need some adjustments around the edges, most regard the basic structure of punishment as sound and the legitimacy of punishment as obvious. Its common and unquestioned endorsement notwithstanding, the legitimacy of punishment is far from obvious. After all, *punishment* involves the intentional infliction of some degree of suffering, and typically *against* the wishes of the person punished. In most cases, such pain-causing behavior is a clear instance of profoundly *bad* behavior. What is it about the category of *punishment* that transforms otherwise bad behavior (the intentional infliction of suffering) into something morally acceptable or even morally mandatory?

Attempts to answer that question are legion, ranging from appeals to God's commands to claims of utility, from retributive to expressive, from fairness to intuitiveness. Recently some have argued that punishment cannot be *justified*, but that is because punishment is so basic that it requires no justification: it enjoys the privileged status of being one of the "basic moral norms" that we must accept "without justification" (Nichols 2013, 43). The sheer number of proposals marks the difficulty of finding a satisfactory answer. The reason these many efforts at establishing the moral legitimacy of punishment have failed is simple: the project is impossible because punishment is inescapably unjust.

Endeavoring to prove the counter-intuitive claim that punishment is inevitably unjust will require examination of arguments made in favor of punishment, as well as the reasons why punishment is unjust. But the immediate focus is not on refuting the claims of punitive legitimacy; rather, the focus is on *why* it is so widely believed that punishment *must* be just. The belief that punishment is just is deeper and stronger than the philosophical and legal *arguments* for the justice of punishment. Many are convinced that at least one of the arguments to establish the justice of punishment is sound; but even they must acknowledge that *belief* in that legitimacy far exceeds the strength of the *arguments* in its favor. The first question to be explored—prior to examining some of the key philosophical arguments offered to support the justice of punishment—is *why* the belief in just punishment is so deep and pervasive. The final question is what would take the place of the just punishment system, and what the effects would be—both social and psychological—of rejecting belief in the justice of punishment. In order to discover those effects it is essential to understand the nature and depth and conditions of that belief. So the immediate question is a basic one: *why* the deep and confident belief that punishment is just?

## The Moral Responsibility System

Punishment is just because when morally responsible persons do something wrong, then punishment is their *just deserts*. Punishment is just because it occupies a secure place in the moral responsibility *system*, and that system was constructed to make the infliction of punishment just.

The moral responsibility system has been a useful system, and a good replacement for the honor system. Compared to the honor system, there is no doubt that belief in moral responsibility actually *prevented* some harms. Suppose that Harry Hatfield has wronged me—insulted and dishonored me, or harmed a member of my family or a close friend—but before I have the opportunity to attack Harry, he dies of natural causes. Under the honor system, it is legitimate, even morally mandatory, that I harm or kill one of Harry's close friends or relatives (resulting in one of Harry's relatives killing one of my friends or relatives, and so on). Under the moral responsibility system, no matter how vile Harry's behavior, it is morally wrong to exact vengeance on Harry's innocent son. So the moral responsibility system served a useful function in getting us beyond the honor system. But like many useful systems, it has endured long after its usefulness has passed. It is a moribund system, and the vigor and variety of its defenses are inversely proportional to its plausibility. Instead of making good use of research developments, its proponents challenge the research, or claim that it is inconsequential, or insist that we must ignore it.

The moral responsibility system hangs on primarily because of fear of what might replace it (or because of the greater fear that we have *nothing* with which to replace it). If we abandon moral responsibility, we lose our reactive participant attitudes (Strawson 1962); without moral responsibility, there would be no special protection of the innocent (Smilansky 2000, 152); in the absence of moral responsibility, we become insignificant or even disappear as genuine agents (Dennett 2003, 287); without moral responsibility, there is no human dignity (Morris 1968; Moore 1997, 149); without moral responsibility, we could have no moral or legal order; without moral responsibility, we would turn to Clockwork Orange brutality. When new developments call moral responsibility into question, we are cautioned against looking too closely or carefully, lest we slide into metaphysical megalomania (Fischer 2007, 67), or possibly vanish altogether (Waller 2015a, Chapter 9). But these horrible warnings are bogus, and are designed to keep us from looking hard at the flaws of the moral responsibility system—flaws that are obvious on close scrutiny. The moral responsibility system is a relic of a bygone system of belief, and at this point it serves no useful purpose and causes enormous harm. The more zealously the moral responsibility system is embraced, the more harm it causes: harms of inegalitarian distribution of goods, reduced opportunity and diminished genuine freedom, and a retributive justice system that is massive, cruel, and short-sighted. Since moral responsibility is our only refuge we keep patching it up and try to ignore its rotten foundation.

## Seeking a New System

There is a marvelous old comic strip—a long-time favorite among logicians—from *The Wizard of Id* series. The first panel shows the unscrupulous shyster lawyer, Larsen E. Pettyfogger, addressing an unhappy prisoner who is locked behind bars. Pettyfogger offers the desperate prisoner hope, encouraging him not to despair, and assuring him that: "If I can't have you out in three days, my name's not Larsen E. Pettyfogger." Pettyfogger then discovers that the prisoner is charged with the one crime that cannot be bought off or fixed in the Kingdom of Id: the crime of cursing the king. Recognizing that he will not be able to beat the prisoner's rap, Pettyfogger pushes on to the absurd conclusion of his valid *modus ponens* argument: "Gone, just like that, a fortune in letterheads." Some might suppose that this book, like the Kingdom of Id comic strip, is an exercise in drawing an absurd conclusion from an absurd premise, while doggedly following the logic of the starting premise. The starting premise is the total rejection of moral responsibility; and the absurd conclusion is that punishment is invariably unjust. Indeed, Saul Smilansky (2011) offers an argument along similar lines, and concludes that it is a *reductio ad absurdum* that shows the falsity—or at least absurdity—of the initial premise (the denial of moral responsibility).

Is the denial of the moral legitimacy of punishment a *reductio* of the rejection of moral responsibility, or is it instead—when the claim is judged *without* the burdensome assumptions of the moral responsibility system—an opening to a better overall social system? Answering the difficult question—what do you do about punishment if you reject moral responsibility?—involves rejecting some basic assumptions (some respected philosophical principles as well as some deep assumptions that rarely emerge into consciousness) and rejecting the moral responsibility system based on those assumptions; and it requires examining a newly emerging system that might replace the moral responsibility system, much as the moral responsibility system replaced the honor system. Seen from *within* the moral responsibility system and its basic assumptions, the proposed claim—punishment is *always* unjust—is indeed a *reductio* of the denial of moral responsibility. Is there another perspective that makes recognition of the inevitable injustice of punishment a plausible and even promising path?

The moral responsibility system is a system that was developed in another era, and is based in beliefs that are no longer plausible within scientific naturalism. It thrives in a setting of miracles and deities, and contemporary scientific naturalism has destroyed its natural habitat. This is not a proposal to revise the moral responsibility system. It is a proposal to abandon it entirely, and dispose of the debris that is left behind. However, this is not a *proposal* of a new *system* to replace the obsolete moral responsibility system. Rather, it is a *report* of the process by which that new system is now emerging, and why it is a superior system. Because the old moral responsibility system continues to frame our beliefs and distort any picture of a new and different system, it is important to be clear on what the new system is not, and on the ways the moral responsibility perspective distorts our understanding of the newly emerging system. This book does *not* build a new system. The foundation of the new system is already in place. It is the product of extensive empirical research and practical application, and was laid by criminologists, psychologists, and workplace engineers—not by philosophers, and certainly not by *this* philosopher. This book is an effort to clear away the moral responsibility debris that obscures that newly emerging system, show how the troubling question—what do you do about punishment?— is answered in that system, and focus philosophical attention on this promising positive system.

John Locke (1690) counseled that philosophers should be content with modest ambitions: "It is ambition enough to be employed as an under-labourer in clearing the ground a little, and removing some of the rubbish which lies in the way of knowledge." But clearing the ground of the moral responsibility system, and the enormous debris that it leaves behind, is a substantial project. In some respects, the task must be even more ambitious: it must also involve at least a sketch of a system that can replace the moral responsibility system. As Thomas Kuhn (1962) pointed out in another context, we are unwilling to relinquish a large theoretical system until we have a promising replacement in view. Philosophers will cling to the moral responsibility wreckage until we can latch onto something more promising. Rather than abandon the flawed moral responsibility system, there are extensive efforts to patch it up, make revisions, and preserve the basic elements of the system. Following an account of why punishment is invariably unjust (in Chapter 2), Chapter 3 examines some of those newly revised editions of the moral responsibility system, and rejects those "Tychonic" variations of moral responsibility and just deserts. Sources for the powerful belief in the justice of punishment are explored, followed by examination of some of the attempts to provide a just basis for punishment. The account of the developing system—the system in which moral responsibility, just deserts, and just punishment are rejected—is found in the final four chapters.

# 2   The Unjust Necessity of Punishment

When moral responsibility is rejected, what do we do about punishment? The basic claim of this book is that although punishment is *necessary* (for at least the foreseeable future), it is never morally *just* (apart from some narrowly utilitarian perspective). Or more precisely, we may be *justified* in punishing, but the punishment itself is *unjust*. Genuinely just punishment would require a foundation of moral responsibility and just deserts, and that foundation does not exist. The emerging system that will someday (I hope) *replace* the moral responsibility system offers a fresh and fruitful answer to the question of what to do about punishment. It is not a *comfortable* answer, but that is a point in its favor. Before examining the basic building blocks of that system it is important to look deeper into the *unjust necessity* of punishment; and prior to that inquiry there are some potential misunderstandings to clear away.

## Real Moral Badness

First, consider the claim that there is *no* moral responsibility whatsoever and punishment can *never* be just. One might suppose that such a claim must be based on the assumption that there are never any morally bad acts. Given the pervasive and powerful moral responsibility framework, this is not a surprising misunderstanding; but it is a misunderstanding, nonetheless. Within the moral responsibility *system*, it seems obvious that anyone who commits a morally wrong act *must* be morally responsible for that act, and therefore justly deserves punishment. Within that system, if a bad act is not an act for which the actor is morally responsible, that must be because the actor is somehow excused, or perhaps incompetent; and in that case, the "bad act" is not really a morally bad act at all. Imagine a small child who plays with matches, having no understanding of the danger involved, and causes a terrible fire. The result may be very bad, perhaps even tragic; but there is no morally bad *act* involved, because the terrible event was not the product of the bad intent of a morally competent actor. From *within* the moral responsibility system, it is reasonable to conclude that without moral responsibility there could be no moral actors. For example, C. A. Campbell

(1957, 167) confidently claims that the denial of justly deserved praise and blame entails denying "the reality of the moral life"; and Susan Wolf asserts that in the absence of moral responsibility "we must stop thinking in terms of what ought and ought not to be" (1981, 401). Given the assumptions of the moral responsibility system, if a moral *actor* (without excuse) performs a morally bad or good act, then that actor is *morally responsible* for the act; and by *modus tollens*, if no one is ever morally responsible then no one can act morally or immorally. This may be true within the assumptions of the moral responsibility system (Waller 2015a); but the position taken here *rejects* the moral responsibility system and its assumptions.

Freed from the stifling system of moral responsibility, it is clear that denial of moral responsibility is *consistent* with the existence of morally bad (and good) acts. In the fifteenth century, Lorenzo Valla—one of the greatest among the Italian humanists—wrote his famous *Dialogue on Free Will*, in the course of which he noted that for his own unfathomable reasons, God:

> created the wolf fierce, the hare timid, the lion brave, the ass stupid, the dog savage, the sheep mild, so he fashioned some men hard of heart, others soft, he generated one given to evil, the other to virtue, and, further, he gave a capacity for reform to one and made another incorrigible.
> (1443/1948,173)

But whether made virtuous or evil, corrigible or incorrigible, each man performs moral or immoral *acts* from his own character and will and choice (even though for Valla there can be no question of thwarting God's plan or being a morally responsible source of such acts). In the nineteenth century, John Stuart Mill insisted that the rejection of moral responsibility is fully consistent with "the highest and strongest sense of the worth of goodness, and the odiousness of its opposite" (1865/1979, 456). Among contemporary philosophers, Harry Frankfurt found no conflict between denying moral responsibility and making judgments of moral distaste and moral contempt (1973, 79); while according to Jonathan Bennett, denial of moral responsibility and just deserts would pose not "the slightest threat to the value-system according to which we judge some actions to be good or right or successful and others to be bad or wrong or failures" (1980, 31).

When we set aside the deep assumptions of the moral responsibility system, we have no difficulty making moral *judgments* independently of questions of moral responsibility. Robert Harris was a cruel and remorseless murderer, who—with clear intent and careful premeditation—callously murdered two young men in order to steal their car. When we examine his intelligent and purposeful act, clearly the act was a terrible moral wrong. When Gary Watson (1987) tells us of the remarkably brutal conditions under which Harris lived his entire life, we may well doubt his *moral responsibility* for his murderous act, but that additional knowledge does not change our recognition of the murder as a morally bad act. The claim being made here is that no one *ever* justly deserves punishment; it is *not* the claim that no one ever commits a morally bad act. Sadly, morally bad acts occur in great number and variety.

## Punishment is an Unjust Necessity

No one is ever morally responsible for his or her acts, and no one ever justly deserves punishment; however, punishment is—and for the foreseeable future will remain—a necessary part of our society. Punishment, then, is an *unjust necessity*. As Saul Smilansky emphasizes, this poses a hard question for those who deny moral responsibility and just deserts: "How, then, can hard determinists deal with the need to punish, when coupled with the obligation to be just?" (2016b, 593)

The basic grounds for claiming that punishment is *unjust* are simple enough, needing only two steps. First, just deserts (including punitive just deserts) require moral responsibility; and second, no one is ever morally responsible. Consider the first claim, that just deserts require moral responsibility. We might offer a variety of justifications for punishment without appealing to moral responsibility: a deterrence justification, for example. In cases of "strict liability," at least some legal theorists regard the punishment imposed as legitimate and justified even when it is evident that the punished individual is not morally responsible. But if we are claiming that the punishment of Joe is *justly* deserved, that requires a basis in moral responsibility. It may be useful and even beneficial to punish when the punishment is *not* just; but the fact that something is beneficial does not make it *just*. If torturing an innocent child prevented harm or disease to millions of other innocent children, then it might be beneficial to engage in such torture (we might even say that such an atrocious act is *justified*); but even if utilitarians would count it as morally legitimate, that would not make the act of torturing the child *just*: it would remain a monstrous *in*justice to that child, whatever the overall benefits. If it seems strange to suppose that an unjust act could be (at least in some sense) justified, consider the question from the opposite direction. D. J. Galligan (1981) and Douglas Husak (1992 and 2000) believe in retribution, and believe that retributive punishment is *just*; but they have doubts that institutions of retributive punishment are *justified*, because they require enormous resources, they involve human and social costs (especially the severe costs involved in wrongful conviction of the innocent), and they are likely to result in abuse of authority.

The second claim is that *no one* is ever morally responsible. That claim obviously is controversial. I have argued for it elsewhere (1990, 2011 and 2015a), and abler philosophers have offered better arguments, so I will not repeat those arguments here (beyond baldly claiming that justified belief in ultimate moral responsibility requires either miracles or principled myopia, neither of which is consistent with a scientific naturalist world view). But in this context, it is worth noting why concern with punishment—when combined with our nonconscious belief in a just world—helps prop up our deep belief in moral responsibility and *just* deserts.

We *must* punish. For some, punishment is a positive good: it restores the moral balance, or affirms the unique godlike status of humans, or celebrates and protects human dignity. For others punishment is a sad necessity, and one that we should eliminate entirely if possible (an outcome we fervently desire but do not foresee). On both sides of that divide, there are many who believe that much less *severe* punishment (particularly less severe than the gross excesses of the U.S. justice system) is not only desirable but also quite possible and would have great advantages; but in any case, there are few who doubt that some form of punishment is a present necessity. (Of course, there are some who believe that we can eliminate punishment and substitute various forms of nonpunitive "quarantine"; but that is an issue to be discussed in Chapter 10.) For the present discussion I will assume that even the most comfortable possible "quarantine" program would involve some coerced punitive elements.) So it is generally agreed that we *must* punish.

Conscious recognition of the necessity of punishment then combines with a generally *non*conscious belief in a just world (discussed in Chapter 5). The deep nonconscious belief in a just world makes it seem obvious that "ought implies can": That is, anything that is *obligatory* must be something we *can* do. Since ought implies can, then if we *ought* not-punish, then we *can* not-punish. Applying *modus tollens*, it is *not* the case that we *can* not-punish (we must punish, punishment is unavoidable), therefore it is *not* the case that we ought not-punish; that is, punishing must be morally legitimate, and for punishment to be morally legitimate it must be justly deserved. So we have an easy justification for the punishment that we *must* inflict: those punished are receiving their *just* deserts. But in this case, our implausible belief in just deserts and moral responsibility is supported by a foundation—belief in a just world—that is even more implausible (and *obviously* implausible when we fish it up from the nonconscious depths and scrutinize it). It is not difficult, then, to understand why belief in just deserts and the moral legitimacy of punishment are so deeply entrenched, but that psychological explanation of the belief does not support its plausibility. To the contrary, it "explains away" the deep sense that inflicting punishment on wrongdoers *must* be just.

## Justified but Unjust

It is one thing to *justify* punishment; but something else entirely to prove that punishment is *just*. Too often arguments slide easily from one to the other, without marking this important difference. But an important—and clear—difference it is. Utilitarians might argue that on their view the difference disappears, and that may be true; but if so, the loss of that distinction is a flaw in the utilitarian model. The line between punishment being *justified* and being *just* is clearly marked, even though the *contents* of both categories may be in dispute. There is a vile—and deeply disturbed—individual who has planted an enormous bomb somewhere in Indianapolis, it will detonate in a few minutes, and the seconds are ticking away. This murderous individual delights in the idea of killing and maiming hundreds or perhaps thousands, and neither incentives nor torture has any effect in convincing him to reveal the location. This mad bomber has only one emotional attachment: his beloved six-year-old daughter. If we subject this innocent child to torture, the bomber will reveal the location of the bomb and many lives will be saved. Are we *justified* in inflicting severe pain on this innocent child? I'm not sure, but I am willing to consider the possibility that this cruel act—in these horrific circumstances—*might* be *justified*; but there is no possibility that this cruel act is *just*. In like manner, there may well be circumstances when punishment can be *justified*; it does not follow that the justified punishment is *just*, or that the person punished is being treated in a fair and just manner, and certainly it does not follow that the justified punishment is therefore *justly deserved*.

Even if we could *justify* punishment on utilitarian grounds, the punishment of the individual would be unjust. Kevin J. Murtagh (2013) develops a utilitarian justification for punishment, insisting that—even if we deny moral responsibility and just deserts—we can justify harsher treatment than the harsh treatment approved by Derk Pereboom (2001). There may indeed be conditions in which considerations of utility, as Murtagh insists, override considerations of just deserts: "I think that it is relatively clear that the principle of utility will *at the very least* occasionally 'trump' the principle of justice and allow for at least limited punishment" (Murtagh 2013, 237; italics in original). My concern is that such utilitarian calculations can make us too comfortable with imposing punishment on those who do *not* justly deserve such punishment. It is very important—both for ethical and motivational considerations—to recognize that punishment is always unjust (even if sometimes *justified*), that unjust punishment is an egregious wrong, and it is a wrong that should be committed with great reluctance and profound sorrow in the face of cruel necessity.

The deep concern with avoiding unjust punishment is perfectly legitimate; David Boonin (2008, 213) describes the infliction of unjust punishment as "morally repugnant," and that is an apt description. However, it is better to acknowledge the fundamental inescapable *injustice* of punishment, rather than struggling to make the "punishment" (or whatever we wish to call it) *just*. If punishment is *just*, then our deep distress with unjust punishment is eliminated; but our distress at unjust punishment is valuable. It holds the strong "righteous retribution" motive in check, and instead motivates dedicated efforts to reduce both the necessity for and the infliction of *unjust* punishment.

Punishment is unjust, but it is also necessary. By whatever name we call it, there are some people who are so dangerous that they must be coercively restrained and isolated for our protection. In a decent society, we will endeavor to make this isolation as painless as we reasonably can—Norway does a good job of this, while falling well short of five-star resorts—and we will aim at rehabilitation and release rather than hopeless warehousing or the barbaric act of execution. There will be no effort to cause pain for the sake of causing pain, but punitive measures—including coercive deprivation of freedom—will still be involved.

## Essential Mild Unjust Punishment

At a much milder level than incarceration, we will continue to require mild punitive processes in order to promote a well-functioning society and optimum social relations. Numerous studies have confirmed the need for "punitive measures" against cheating in social contexts and cooperative social enterprises (Fehr and Gächter 2000, 2002; Keltner and Haidt 2001; Gächter, Hermann, and Thöni 2010; Nichols 2015, 158–161); however, there have been some challenges to such studies, particularly to claims that the studies provide evidence that punishment (and "altruistic punishment") played an essential role in the evolution of group cooperation (Baumard 2010). Such studies indicate that—unless and until we can find some nonpunitive substitute—a well-functioning social network will probably need punitive measures against cheating. If it is true that the optimum functioning of social systems requires penalties for those who wish to take unfair advantage, then there will be good reason to incorporate such punitive measures. But it does not follow that those who cheat—and who then suffer from the necessary punitive measures against cheaters—*justly deserve* to suffer such punishment. In order for a child's well-functioning nervous system to protect her body against severe damage, it is essential that the child feel *pain* when accidentally encountering a hot stove. The pain is valuable for the child, just as the cheater's painful penalty is valuable for the social structure; in neither case does that show anything whatsoever about whether the pains suffered are justly deserved—unless, of course, one is fortunate enough to be living in a just world in which all pains suffered and pleasures enjoyed are justly deserved (a world very different from the natural world in which we live and breathe and have our being).

Pamela Hieronymi develops a valuable analysis of the mundane but important social sanctions that occur informally in our daily lives. These are the business of neither the criminal justice system nor of the rule-governed formal processes for penalizing cheaters and others who commit minor infractions. Rather, Hieronymi focuses on the relatively mild social sanctions manifested in distrust and resentment toward those who act in ways that are harmful, insensitive, and perhaps manipulative. She acknowledges that reacting with resentment and distrust toward those who act selfishly and insensitively may cause pain for the objects of resentment; however, she maintains that the reaction is legitimate and the pain imposed is fair and just. Hieronymi argues that:

resentment and indignation are like distrust. Though distrust also carries a special, characteristic and burdensome force or significance, and though it may be unfair that a person has suffered from formative circumstances that render her generally unreliable and so leave her systematically subject to constant distrust, those who interact with her cannot be unjustified in distrusting her on these grounds. The distrust simply marks the fact that the untrustworthiness is known. Its force is inherited from the significance of untrustworthiness. Likewise, it may be unfair that a person is subject to formative circumstances that render her unable to show proper regard for others and so leave her systematically subject to other's resentment and indignation. But, once it is granted that the relations in which she stands are of a certain quality, the attitudes which simply acknowledge those facts cannot be unfair.

(2004, 136)

Hieronymi's subtle analysis makes a number of excellent points. First, it is legitimate to feel resentment toward a colleague who treats people in a demeaning manner; indeed, we should be concerned if someone does *not* feel such resentment. To take the most obvious example, suppose you have a white co-worker who is profoundly prejudiced, and consistently treats one of your black colleagues in a demeaning and condescending manner. If your black colleague does not feel resentment, then you would be concerned that she is lacking in self-respect and self-confidence; and if *you* are not angered at this vile behavioral pattern, then we would surmise that you approve or at least are not bothered by such despicable racist behavior. As Damasio (1994) notes, if one does not feel such anger, it is unlikely that one has strong value commitments that condemn racism. We should certainly not attempt the impossible task of eradicating such angry feelings; indeed, we should not attempt it even if it were possible. If Damasio is right, then those feelings—Kant's claims to the contrary notwithstanding—are probably inseparable from our strong value commitments. Even when we recognize that a feeling is vile—such as racist feelings—research has shown that it is very difficult to eliminate (Devine 1989; Dovidio, Kawakami, and Gaertner 2002; Quillian 2006 and 2008; Lane et al. 2007), though we wish we could. The feeling of deep resentment against racist behavior is, on the other hand, *not* a feeling we should wish to eliminate. But while such feelings are essential, it does not follow that we should act on them. That is hardly extraordinary. There are many important feelings we should not wish to eliminate, but that we do not regard as consistent guides to good behavior. The feeling of strong and special affection for family and friends is good, and we legitimately have special feelings for their success and well-being; but *acting* on such feelings to give a job to an unqualified friend in preference to a well-qualified stranger is not an exercise of virtue.

In the case of our racist colleague, it is good that we feel disgust toward his behavior; and as Hieronymi notes, it is legitimate and accurate to judge the behavior morally vile, and we probably cannot—and in this case, probably should not—avoid some overt indication of that deep disgust, which will be unpleasant or even painful for our racist colleague. It is legitimate and important that your racist colleague be shown that such behavior is widely regarded with strong disgust. After all, your racist colleague may come from a background and culture of pervasive racism in which such behavior is an approved norm, and it is important to bring home to this colleague that you and others find such behavior morally repugnant and unacceptable. That expression of moral disgust—which involves pain for our racist colleague—is certainly *fair* in the sense that it is directed at an appropriate object of disgust; and it may well be beneficial for the improvement of society and for the improvement of our colleague's character and behavior. All of this is true. It does not follow that our racist colleague *justly deserves* to suffer the pain involved in these expressions of disgust: not even if they are inevitable, and not even if they are beneficial (our racist colleague may have been profoundly conditioned to racism in a pervasively racist society, and never had the opportunity to question those racist values). Some punitive measures may be inevitable and sometimes valuable in social situations. That does not make them just, or justly deserved.

It is true—as Hieronymi emphasizes—that directing social opprobrium at an arrogant and abusive (or racist) co-worker is *fair*; that is, it is fair in the sense that the expressions of resentment and even disgust are directed at a target who has genuine moral flaws. But it does not follow that such socially punitive pressures are fair and just in the sense that they are *justly deserved*. The socially punitive pressures on the bad co-worker may be beneficial and necessary, and they qualify as punishment; as John Tasioulas (2006, 295) notes: "Even purely formal censure constitutes hard treatment, since condemnation is meant to be experienced as unwelcome." But our co-worker does not *justly deserve* such punishment, any more than the inquisitive and adventurous child who benefits from a slight burn justly deserves to suffer.

This claim is so directly counter to our "common sense" system of moral responsibility that a clearer though less plausible example might be helpful. Suppose that a wonderful unbiased white colleague is given a potion by the philosophically proverbial mad scientist: a potion that causes her to become profoundly racist, and to treat our black colleagues in a demeaning manner. Suppose further that by inflicting some degree of unpleasant or even painful social opprobrium on this transformed colleague we can eradicate the effects of the drug, and the prejudice of our colleague will be eliminated (would that eliminating prejudice were so simple). In this case our feelings of disgust would be appropriate, our expressions of disgust would be largely unavoidable, and the social opprobrium would serve a good purpose. But we would not suppose that our unfortunate colleague *justly deserves* such suffering. To the contrary, we would think—in Levy's (2011) phrase—that our colleague is *doubly* unlucky: unlucky to have received the vile drug, and then unlucky to be subjected to punitive measures. In the case of our drugged friend, the causes of her moral flaws are clear; in the case of the nasty colleague, the deeper causes of her flaws are much more difficult to discover—and holding her morally responsible makes them even more difficult to discover, since when we attribute moral responsibility we block deeper inquiry into causes.

Both the "naturally" nasty colleague and the "drug-induced" nasty friend are genuinely bad, and both may benefit from social sanctions against their behavior, and such sanctions are necessary in both cases. The only difference in the two cases is that the drug causes are impossible to ignore, and that makes the basic *unfairness* of punitive intervention painfully obvious. It is certainly accurate—and fair, in that sense—to say that Robert Harris is brutal and dangerous, and must be isolated for the protection of society. But it is still the case that it is unjust that he be subjected to this unavoidable treatment.

Saul Smilansky makes clear the basic unfairness of criminal punishment when viewed from the moral responsibility-denying hard determinist perspective:

> According to a hard deterministic interpretation, our criminal is but a *victim of the circumstances* that molded him and the forces that operated through him, all ultimately beyond his control. . . . For this person to end up, because of any of his actions, worse off than anyone else is thus grossly unfair. We may have some consequentialist or other form of justification for preferring certain social arrangements, but if he pays the price, then what we are doing is not fair *to him*.
>
> (Smilansky 2016a, 142; emphasis in original)

Furthermore, such unjust and unfair punishment is sometimes *necessary* for protecting and maintaining society. Smilansky (2011) regards the combination of those facts as leading to a *reductio* of the denial of moral responsibility. Instead, it is a *reductio* of belief in a just world.

## Dennett on Punishment

Daniel Dennett believes we can give "just deserts" a consequentialist reading that preserves just deserts without the retributive harshness. Dennett acknowledges that there are powerful emotions involved, but maintains that they can be channeled into controlled and positive paths:

> I agree . . . that our retributive desires have an ancient and amoral source in our evolutionary past but I don't "rest my case" on them; I argue . . . that we have devised ways to harness them—tame them, direct them down *justifiable* channels—in order to secure something very valuable: a secure and civil society in which people are held responsible for their promises and the other deeds they do "of their own free will."
>
> (Dennett 2012)

But our retributive desires are not so easily harnessed and tamed. Cultures that attempt to make extensive use of those "tamed" retributive emotions—in the form of just deserts for what we do of our "own free will"—wind up with harsher punitive practices: punitive practices (as described in Chapter 7) that go far beyond any consequentialist justification. We cannot avoid punishing; but we can avoid believing that punishment is *justly deserved*, and that would be a major step toward controlling those powerful and dangerous desires.

Moral responsibility was contrived to make punishment *justly deserved*. Rather than protecting from abuse, belief in just deserts increases the danger of abuse. When we say that the punishment is not only necessary but *justly deserved*, that fans the flames of anger and makes us comfortable with the infliction of justly deserved punishment. But we are already willing and eager to punish, and we don't need any extra motivation. The strike-back desire (discussed in Chapter 4) is powerful and dangerous (and not very precise). We need ways to control and limit it, not nurture it and make it respectable. The best way of restraining and controlling the strike-back desire is through more knowledge, careful deliberation, and deeper inquiry. That is precisely what moral responsibility and just deserts block, while simultaneously strengthening the desire—and the "right"—to punish.

Dennett makes clear that he is disgusted with the excesses of the U.S. justice system, and that he supports major reform:

> I think that the reforms most pressingly needed are obvious: a drastic diminution in the length of sentences, and indeed the elimination of most incarceration in favor of less drastic penalties, much better enforcement of prisoners' rights, and better programs for reintegrating prisoners into society.
>
> (Clark, Dennett, and Waller 2012, 9)

In Norway the reforms that Dennett desires have largely taken place; in contrast, those reforms are not happening in the neo-liberal United States. As England becomes more stringently neo-liberal and more devoted to moral responsibility, its justice and prison systems are looking more like that of the United States and less like that of Norway (and like the U.S. system, the British system is being condemned by the European Human Rights Commission). A key difference (as discussed in greater detail in Chapters 7 and 13) is that the United States has a strong devotion to belief in moral responsibility, while Norway has a belief system and culture that allows a much smaller role for moral responsibility. Dennett wants to reform our criminal justice system, and on that we are in complete agreement. But Dennett believes we should carry out those needed reforms while keeping our belief in moral responsibility intact. If sociologists like Cavadino and Dignan (2006a and 2006b) are correct, it is the belief in moral responsibility itself that is causing many of the worst problems, and real reform will be facilitated by dropping or at least minimizing the commitment to just deserts and moral responsibility.

Dennett notes (2012, 10) that in *Against Moral Responsibility* (Waller 2011) I "applaud Gilligan's restraint-only institutions, with education and other programs offered." I do indeed, and would add Norway's Bastoy Island to the list of programs I applaud. Dennett then states that I fail to "notice that this is still punishment, and still needs the justification of some kind of desert. We don't send people there unless they are found guilty." I agree that such programs are still punishment, and we do need careful checks on coercively sending people to these programs (as discussed in the final chapter); and we need strong *justification* for such coercive acts (and I should have made that clearer in *Against Moral Responsibility*). But we do not need the justification of *just deserts*. We must punish. That is sad but true. But we do not have to suppose that the punishment is *just*, for that makes us comfortable with a punitive process that we *should* find deeply distressing.

Punishment cannot be eliminated, neither in the United States nor in Norway; but if we want a justice system that avoids the excesses, the cruelties, and the deep unfairness of the U.S. system, an important step in making such reforms is reducing—and ideally, eliminating—the commitment to belief in *justly deserved* punishment. Punishment is necessary, and it can be *justified* as a sad necessity, but it can never be *just*. The most promising path to a better justice system requires recognition of that distressing fact. We live in an unjust world. Life—as Dennett agrees—is not fair. In our unjust and unfair world, punishment may be necessary and justified, but that does not make it fair and just. Recognizing that disturbing fact, and learning to live with the cognitive dissonance it generates, is a vital step toward developing the least punitive, most effective, and fairest system we can contrive.

## Facing the Injustice of Punishment

What are the benefits of recognizing the injustice of punishment? First, it checks the righteous retribution tendency to *over* punish and celebrate the result: "he really got what was coming to him!" There is an important difference between celebrating punishment as righteous retribution and regretting punishment as an unavoidable but unjust necessity. Michael Corrado clearly marks that difference:

> If we saw prisoners as human beings made to suffer for the benefit of others, surely we could not be so callous in our treatment of them. But if they are sinners who deserve to suffer, then it is an entirely different matter.
>
> (2001, 275)

We cannot now change the necessity of punishment, nor can we—or should we—eliminate the emotional reactions that prompt the punitive efforts. But we can change our attitude to punishment itself. Punishment is *necessary*, but it remains important to recognize that punishment is *unjust*.

Some may regard this as too fine a distinction, or even a distinction that marks no real difference. What does it signify? We should still punish, but now we should feel bad about it? We should not feel *guilty* about it; but yes, we should feel bad about it: feeling bad is a valuable and appropriate response. That is, one should recognize that those who are punished do not deserve such punitive responses, necessary though they be. When we *reject* moral responsibility and acknowledge that punishment is *never* just, then when we must punish we recognize punishment as a problem instead of a solution. That is a much better and more productive attitude than the common feeling of righteous retribution, which blocks understanding and prevents consideration of better alternatives. Moral responsibility was designed to *fix* our cognitive dissonance by making punishment *justly deserved* and preventing us from looking harder and deeper at the real problems. A system that makes us comfortable with punishment by blinding us to injustice is not a system worth preserving.

It is painful to recognize that we do not live in a just world, and especially painful to realize that we cannot avoid being unjust operatives in that world; but it is disastrous to contrive schemes to hide that knowledge from ourselves, whether by "self-making" schemes or "godlike first cause powers" or by blocking deeper inquiry into the causes of character and behavior. When we hold morally responsible, we are looking for a place to *stop* inquiry. To hold someone morally responsible, we must reach a point at which we can say—as Adina Roskies (2012) emphasizes—"the buck stops here." At that point, no deeper inquiry is allowed (it is treated as irrelevant). Belief in moral responsibility is a powerful narcotic that blocks the pain we *should* feel when engaging in unjust but unavoidable punishment. It is better to abjure any painkillers—especially those that mask symptoms and block deeper inquiry—and deal with the real problem. That pain can motivate us to *fix* the causes of the behavior we must punish and thus *minimize* our pain in inflicting unjust punishment rather than masking it.

In T. S. Eliot's *Burnt Norton* a bird warns that "human kind cannot bear very much reality." Given the many efforts human kind make to avoid facing reality—deities by the score, miracles in abundant variety, persecution of Copernicans, denial of Darwinism, rejection of evidence of global warming, fervent belief in a just world, devotion to special godlike powers of free will, and deep commitment to moral responsibility—Eliot's bird seems quite perceptive. Though the comforts of such avoidance are considerable, the perils are greater. The problems that stem from belief in miracles and deities are obvious, while the problems that arise from belief in a just world and belief in moral responsibility will be discussed in later chapters. But the advantages of rejecting moral responsibility and just deserts—and forgoing the comfort as well as the self-satisfaction they provide—are also significant. We will treat those we *must* punish in a more humane manner; and we will seek *without limits* the causes of destructive behavior and flawed character, find better ways of preventing such problems and character flaws, and develop effective reform measures: measures that will examine both the larger social context as well as individual development and circumstances. The cost of more blame is less understanding. That cost is paid not only by those who are subjected to punishment, but also by the society inflicting the punishment: the problems are left intact, and the harmful behavior continues. As is typically the case, the cost of actually *fixing* the problem is much less than the cost of repairing the damage when the cause of the problem is ignored.

Painful as it is, it is better to acknowledge that we must punish, that punishment is unjust, and that we cannot avoid playing our part in an unjust world. In order to believe that a person is morally responsible and a legitimate target of just deserts, it is essential that one place limits on inquiries into *why* the person behaved as he or she did; for if those inquiries proceed, they soon find deeper causes that raise serious doubts about moral responsibility and just deserts. Those deeper inquiries are more valuable than the moral responsibility analgesic they replace. Aaron was an abused child, and he does not now exhibit violent tendencies. Bob has a genetic abnormality (a defective MAO-A gene) sometimes associated with violent behavior, but he does not now exhibit violent tendencies. And Carla has Bob's genetic abnormality, and was—like Aaron—an abused child, but she is not violent. So if we stop there, it seems as if neither abuse nor the genetic abnormality—not even in combination—is the deep cause of David's violent behavior, so he is morally responsible. But when we look deeper still, we find that *male* children who have the genetic abnormality *and* suffered early childhood abuse are at greatly increased risk of adult violence (Tancredi 2007, 303–304). Sometimes looking deep is essential, but typically the challenge to moral responsibility does not require such deep inquiries. We need not look deep to find differences in need for cognition, situational factors, self-efficacy, and ego depletion; we need only modest curiosity, which compatibilists are at pains to suppress. It is not only the deep inquiries that are off-limits on the plateau of moral responsibility, but also the relatively shallow ones (Waller 2011, 223–233). What is "lost" when we deny moral responsibility is the blocking of inquiry, both shallow and deep.

When we give up moral responsibility, and break through the barriers it erects against deeper inquiry, then we can discover and understand and *improve* the deeper causes that shape both virtuous and vicious character, and thereby *reduce* the necessity for unjust punishment. Children grow up in conditions that we know shape crime—conditions of lead poisoning, inadequate nutrition, poor schools, few successful role models, few or no opportunities for meaningful or even living-wage work—and we blame the individuals who become criminals and ignore the conditions that cause crime, leaving those environments in place to produce more crime. Blocking inquiry is not a good procedure if we want to understand how both flaws and virtues were shaped, and the steps we must take to shape more self-controlled, empathetic, considerate, creative people; and blocking inquiry is not the procedure we must adopt if we want to *understand*—as opposed to merely condemn and punish—why some people become violent, mercurial, callous, and inconsiderate while others are empathetic, self-controlled, and resilient.

Sometimes—perhaps quite often—we will discover that the flaws are not in our stars, nor in ourselves, but rather in our social environments. We need to make changes, but not so much changes in individual character as changes in the environments in which individuals live. If a young man lives in an environment in which he is constantly humiliated, where he is frequently subjected to "stop and frisk" indignities, where he cannot get effective educational training, and in which there is no positive path available for personal success, then perhaps the problem is not in the person but in the society. When we insist on the narrow and limited focus of individual moral responsibility, then it seems plausible—even obvious—that the problem is in the individual young man, and our "solution" is to "get tough" and punish more severely. Closer scrutiny would make it obvious that the problem is not in the rebellious young man, but in the grossly unfair and discriminatory system he is rebelling against. In such cases, *punishment* distracts us from the real problems in our society, and by blaming and punishing the victims of those problems we are prevented (or protected) from examining the actual problems.

We must not become comfortable with punishment. That is the great wrong of moral responsibility. When we can appeal to moral responsibility and just deserts, punishment becomes not only morally acceptable, but morally required; not a disturbing problem, but a positive good; not a troubling misfortune, but a celebration of personhood; not a deeply unfortunate wrong, but righteous retribution. Why should we look for ways to minimize and reform punishment, if it is not only morally good but positively ennobling? Belief in punitive just deserts not only blocks deeper inquiry, but vilifies it. Discovering deeper causes that explain why a malefactor chose the path of violent crime diminishes the respect due the criminal and his deliberative godlike power of free choice; in contrast (as C. S. Lewis celebrates it): "to be punished, however severely, because we have deserved it, because we 'ought to have known better,' is to be treated as a human person made in God's image" (Lewis, C. S. 1971, 246).

## The Illusion of Just Deserts

One philosopher clearly recognizes the implausibility of moral responsibility and the injustice of punishment, but insists on keeping that knowledge hidden: hidden, that is, from the masses, but not from himself and his fellow philosophers. Saul Smilansky recognizes the basic injustice, but maintains that the injustice is unavoidable, and that we must sustain the *illusion* that moral responsibility is justified by libertarian free will (though in fact libertarian free will is implausible) and that punishment is just. Smilansky describes the situation in graphic terms and with remarkable clarity:

> The Fundamental Dualism [the disturbing truth of hard determinism together with the required illusion of libertarian free will and moral responsibility] means that in practice we commit horrendous injustice on a daily basis, and must do so: to follow Control Compatibilist Justice is often to amplify Ultimate Injustice (injustice from the ultimate hard determinist perspective), and vice versa. At best, Compatibilist Justice is a kind of 'justified injustice', indefensible at the ultimate level. But since Compatibilist Justice is applicable to most areas of social and even personal life, e.g., whenever people are punished, the scope of injustice is overwhelming. Were we to attempt to follow more closely the hard determinist perspective, injustice would soon follow in terms of the compatibilist perspective. . . . This type of injustice, following from the basic dualistic ethical structure of free will related morality, to a large extent *cannot* be overcome; I call it Structural Injustice. . . . Flowing as it does from the basic ethical structure of the free will issue, such injustice is a part of the human condition.
>
> (2000, 256–257)

Smilansky begins this section of his book with a quotation from William Goldman: "Life is not fair, and it never has been, and it's never going to be." That is a hard and honest look at the falsity of our comforting belief in a just world. It is obvious that however painful that truth may be to Smilansky—it is a painful truth for any decent person to acknowledge, and Saul Smilansky is a very decent person—Smilansky is capable of facing it, and continuing to live a full rich life, complete with reactive emotions and friendships and loves. Still, it *is* an uncomfortable truth. Suppose we offered Smilansky a pill that would guarantee to him the comforting illusion that he recommends we sustain in others: take this potion, and you will no longer have doubts about libertarian free will, you will have complete faith in our retributive justice system, and you will enjoy confident certainty that the world is basically just. Smilansky would scorn such an offer, and for good reason: whatever some may suppose to the contrary, ignorance rarely equates to bliss. Instead, ignorance is more often an opening to exploitation and abuse. Belief in a just world is a comforting but false belief. It results in blame of victims, as well as self-blame for our misfortunes. Illusions may be comforting, and there is no question that they can provide some benefits (belief in a just world certainly does). But those benefits come at too great a price. Saul Smilansky no doubt has generous motives for the illusion he wishes to protect and foster; but few illusion-mongers are so selfless and trustworthy.

What the illusion of just deserts mainly preserves is the smug feeling of righteousness for those in positions of privilege, along with the system that maintains those privileges. The illusion of robust moral responsibility may comfort the comfortable (who gain a disproportionate share of the "just rewards" while feeling self-satisfied outrage at those who receive their "just deserts" in the form of punishment or deprivation); but it afflicts the afflicted. Reform is blocked by the illusion that our punitive practices are actually just: why reform a just system? If instead we look honestly at the injustice of "just deserts," and acknowledge the injustice in which we are participants, then the unpleasantness may act as a powerful stimulus for effective change. We cannot eliminate injustice, but we can reduce it. At the conclusion of a recent essay, Smilansky recommends "a complex view" combining the hard determinist rejection of moral responsibility and just deserts with a compatibilist view that treats at least some punishment as justly deserved:

> Our conclusions should lead to a re-evaluation of the compatibilist interpretation of moral life, as a richer, more plausible, and safer interpretation than hard determinism. This needs to be combined with a hard determinist acknowledgment of the deep injustice and tragedy involved in punishment, in light of the absence of libertarian free will.
>
> (2016b)

Placing an overlay of compatibilist comforts on our recognition of "the deep injustice and tragedy involved in punishment" makes it more palatable; but the deep injustice of unavoidable punishment should be faced with no compatibilist comforts. There is a powerful and constant temptation to convince ourselves that punishment is justly deserved. We need no help in finding ways to mask the troubling truth that punishment is never justly deserved: Philosophers have been very creative in that endeavor. Rather, the real challenge is in viewing that deep injustice honestly, so that distress at punitive injustice will motivate the difficult work of changing the harmful causes and *reducing* the need for unjust punishment.

Smilansky notes (in the same essay) that:

> Hard determinism as a moral position thus ought to hold that no one deserves to be made to suffer, or to be made worse off than another, and hence that it would be *unjust* to do so.
>
> (2016b, 596)

Smilansky is precisely right. Punishment is *unjust*, and inescapable, and we live in an unjust world in which we cannot avoid being part of unjust punitive processes. That is a tragedy, as Smilansky makes clear. Smilansky characterizes me as a "happy hard determinist" (2016b, 598): one who believes that rejection of moral responsibility will have positive effects. That is not quite accurate: I concur with hard determinists in rejecting moral responsibility but then part ways with hard determinists (Waller 1990) because rather than rejecting free will I believe there is great value in a natural animal free will (Waller 2015b) that does not support moral responsibility (discussed in Chapter 14). But in any case, I am not a happy hard determinist who believes that denial of moral responsibility will result in a just world in which all wrongs can be eliminated. Rather than a happy hard determinist, that would be an irrationally exuberant hard determinist. I believe that we will be better off—and ultimately happier—if we face the painful reality of unjust but unavoidable punishment, rather than hiding that disturbing truth behind false belief in just deserts and righteous retribution.

Punishment cannot be eliminated, and punishment was, is, and always will be unjust. That is a sad and genuine problem that can be ameliorated but (so long as punishment is necessary) never solved. The effort to find an account that will make punishment *just*: that is also a severe problem, but it *can* be solved. When we recognize that the project is futile as well as harmful, we can give up that hopeless and harmful quest.

# 3 Tychonic Moral Responsibility

Deeply entrenched systems are difficult to renounce. By the end of the sixteenth century the Ptolemaic view was under increasing challenge, but the Copernican system—claiming that the Earth is *not* the fixed center of the cosmos—seemed impossible to accept, and the Ptolemaic system seemed impossible to relinquish. The Tychonic System—developed by the Danish astronomer Tycho Brahe—became an attractive alternative: the Earth remains the fixed center, and the Sun orbits around the immobile Earth, but all the other planets orbit around the Sun. The Tychonic system incorporated elements of the Copernican challenge to the Ptolemaic view while retaining as much as possible of geocentrism, and was adopted by the Church as well as many astronomers.

William James noted the strong desire to retain as much as possible of our older belief system when we encounter information that requires changing our views. When we incorporate a new idea into our beliefs, we strive to make the new belief fit as comfortably as possible with the old system; we preserve:

> the older stock of truths with a minimum of modification, stretching them just enough to make them admit the novelty, but conceiving that in ways as familiar as the case leaves possible. . . . New truth is always a go-between, a smoother over of transitions. It marries the old opinion to new fact so as ever to show a minimum of jolt, a maximum of continuity.
>
> (1907, 35)

But as Thomas Kuhn (1962) reminded us, there are times when systems should be junked rather than patched up or remodeled. The moral responsibility system did not modify the honor system, but replaced it. The moral responsibility system was better, certainly, and in some respects was a very useful system; but its period of usefulness has run out, it blocks better ways of understanding and improving human behavior, and it should be razed rather than repaired. There is a new system developing that is a major improvement over the moral responsibility system. In order to gain the advantages of that new system it is necessary to reject the moral responsibility system in its entirety, with no Tychonic compromises.

## The Attempt to Make Punishment *Just*

One of the earliest substantive discussions of moral responsibility is found in Aristotle, and in Aristotle the various pieces fit together to make a consistent moral responsibility system. Aristotle lived in a world that was morally well-ordered, with an omniscient God of perfect rationality providing the inspiration if not the direct guidance for this morally well-ordered world: a world in which a life of virtue was a reliable path to genuine happiness, and humans had the capacity to emulate God's sublime rationality (or at least the capacity to aim in that godlike rational direction). In such a world, ordered by a just God, punitive processes must be just.

The Aristotelian system was an enormous change. As Bernard Williams (1993) notes, the common Greek view—as voiced by the dramatists—made no assumption of a just world. To the contrary, the gods were more likely to play dirty tricks than maintain justice, and bad things could and did happen to good people. In another era, the jealous god who worked out a special deal with Abraham was obsessed with receiving exclusive devotion from his people, but exhibited little concern for justice. Consider those who had the misfortune of being in the path that the Israelites took to the Promised Land: this jealous god of the Israelites commanded that they be put to the sword and "spare not one," men, women, and children alike. Even with his favorites, there was little concern for their "just deserts." If you doubt that, ask Job, a "righteous and upright man," whose family was killed, his possessions stolen, and his body covered with painful bleeding boils "from the soles of his feet to the crown of his head," merely because of a silly argument between God and Satan.

When the Christian God becomes omniscient and omnipotent, and is no longer an arbitrary and tempestuous god who plays favorites and is easily provoked to wrath, then the world governed by this God and the punishments he inflicts must be *just*; and this problem becomes especially acute when God starts dealing out mass punishments of eternal gruesome torture. Augustine and Aquinas struggle with the problem, with little success; Lorenzo Valla and—a century later—Martin Luther rule the problem impossible, and insist that it is blasphemous to seek a rational answer for something that must be accepted on blind faith.

Pico della Mirandola, having more imagination and less respect for Christian orthodoxy, proposed a "solution" that has remained popular to this day with libertarian philosophers and evangelical Christians: God grants to all humans—God's last and favorite creation—a special godlike first cause power of making choices that have *no* causal antecedents. Compatibilists, as well as some noteworthy contemporary libertarians—such as Robert Kane—renounce the miraculous powers of being "self-caused" from scratch; and few philosophers of any variety believe in a just God who runs a just world. But the remarkable thing is that having given up the special free will support system for moral responsibility, *and* having long since stopped believing in an omnipotent just God who orders a just world, most philosophers *continue* to believe in the moral responsibility system that was invented to place unavoidable punitive measures in the category of *morally just* acts.

In our nonjust world (as described in greater detail in Chapter 5), devoid of any deity that imposes a just order, it is not surprising that there should be some *unjust* acts that *cannot* be avoided. Some instances of punishment fall into that unfortunate category. Sometimes we *must punish*, even though no one justly deserves punishment. We cannot have perfectly clean hands in this world that is *not* perfectly just. Nietzsche noted that it takes philosophers a very long time to fully realize that God is dead, and one illustration of Nietzsche's observation is the persistent philosophical belief that there *must* be moral responsibility that will make punishment *morally just*. Having given up the support system, as well as the belief in a just world governed by a just God—the basic motive for a *just* system of punishment—why should we suppose that we can keep moral responsibility, or that we should even want to do so? We no longer live in a just world governed by a just God, and there is no need to justify God's ways to man.

We have struggled to keep the moral responsibility system, and even those who recognize that we cannot justify moral responsibility strive to keep something comparable. But it is better to recognize that the whole project is fundamentally misguided. It is an effort to justify what cannot be justified, and part of a system—including a god-governed just world and godlike free will—that is incompatible with our naturalistic world view. We should take comfort from the fact that we are not required to reconcile a cruelly punitive God with the godly virtue of being just—a project that Valla (1443/1948) long ago recognized was impossible (and consigned to mysteries beyond mortal understanding). This world is not just, and it is better to face that unpleasant fact than contrive moral responsibility accounts that provide just world comfort at the price of blocking deeper understanding and better systems.

## The Tychonic Temptation

Even among those who have been the most powerful critics of moral responsibility, there is a tendency to keep as much as possible of that moribund system. Derk Pereboom is a stalwart opponent of moral responsibility; nonetheless, even he sometimes suffers from the Tychonic tendency. Rather than rejecting blame altogether as part of the obsolete moral responsibility system, Pereboom favors "a notion of blame that has a more pronounced forward-looking aspect" (2014, 131). One of the virtues Pereboom claims for his model is that "while it is revisionist relative to widespread and historical punitive practice," it is nonetheless "sufficiently continuous with traditional and current policies to count as part of our general moral practice of holding people morally responsible" (2014, 156). Pereboom cites Moritz Schlick and J.J.C. Smart as positive models, who "claim that given determinism, a kind of blame that can be retained is indeed forward-looking: the justification and goal of such determinism-friendly blame is to moderate or eliminate dispositions to misconduct" (Pereboom 2014, 132). David Hume offered a moral responsibility justification along the same "forward-looking" lines:

> All laws being founded on rewards and punishments, it is supposed as a fundamental principle, that these motives have a regular and uniform influence on the mind, and both produce the good and prevent the evil actions.
>
> (1748/2000, 74)

Moritz Schlick, who credits Hume and is in turn credited by Pereboom, develops that model further:

> Punishment is concerned only with the institution of causes, of *motives* of conduct, and this alone is its meaning. Punishment is an educative measure, and as such is a means to the formation of motives. . .
>
> Hence the question regarding responsibility is the question: Who, in a given case, is to be punished? . . . Consideration of remote causes is of no help here, for in the first place their actual contribution cannot be determined, and in the second place they are generally out of reach. Rather, we must find the person in whom the decisive junction of causes lies. The question of who is responsible is the question concerning the *correct point of application of the motive.* . . . It is a matter only of knowing who is to be punished or rewarded, in order that punishment and reward function as such—be able to achieve their goal.
>
> (1939, 152–153)

Daniel Dennett proposes a similar justification for the moral responsibility system, insisting that "*holding people responsible* is the best game in town" (1984, 162, italics in original), and this is how that game is played:

> Instead of investigating, endlessly, in an attempt to *discover* whether or not a particular trait is of someone's making—instead of trying to assay exactly to what degree a particular self is self-made—we simply *hold* people responsible for their conduct (within limits we take care not to examine too closely). And we are rewarded for adopting this strategy by the higher proportion of "responsible" behavior we thereby inculcate.
>
> (1984, 164, italics in original)

J.J.C. Smart—cited by Pereboom as a proponent of forward-looking moral responsibility—gives this account, along with a dramatic example of how it works:

> When in a moral context we say that a man could have or could not have done something we are concerned with the ascription of responsibility. What is it to ascribe responsibility? Suppose Tommy at school does not do his homework. If the schoolmaster thinks that this is because Tommy is really stupid, then it is silly for him to abuse Tommy, to cane him or to threaten him. This would be sensible only if it were the case that this sort of treatment made stupid boys intelligent. . . . The schoolmaster says, then, that Tommy is not to blame, he just *could not* have done his homework. Now suppose that the reason why Tommy did not do his homework is that he was lazy. . . . In such a case the schoolmaster will hold Tommy responsible, and he will say that Tommy could have done his homework. By this he will not necessarily mean to deny that Tommy's behaviour was the outcome of heredity and environment. . . . If Tommy is sufficiently stupid, then it does not matter whether he is exposed to temptation or not exposed to temptation, cajoled or not cajoled. When his negligence is found out, he is not made less likely to repeat it by threats, promises, or punishments. On the other hand, the lazy boy can be influenced in such ways. Whether he does his homework or not is perhaps solely the outcome of the environment, but one part of the environment is the threatening schoolmaster.
>
> Threats and promises, punishments and rewards, the ascription of responsibility and the nonascription of responsibility, have therefore a clear pragmatic justification which is quite consistent with a whole-hearted belief in metaphysical determinism.
>
> (1961, 302)

Pereboom generously credits Smart with offering a forward-looking account of moral responsibility, though there are some clear differences between the forward-looking moral responsibility of Smart and that of Pereboom: Pereboom does not favor caning lazy students. But there are also some points in common. What Smart and Pereboom have in common is something that forward-looking moral responsibility tends to share with the backward-looking "just deserts" moral responsibility that Pereboom rightly rejects: the disinclination to examine at greater depth the history that shaped character and ability. The problem is not only that the schoolmaster's caning is cruel, and that even if it is short-term effective it is likely to have very bad side effects (such as the development of an authoritarian personality, or a student who does the work but vehemently hates it and leaves school as soon as possible). The deeper problem is that this quick and easy use of punitive methods blocks inquiry into better methods that would be more effective and do not generate other problems. The caning will in many cases be profoundly counterproductive, and exacerbate rather than correct the boy's laziness. We must ask *why* the lazy boy is lazy, and it is precisely that deeper query that all forms of moral responsibility hinder. If the lazy boy is suffering from learned helplessness, or a weak sense of cognitive self-efficacy, the caning—and even mild rebukes, which the forward-looking model of Pereboom is more likely to countenance—may deepen the problem.

Derk Pereboom's work is wonderful, and his arguments against moral responsibility are a unique and powerful contribution to the struggle against just deserts and *basic* moral responsibility. By my reckoning, Pereboom is the victor in the war against basic moral responsibility; but he is a victor who is too gracious to the fallen foe. Rather than battering down its walls and sowing salt in its fields (my own preference) Pereboom adopts a *forward-looking* model of moral responsibility in which some central elements of the moral responsibility system survive. Pereboom offers a nice illustration of how his "forward-looking" responsibility might function:

> Suppose someone acts badly, say by disseminating defamatory fabrications about his political rivals. One might then confront him by asking what good evidence he has for his allegations, and supposing he cannot produce it, one might indicate to him that his behavior is immoral and that he should cease to be disposed it. . . . This process might be harmful to the wrongdoer in various ways—it might, for instance, cause psychological pain. . . . But inflicting this harm is justified first of all by the right of the defamed to protect themselves and to be protected from this type of aggression and its consequences. In addition, one might have a stake in reconciliation with the wrongdoer, and calling him to account can function as a step toward realizing this objective. Finally, we also have an interest in his moral formation, and the moral address described naturally functions as a stage in this process. Blame grounded in this way is essentially forward-looking, since its aims are future protection, future reconciliation, and future moral formation.
> (Pereboom 2014, 134–135)

Pereboom's forward-looking moral responsibility is a gracious concession to the proponents of moral responsibility, but the result is a Tychonic system of moral responsibility that preserves elements of the just deserts moral responsibility system—a system that is not worth preserving in whole or in part. Certainly, this is an improved version of moral responsibility, but it still aims at making blame and painful punishment *just*. As a result, this forward-looking responsibility does not make optimum use of the best processes for understanding and improving behavior.

## Forward-Looking Moral Responsibility

"Forward-looking moral responsibility" is an appropriate name for Pereboom's model. First, it shares a basic aim of the traditional moral responsibility system: to show that infliction of punitive processes can be *just*. The moral responsibility system was invented for that purpose. Second, in order to preserve the plausibility of moral responsibility and just deserts, the focus must be exclusively *forward*: looking back into the deeper causes of behavior soon reveals the *unjust* nature of punitive just deserts.

Other proponents of "forward-looking moral responsibility" recognize that in order to preserve just deserts, the focus must be exclusively on future benefits of punitive measures while assiduously avoiding scrutiny of the deeper causes of the punished behavior. Thus, Schlick insists that "consideration of remote causes is of no help here"; Dennett rejects the "endless investigation" that attempts "to *discover* whether or not a particular trait is of someone's making"; and Fischer (2012) deplores the "metaphysical megalomania" that impels us to investigate the deeper causes of character and behavior, insisting that we instead "play the cards that are dealt us" and not worry about the deeper causes of the good and bad cards.

Obviously, there are benefits to "looking forward." It is worth emphasizing that even if you were dealt a bad hand, there are now steps you can take to improve your prospects of success. But we don't need a notion of "forward-looking responsibility" to establish that. "Forward-looking responsibility" still smacks of "if now you fail, it's your fault." In particular, it encourages the idea that we're being fair because "we don't care what your past was, it's what you can do now that counts." But the past, as William Faulkner noted, is never really past: it is what shapes our capacity for present fortitude, our present sense of self-efficacy, our present level of education. "Forward-looking" is a program for shaping better character and behavior, which is good; but to the degree that it tries to mimic moral responsibility it goes wrong (particularly when it attempts to serve the moral responsibility function of making punishment just). The moral responsibility model is a model for miracles and gods; it is not a model that we can fit into the naturalistic system. We should not put new wine in old skins.

Pereboom wants to preserve the idea that punishment can be *just*. That requires that we never look backward into the deeper causes of behavior and character, and that limitation deprives us of the knowledge necessary to most effectively improve behavior. We need to know that this person's history involved trauma, learned helplessness, weakened self-efficacy, ego depletion; and we need to know the history of childhood lead poisoning; and looking even deeper into that history, we must understand the effects of fetal exposure to alcohol and nicotine, as well as genetic factors. We also need to examine the *situation* in which the bad behavior occurred. *Effective* forward-looking programs require extensive in-depth *backward*-looking studies. The more extensive and effective those backward-looking studies are, the less plausible anything resembling moral responsibility becomes.

Punishment is sometimes *justified*, because it is the better choice between two evils; but that does not make it just. Consider an extreme case. We are justified in confining a dangerous and hate-driven murderer like Robert Harris (Watson 1987). Whether we call it prison or quarantine, that involves an unpleasant and coercive confinement that is done for our protection rather than his benefit. But when we learn of his brutal and affection-deprived infancy and childhood, succeeded by a cruel adolescence filled with taunts and sexual abuse, it calls into question any claim that such punitive treatment—no matter how minimally unpleasant we make the confinement—is *justly deserved*. To the contrary—as Neil Levy (2011) emphasizes—such treatment involves a second dose of bad luck for Harris, in which his unfortunate youth is followed by an unpleasant confinement that he does not justly deserve. Confining Harris is not just; rather, it is an unjust necessity in our unjust world. Pereboom focuses more on milder wrongs and milder punitive measures. If these are effective, they may be *justified*; but again, that does not make them *justly deserved*.

The basic problem with both forward-looking and backward-looking moral responsibility is its impossible goal of making punitive measures just, and that problem is one that will be discussed further in later chapters. But stemming from that problem is a second problem in Pereboom's forward-looking model: it strives to be a reassuringly close match with our traditional moral responsibility model. Punishment and reward cannot be eliminated (and in the case of reward, there is no reason to suppose that would even be a desirable ultimate goal); and so there will be some instances in which the use of punishment and reward will bear some resemblance to the procedures championed by the just deserts system of moral responsibility. A hardened murderer such as Robert Harris must be confined for our protection, and isolated from society. There will of course be substantial differences, as Pereboom rightly emphasizes: Whether we adopt Pereboom's forward-looking model, or abandon the notion of moral responsibility altogether, we will not suppose that Harris should be dragged into an execution chamber and ritually killed; and we will strive to make the confinement (or "quarantine") of Harris as painless as possible, consistent with the requirements of public safety; and we will emphasize the importance of working to rehabilitate Harris, rather than intentionally aiming at his suffering. At the other end of the punitive spectrum we will still make use of mild social sanctions, which can sometimes be valuable in controlling unpleasant behavior and promoting positive behavior. And of course we must positively reinforce (or "reward") behavior that should be promoted and sustained. Pereboom acknowledges that there will be important differences (as he emphasizes when he insists on a quarantine rather than a punitive incarceration model when confinement is unavoidable). However, he also promotes the idea that forward-looking moral responsibility can and should roughly *match* the procedures of traditional moral responsibility. But any similarities between the practices of the just deserts system and a system that rejects just deserts are accidental, rather than essential. When we reject just deserts, then the resultant process of shaping character and behavior will bear little resemblance to that supposedly justified by claims of just deserts (Waller 1989).

Consider the spouse who never helps with household chores. If the overburdened partner blames and complains, there is likely to be little progress. If one instead praises small efforts, there will be more such efforts—even though those efforts are small, and not very "deserving" of praise. The spouse who is doing all the work may not feel much like praising, but more like blaming, and the moral responsibility system fosters that (though the inclination is already there to be fostered). Why should he be *praised* for paltry efforts, when I do so much more? If instead of blaming and shaming we look at his history and understand that he was spoiled, then we can start to deal with the real problem in the most effective manner. That is not to suggest that feeling the resentment is *wrong*: the overburdened partner does have a legitimate grievance. Nor is it to suggest that the resentment should never be expressed—in some cases it may be beneficial to make the lazy partner aware of the problem (if your partner was constantly pampered by doting parents, he may not really understand the nature of his flawed behavior or even recognize that it *is* a flaw). Or perhaps your spouse feels incompetent to help; then praising second-rate work may be positive, though it flies in the face of "just deserts."

Consider the lazy boy who is caned by Smart's forward-looking schoolmaster. The *effective* schoolmaster may need to praise minimal efforts, and withhold praise from a fellow student's much greater efforts if the latter student is on this occasion performing substandard work (work that is still far superior to that of the lazy boy's best efforts). That is not to say that responding in more traditional punitive ways is never effective: obviously it is, or such behavioral patterns would not have developed. But they often are only short-term effective, with unfortunate side effects. Of course, the schoolmaster may feel better as a result of inflicting severe punishment on the frustrating lazy student, even if it has no positive effect whatsoever in shaping a better student, and even if it makes the student worse: when we are frustrated, the desire to pass the pain along (as described in Chapter 4) is powerful.

This is not to suggest that "forward-looking shaping" in the form of reward and mild punishment and social conditioning is ineffective, nor that we can dispense with it. But we can employ it more effectively and find better means of dealing with behavioral problems when we look carefully at the deeper causes and renounce any purposeful correspondence to the methods endorsed by the moral responsibility system. The optimal social conditioning for the person mired in learned helplessness will be very different from that of the person high in self-efficacy. We must look hard at the past, and all forms of moral responsibility—both backward-looking and forward-looking—discourage that deeper scrutiny. Being "continuous with the moral responsibility tradition" is not a point in favor of Pereboom's forward-looking model, but a reason to doubt it. Myopia is a basic element of the moral responsibility system (Waller 2015a, Chapter 12), and a good reason to reject the entire system rather than trying to patch it up.

## Reason and Moral Responsibility

An emphasis on *reason* is an essential element of Pereboom's forward-looking account of moral responsibility. Pereboom mentions John Martin Fischer, Susan Wolf, Michael McKenna, and Dana Nelkin as philosophers who place great emphasis on the importance of reason in their accounts of moral responsibility; and he notes that his own account also makes important use of reason, even though it focuses responsibility forward rather than backward:

> These philosophers all see some type of attunement to reasons as the key condition on basic-desert or reactive-attitudes-involving moral responsibility, while I instead view it as the most significant condition for a notion of responsibility that focuses on protection, reconciliation, and moral formation.
>
> (2014, 136)

By focusing on *reasoned* behavior Pereboom maintains a connection with traditional moral responsibility. We must be very special rational creatures if we are to be the unique creatures to which moral responsibility applies. Abandoning moral responsibility entirely means eliminating that distorting influence, which empowers us to examine more effectively what is actually motivating the behavior (the motivation is not likely to be rational, even when the actor supposes it to be). Reason—reflective deliberation, System 2 reasoning, higher-order reflection—is a wonderful thing. Like many wonderful things, it is comparatively rare (Kahneman 2011). Reasoning that rises above rationalization (in support of a conclusion favored for no rational motives) is rarer still (Haidt 2001, 2012). Making reason the keynote of behavior exaggerates its power as well as its range. Most of our behavior is *not* reflectively based; and even when it is, much of the "reasoning" is rationalization. Bad behavior may sometimes be corrected through a process of rational engagement, and when that happens it is worthy of celebration; but it is much more likely to be corrected through a process of emotional intervention or by changing the environment in which the behavior occurs. For every racist or sexist who repudiated racism or sexism as a result of "rational conversation," there must be scores who changed as a result of empathetic relations or a changing environment in which such feelings are the object of social disgust rather than social reinforcement.

Reason has long been part of the moral responsibility armament: Susan Wolf (1990) makes super rationality (that unswervingly tracks the True and the Good) essential for moral responsibility, John Martin Fischer (1994) requires reasons-responsiveness, and Harry Frankfurt (1971) demands higher-order reflection. This emphasis on higher-level rationality is there for two reasons. First, as Fischer and Frankfurt insist, moral responsibility is what makes humans unique (in another era, it would be what makes humans God's special creation) and radically different from other animals. The plausibility of this radical distinction in a post-Darwinian godless world may have problems of its own, but the point here is that it is implausible as the key element of a forward-looking account of how to change character for the better. If one wishes to keep a similarity to traditional moral responsibility accounts, reason is a good bridge. Whether it can function well as a means of promoting "protection, reconciliation, and moral formation" (Pereboom 2014, 136) is another matter. There is no doubt that reason can provide some benefits; but it is hardly the first tool one would choose for those projects. Indeed, depending on the power of reason for such changes may often be counterproductive: if a person can respond to reasons, we need not worry much about the environment or history, since reason conquers all. In this context, it stands in for the traditional libertarian power of creative will that removes any need for careful scrutiny of history: one can reason, one is on the plateau of competence (Waller 2011, 223–232), and so reason must be sufficient (and history, situations, and circumstances are irrelevant).

The common emphasis on reason keeps Pereboom's account of forward-looking responsibility connected to the backward-looking basic desert account of moral responsibility (rational competence grounds backward-looking moral responsibility, and rational processes are the preferred method for facilitating forward-looking responsibility); but that is not a connection worth maintaining. If we abandon the whole system of moral responsibility, and focus on ways to actually enhance "protection, reconciliation, and moral formation," then reasoned deliberation will be of some use (but very limited, since rationalization is more likely than unbiased deliberation); but we will not be tempted to suppose that reason can be the primary element in our program to promote better behavior.

## Revisionist Moral Responsibility

The outstanding and resourceful champion of Tychonic moral responsibility is Manuel Vargas, who makes his Tychonic commitment perfectly clear:

> Taken as a whole, the responsibility norms and their attendant social practices, characteristic attitudes, and paradigmatic judgments constitute what we can call *the responsibility system*. The challenge for a systematic

revisionist about free will is to tell a story about the justification of the responsibility system, and, in particular, the responsibility norms, that will give us some principled grounds on which to offer a naturalistically plausible and normatively adequate account of moral responsibility.

(2007, 154)

Vargas' *revisionist* account of moral responsibility explicitly aims at preserving a modestly modified version of moral responsibility:

> Whatever else they do, our concepts of free will and moral responsibility are important for helping us to organize, track, and justify different ways of treating each other. If we can show that there is something that plays these roles, that does the work that is supposed to be done by these concepts, this may be a good reason to believe that free will and moral responsibility exist, even if they are somewhat different than we tend to have thought. At the very worst, it would show that there is something that is functionally equivalent (or nearly so) to free will and moral responsibility.
>
> (2007, 147)

But we do not want a system that will "justify different ways of treating each other" when that makes punishment justly deserved and the infliction of punishment just.

In Vargas' revisionist account of moral responsibility, the emphasis is on how moral responsibility practices shape better behavior. Vargas makes no appeal to special godlike powers of first cause self-creation, but instead rests his case for moral responsibility practices on their success in shaping better character and behavior:

> The responsibility-characteristic practices, attitudes, and judgments are justified inasmuch as they, on the whole and over time, tend to contribute to our better perceiving and appropriately responding to moral considerations. It is plausible to think that our responsibility-characteristic practices, attitudes, and judgments have this effect. Think about moral praise and blame: they tend to get creatures like us to pay better attention to the moral considerations recognized in our sociohistorical context and they provide incentive for us to act accordingly. Since they are reasonably effective at doing this, it is plausible to think that the responsibility system is by and large justified. To be sure, there are likely aspects of our current norms that are less than fully ideal. It would be unduly optimistic to assume that the exact norms that have the most currency in our society just happen to be the normatively ideal norms. Nevertheless, it is plausible to think that the bulk of our responsibility-characteristic practices, attitudes, and beliefs can be justified in this way.
>
> (2007, 155–156)

It is *plausible*, for they do so contribute; but while being a plausible thought, it is a false one. The "responsibility norms and their attendant social practices, characteristic attitudes, and paradigmatic judgments" have now become crude and inefficient tools that block the adoption of better methods and cause unnecessary suffering. And they carry some unpleasant baggage. The problem runs deep: it is not that we don't have exactly the right arrangement of moral responsibility norms, but rather that the system itself is badly flawed, and fine tuning will not fix it.

What Vargas offers is valuable in many ways: we do need to think carefully about the best ways of shaping the behavior that the moral responsibility system purportedly *aims* at shaping; and some elements of social punishment and praise could be useful in that regard. There is nothing inherently wrong with forward-looking models of shaping positive behavior. The emphasis on personal development and against fatalistic helplessness is good. The problems start when we try to make them do the work of moral responsibility: the work of making the infliction of punishment *just*. Keeping the "just deserts" element of moral responsibility is not a way of achieving a better system. To the contrary, it makes that system not only less effective but also morally harmful.

The basic problem with the revisionist view is the deep assumption that it is desirable to keep something that closely resembles moral responsibility practices. That is no more plausible than supposing that germ theory must be compatible with belief in black bile. The fact that a model was the best we could do with cruder understanding is no grounds for keeping it when we gain greater knowledge. Moral responsibility was once a useful model, and perhaps the best we could do. It no longer is, and it is counterproductive to promote the illusion of its special benefits. When we had no way of looking deeper, then a justification for not looking deeper offered comfort at no great price. But that comfort is now bought at a dear price: the price of blocking inquiries that are both possible and valuable.

The Tychonic versions of moral responsibility championed by Pereboom and Vargas are improvements: they make no appeal to mysteries, they focus on positive results, and they seek to minimize punitive measures. But both suffer from one severe flaw, which is the result of a commitment to some form of the widely revered moral responsibility system: they are motivated by a desire to make punishment *just*. It is time to renounce the impossible goal of the moral responsibility system—in both its retributive and its Tychonic versions—and acknowledge the disturbing fact that punishment is necessary and unjust. When we "quarantine" we are doing so for our own good, not primarily for the good of the individual quarantined. It is better to recognize what we are doing, that we do not live in a just world (Chapter 5), and that punishment is sometimes unavoidable but always unjust.

It is true that we cannot do without punishment; that was the whole point of contriving a moral responsibility system that would provide *moral justification* for punishment. But we should recognize that though we must punish, punishment is never justly deserved. There is, sadly, a place for punishment, and it is probably a place that cannot be vacated for many years, if ever. But the problem with the moral responsibility system is that it is contrived to make punishment *justly deserved*, and that has no advantages whatsoever—except in comforting those who do the punishing, and further damaging those on whom punishment is inflicted. Punishment is probably necessary; in very limited use, it is probably useful; but it is never just.

## Free Will Without Moral Responsibility

My intrepid allies in the battle against moral responsibility—some of whom I have perhaps insulted by claiming that they are too willing to accept remnants of the moral responsibility position—might turn the tables and suggest that I am the one promoting Tychonism, since I want to retain free will (Waller 2015b). Not so. Deep in the moral responsibility system is the belief that moral responsibility cannot be divorced from free will. Vargas insists that "I am following the bulk of the literature, both current and historical, in supposing that free will is the freedom condition for moral responsibility." (2007, 153) And indeed the deep conviction that free will and moral responsibility are inseparable is an integral element of the moral responsibility system. For C. A. Campbell free will is the essential foundation for moral responsibility:

> It is not seriously disputable that the kind of freedom in question is the freedom which is commonly recognised to be in some sense a precondition of moral responsibility. Clearly, it is on account of this integral connection with moral responsibility that such exceptional importance has always been felt to attach to the Free Will problem.
>
> (1957, 159)

Peter Van Inwagen agrees, claiming that knowing we are morally responsible suffices for certainty regarding free will:

> If we do know that moral responsibility exists, then we should have no doubt about whether we have good reason to believe we have free will.
>
> (1083, 209)

Willard Gaylin keeps the close connection but switches the order, making free will a sufficient condition for moral responsibility: "Freedom demands responsibility; autonomy demands culpability" (Gaylin 1982, 338). Walter Glannon combines free will and moral responsibility into a logical equivalence: "Autonomy and responsibility are mutually entailing notions" (1998, 45).

If one supposes that denying moral responsibility entails denying free will, that is because one has accepted a basic principle of the moral responsibility system. Severing free will from moral responsibility—and preserving a natu-ralistic account of free will while eliminating moral responsibility—is not saving an element of the moral responsibility system; rather, it is a more thorough *rejection* of that system, which rejects not only moral responsibil-ity but the deep assumption that moral responsibility and free will are insep-arable: that free will *exists* to justify moral responsibility. That assumption has distorted our understanding of free will, while commitment to moral responsibility has blocked deeper inquiry into natural free will (as discussed in Chapter 14).

Others might claim that I also want to keep a "Tychonic" version of moral responsibility, since I favor (what I have called) "take-charge respon-sibility": a broader version of H.L.A. Hart's (1968) role responsibility, which includes "taking responsibility" not only for socially defined roles but also for making decisions concerning our own lives. But this is in no way a version of moral responsibility, nor a substitute for moral responsibility; it does nothing whatsoever to justify any claims or ascriptions of just deserts; and it is carefully distinguished—both in Hart's version and my own—from anything resembling moral responsibility. Indeed, the whole point of that discussion is to make clear that valuable take-charge responsibility is *noth-ing like* moral responsibility, and the two should not be confused. But that is a subject for Chapter 13.

Punishment existed long before the invention of moral responsibility, and we will continue to have punishment when the moral responsibility system is relegated to the cupboard of obsolete philosophical systems, alongside occasionalism and social Darwinism and theological voluntarism. Moral responsibility serves one basic function: it makes us comfortable with inflict-ing punishment by reassuring us that our punitive measures (which need little encouragement in any case) are genuinely *just*. Getting comfortable with punishment is not a virtue, and a system that makes us comfortable with inflicting unavoidable punishment is not a system we should cherish or preserve, in whole or in part.

# 4    The Strike-Back Roots of Retributive Justice

Punishment is enmeshed in complex social, legal, and cultural tangles. We are inclined to think of punishment, especially retributive punishment, as a basic and immediately intuited value. It does have primitive roots, but it is part of a complex system of beliefs. The "retributive desire" which we may imagine to be the primitive basis of our retributive punishment system is actually a highly refined and culturally complex motive.

The primitive desire that fuels retributivism is still present, and still manifested in its primitive form. When the despised rival team scores the winning goal in the final seconds, the passionate fan rips up her program, stomps an inoffensive plastic cup into small pieces, slams a fist into the coffee table, or—unfortunately—takes a punch at a nearby fan wearing the rival's colors. The fan of the opposing team is innocent of having destroyed the home team's hopes, and certainly the shattered plastic cup did nothing to offend; but the last second loss was intensely painful. A popular commercial shows a small boy—playing the part of a well-dressed business executive—speaking on his cell phone, becoming angry, and slamming the phone to the concrete where it shatters with a satisfying explosion. No one has to explain the commercial to us. We've all felt the same way, from the frustrated golfer who wraps his seven iron around a tree to the small child who throws her plate on the floor when offered fruit rather than ice cream. On reflection we may feel foolish; in the immediate circumstances we feel better.

The foundation of belief in moral responsibility and retribution—that existed long prior to the belief in retributivism itself—is the strike-back desire; or more precisely, the desire to "pass the pain along" (Barash 2005; Barash and Lipton 2011). It is found in rats and cats and chimpanzees, as well as in butchers, bakers, and philosophers. It is based in a "strike-back" desire that is not particularly selective. "Displaced aggression" (Potegal 1994; Virgin and Sapolsky 1997)—responding to pain by attacking the most convenient target—is not an aberration, but the basic element of the primitive desire.

## Pass the Pain Along

When we are harmed, we have a strong desire to "pass the pain along" by attacking someone or something. The perceived source of the pain makes a fine target, but often that target is unavailable; and when available, it is often not a desirable target. When the alpha male attacks or threatens me and causes me to suffer, attacking the stronger and very dangerous alpha male is not a salubrious choice. Attacking a much weaker target, lower in the hierarchy, works fine—the pain is successfully "passed along"—with considerably less risk. Even targeting an inanimate object will do.

The legendary Irish warrior, mighty Cuchulain, unknowingly kills his son in battle. When he discovers what he has done, Cuchulain is plunged into profound grief. Conchubar, the king and the leader of the army in which Cuchulain is a powerful warrior, fears that Cuchulain in his deep pain will attack his own army and slay them all. Conchubar orders his Druids to place a spell on Cuchulain, so that when he rises to fight he will attack the sea instead of his comrades in arms. The notion of Druids casting spells is a bit difficult to swallow; but the idea of the grief-stricken warrior attacking *something*—if no enemy is handy, his comrades or even the sea will do—we can easily understand. It is a staple of slapstick comedy: Moe hits Larry, Larry twists Curly's nose, and Curly smashes a table.

Passing the pain along is good for our health (so long as we do not attempt to pass it on by attacking the boss, or a defensive tackle for the Pittsburgh Steelers). When a chimpanzee is attacked by a more powerful individual, he then directs an attack at a weaker member of the group (Kawamura 1967). When rats are placed in a box with an electrified floor grid and shocked, they immediately attack each other; if no other rat is present, a gnawing post serves as a satisfactory substitute. But if there is no target on which to "pass the pain along," the rat suffers increased stress and is likely to develop ulcers (Virgin and Sapolsky 1997; Barash 2005). Barash and Lipton describe the basic process involved:

> Animals—and by all accounts, people, too—who lose a social confrontation experience what is called "subordination stress." Their blood pressure and adrenal hormones go up, while neurotransmitters that influence the sense of well-being go down. But if these same animals have the opportunity to "take it out" on another individual, their stress hormones and neurotransmitters return to normal levels. In short, living things can reduce their own pain-induced stress by passing that pain to another. . . . "A hurts B, B hurts C." By displacing the aggression, B down-regulates his stress and upgrades his neurotransmitters by dumping his pain on someone else, who is then inclined to offload his or her burden, giving rise to "C hurts D," and so on.
>
> (2011, 17)

The primitive emotion is not one of striking back at the source of harm, but striking back at *something* in order to pass the pain along. Rather than the retributive impulse against the wrongdoer being basic, the basic desire is to pass the pain along through aggression at whatever target is readily available. We tend to interpret "displaced aggression" as an aberration, a desperate and anomalous substitute for the desired retributive strike-back at whoever or whatever hurt us. Instead, when we suffer harm the basic desire is to strike at *something*. When striking back is directed at the source of harm, that is primarily because that source happens to be conveniently located and easily attacked. As Michael Potegal notes: "From the perspective of a theoretical distinction between provoker and target, redirected aggression is not a special case; in most cases aggression just happens to be directed at the object that provoked it" (Potegal 1994, 88).

Passing the pain along has deep roots in human cultures. The "mourning wars" among the Iroquois tribes (prior to their Confederation) served a variety of complex social functions, but one important purpose was to pass the pain along: when a member of a tribe died (from whatever cause) the grief was somewhat assuaged by an attack which inflicted suffering or death on a neighboring tribe. In honor cultures, when Arthur insults or injures or kills Benjamin (or a member of Benjamin's family), then Benjamin (or some family member) must pass the pain along with a violent response; but the violent attack need not be on Arthur, the original cause. If Arthur has died before the attack can be made, Arthur's son or brother is a satisfactory target; and if the living Arthur is a rather low-ranking person, then an attack on Arthur's stronger and higher-status brother may be more appropriate.

The general strike-back motive is clear in honor cultures; but while we generally look with contempt at honor cultures, the same desire motivates our supposedly more sophisticated system of "justice." When a horrible crime is committed, we want to strike-back at someone. If we happen to strike the guilty party, so much the better, but almost any available vulnerable target will do. One painfully obvious example is the case of "the Central Park Five." An attractive young investment banker was brutally attacked, raped, and left for dead while jogging in Central Park. There was legitimate outrage, and the outraged feelings demanded a target. The New York police soon supplied one, in the persons of five black and Hispanic youths ranging from 14 to 16 years old. Under harsh conditions and prolonged pressure on each of the isolated prisoners, the police managed to coerce strangely worded and inconsistent "confessions," and all were imprisoned for years in either juvenile or adult facilities. The New York media played its part in this strike-back frenzy, with the *Daily News* running an enormous headline "WOLF PACK'S PREY" over a front page story with a sub heading "Female jogger near death after savage attack by roving gang." Eleven years later one of the five was still in prison, and by coincidence learned of another prisoner—Matias Reyes—who was imprisoned for multiple counts of rape, and whose methods matched those used in the rape of the Central Park jogger. Reyes eventually confessed to the crime: acting alone he had beaten and raped the victim. The DNA evidence confirmed his confession. If anyone had really cared, it would not have been difficult to find the problems in the "confessions" of those convicted; but the public, the police, the media, and the "justice system" instead joined the strike-back frenzy. Donald Trump paid for a full-page advertisement in the *Daily News* advocating the death penalty for the "crazed misfits" whose "civil liberties end when an attack on our safety begins," and no one was much interested in whether the strike-back targets were innocent or guilty.

When we combine the strike-back motive with belief in a just world, things get more complicated. Now the target of our wrath must *justly deserve* such punitive measures. Justifying that claim requires moral responsibility and all its systemic trappings. But the moral responsibility system is a rationalization for something that is believed in at a much deeper—and more primitive—level. That is why the belief in moral responsibility is so much stronger than the *arguments* given in support of moral responsibility (Waller 2015a), and remains in place even if those arguments collapse.

When we seek a justification for our strike-back desire, we are seeking a justification for what cannot be justified. The problem then becomes deeper and the "solutions" more destructive. Attempts at justification careen from miracles to myopia. Desperate efforts produce the notion that moral responsibility makes us *uniquely deserving* of punishment. The just desert of punishment makes humans unique and worthy of special respect and dignity, and denying moral responsibility and the "right to punishment"—it is claimed—destroys human dignity. Starting from an impossible attempt to justify what cannot be justified, the system grows into something cruel and myopic that blocks efforts to develop better alternatives.

## Deep Retributive Emotions

Peter French celebrates (what he calls) the *virtue of vengeance*, along with the emotions at its core:

> Personal and vicarious moral anger can be and ought to be placated by hostile responsive action taken against its cause. Wrongful actions require hostile retribution. That, despite its seeming lack of fit with the body of moral principles upheld in our culture, is actually one of the primary foundations of morality. It is a foundation that is settled in passions, attitudes, emotions, and sentiments, not in reason.
>
> (French 2001, 97)

In this passage, French acknowledges what many philosophers have been loath to admit: the basic belief in righteous retribution and just deserts "is settled in passions, attitudes, emotions, and sentiments, not in reason"; and this is indeed "one of the primary foundations of morality," at least that part of our moral system that incorporates belief in moral responsibility. Philosopher and psychologist William James (1907, 56) was also clear on the basic *non*rational foundation of our belief in moral responsibility, attributing it to an *instinctual* urge: "Instinct and utility between them can safely be trusted to carry on the social business of punishment and praise."

When the moral responsibility system took hold, it was embraced not only by "the folk," but also by philosophers. While the folk might not have worried about whether the system of just deserts and moral responsibility was rationally respectable, philosophers certainly did—and continue to worry about it to this day, proposing a remarkable range of desperate schemes to provide rational grounding for the moral responsibility system. Those efforts to find a rational justification for moral responsibility have been creative, insightful, and often valuable; but—by my lights (Waller 1990, 2011 and 2015a)—they have failed. In any case, this is not the time to review that enormous and ongoing controversy. The point here is only that the effort to find a *rational* foundation for just deserts and moral responsibility was always a dubious undertaking, because the foundation for moral responsibility rests on emotions rather than reason. That does not mean that there could not *also* be rational grounds for the moral responsibility system, but we should not be surprised when a multitude of heroic philosophical efforts fail to discover such grounds.

The experimental philosophy studies of moral responsibility have produced some fascinating and surprising results. When we recognize that the moral responsibility system is based in *emotions* rather than rationality—the moral responsibility system was created to add a patina of moral respectability to powerful strike-back motives—some results no longer seem strange. Experimental philosophy studies offer valuable insights into the "folk" view of free will (is it really libertarian?); but they also demonstrate the enormous power of the strike-back retributive emotions. When we ask subjects to adopt a strict determinist perspective, they tend to conclude—from that abstract perspective—that people cannot be morally responsible and cannot justly deserve punishment (Nichols and Knobe 2007; Roskies and Nichols 2008; Sarkissian et al. 2010). But if instead of asking whether moral responsibility can survive in a deterministic universe, we ask whether—in this same deterministic universe—a specific individual justly deserves severe punishment for a horrible deed (such as murdering his family) then suddenly the concern about determinism is overwhelmed by the desire to punish, and the individual must be held morally responsible (Nichols and Knobe 2007). And we are not studying the responses of chimpanzees, or members of honor cultures, or people adhering to the harsh justice of the Hammurabi code; rather, the subjects of these experiments are typically sophisticated college students and others deeply immersed in the contemporary Western system of justice and ethics.

The responses of the experimental philosophy subjects are strikingly similar to the conclusion drawn by Peter van Inwagen. Van Inwagen is philosophically famous for his arguments *against* compatibilism, and for his vigorous insistence that moral responsibility *requires* a libertarian free will that cannot exist in a deterministic world. But his belief in moral responsibility is so powerful that it overwhelms even his carefully reasoned arguments for the incompatibility of moral responsibility and determinism:

> If incompatibilism is true, then either determinism or the free-will thesis is false. To deny the free-will thesis is to deny the existence of moral responsibility, which would be absurd. Moreover, there seems to be no good reason to accept determinism. . . . Therefore we should reject determinism.
>
> This conclusion is, at least in principle, open to scientific refutation, since it is conceivable that science will one day present us with compelling reasons for believing in determinism. Then, and only then, I think, should we become compatibilists.
>
> (1983, 223)

With the folk, there is not a double set of beliefs concerning moral responsibility: there is a libertarian belief, though not a very deep one. If pushed to believe abstractly in determinism, they are incompatibilists; but move closer to harsh reality, and the strike-back desire—especially when turned into righteous retribution—overwhelms the abstract resistance. This is a powerful emotional motivation that can overwhelm the reflective incompatibilism of the folk. Even more striking, it can overwhelm the carefully and reflectively examined incompatibilist views of a rationally rigorous philosopher such as Van Inwagen, whose powerful rational resistance to compatibilism crumbles in a confrontation with retributive desires. Compatibilism may be reflectively doubtful, but the rejection of moral responsibility and just deserts is emotionally unthinkable.

Experimental philosophers have revealed the deep emotional underpinning of the moral responsibility system; and (as will be discussed later) psychologists have uncovered many of the details of that emotional foundation and its impact on the process of blaming. But Thomas Nagel's work on "moral luck" (1979) remains one of the clearest accounts of the emotion-driven inconsistencies in the moral responsibility system. Nagel noted that we blame more severely for results that were—by chance—worse, even though the *acts* were identical: identical in *what* was done and *why*. Driver A is distracted by a cell phone call and swerves across the center line, but luckily no car was approaching from the other direction. If observed by a police officer, the driver—at worst—will receive a ticket and pay a fine, and quite possibly get off with a stern warning. Driver B does precisely the same thing under precisely the same conditions with exactly the same degree of negligence; but this time, strictly by luck, a car is approaching from the other direction and the collision results in the death of its driver and passenger. Driver B may serve a prison sentence for vehicular homicide, and certainly will have his driver's license suspended—and the same people who think a stern warning was quite enough blame and punishment for Driver A will agree that

Driver B justly deserved the more severe punishment. This makes no sense, when viewed as part of some *rational* model. It makes perfect sense when we consider the actual *emotional* operations of blaming and holding people morally responsible.

The problem gets worse, as psychological research has made clear. We do not objectively observe behavior, and then decide whether and who to blame; rather, we are more likely to decide that some individual should be blamed (because that individual justly deserves *punishment*) and then interpret and classify the individual's behavior in accordance with our blame judgment (Alicke 2000; Alicke, Rose, and Bloom 2011). Since we are uncomfortable blaming and punishing B severely and A hardly at all—for what was the same negligent behavior—there is a strong tendency to interpret the actual behavior differently: Driver B must have been *more* negligent than Driver A (Alicke 1992 and 1994; Alicke and Davis 1989; Alicke, Davis, and Pezzo 1994). And the same process plays out in other ways. If persons C (whom we like, or with whom we easily empathize) and D (whom we do *not* like—perhaps because of cultural or racial or ethnic biases) commit exactly the same offense, with precisely the same evidence against them, we attribute darker motives to D (Alicke and Davis 1989; Alicke and Yurak 1995; Kaplan and Kemmerick 1974; Landy and Aronson 1969). Examples are legion. When a player on my favorite team makes a sliding tackle that results in a foul call and an injury to the opponent, the player on my team was playing hard and perhaps slightly out of control, but there was certainly no intent to injure. When the same scenario plays out in reverse, the offending player was guilty of a flagrant foul and was clearly intending to cause injury. And not only do we *interpret* evidence differently, but we actively seek evidence that supports our blame evaluation and avoid counter evidence (Mazzocco, Alicke, and Davis 2004).

Nagel recognized that the problem of moral luck runs even deeper, and undercuts any confidence that the moral responsibility system is rationally consistent. Not only does moral luck permeate the results of our acts, but moral luck also plays a large part in the type of acts we perform: people of similar *characters* placed in differing *circumstances* act in radically different ways. Using Nagel's example, consider a person of authoritarian tendencies who unreflectively follows the pattern of his culture and is easily led. If he lived in Nazi Germany, he would likely have become an enthusiastic Nazi carrying out acts that are horribly wrong; but if that person—with the same character—were a Canadian shopkeeper, he would have lived a morally decent life. But it was bad moral luck that resulted in growing up and living in Nazi Germany rather than a small town in Canada. Nagel's point concerning the moral luck of circumstances has been further strengthened by the wide range of psychological research on situationism. As we know from Milgram's (1963) authority studies and Zimbardo's (1974) "prison" experiment with Stanford students, *most* of us are quite capable of carrying out horrific acts under the right situational influences, and it is only our fortunate moral luck that has kept us out of situations in which we would have done awful acts.

Nagel goes still further: there is not only moral luck in outcomes and circumstances, but the even deeper *constitutive* moral luck. When we consider the environmental contingencies that shape our genetic legacies (Raine 2013, 242–272) into the people we ultimately become, it is clear that *moral luck* plays a decisive role in our characters and our resultant behavior. Of course, we ourselves play an active role, but the abilities and capacities we bring to that role—including our levels of self-control, our initial intelligence, our confidence, our fortitude, our psychological adjustment—are the product of our good or bad fortune: none of us make ourselves from scratch, none of us choose our vitally important early childhood circumstances nor our genetic makeup.

Moral responsibility blinds us to those causes: we insist that almost everyone "has roughly equal opportunity for success" (Sher 1987, 31–32) though we know it is false; or that "luck averages out in the long run" (Dennett 1984, 95) which is also nothing one could reflectively believe to be true (though it fits well with our deep nonconscious belief in a just world). Belief in moral responsibility makes us insist that we should just "play the cards that are dealt to us" (Fischer 2012, 185) and refuse to look deeper. Rational consistency would insist on deeper inquiry, on recognizing moral luck (Levy 2011) in all its dimensions while scrutinizing the fundamental factors—both genetic and conditioning—that exert a powerful influence on our ultimate characters and behavior. As a system to give an ethical imprimatur to our powerful strike-back emotions (together with our deep nonconscious belief in a just world) moral responsibility functions well; but it functions well *only* if we avoid deeper scrutiny of its nonrational emotional nature.

When we recognize that the moral responsibility system exists to provide ethical cover for our strike-back emotions, then an otherwise curious phenomenon is no longer surprising. *If* moral responsibility functions as a rational process that assigns blame and punishment by scrupulously rational standards—as it is advertised to be—then we would expect that *stronger* commitment to moral responsibility and *just* deserts would be accompanied by a stronger commitment to careful and rigorous efforts to be *certain* that those held morally responsible and subjected to punishment are genuinely guilty of the charges against them. It is painfully obvious, however, that the opposite is the case: the *greater* the belief in individual moral responsibility, the less concern with avoiding mistaken punishment of the innocent (discussed in Chapter 7). It is not supposed to be that way: the myth is that belief in moral responsibility offers special *protection* of the innocent. But the myth portrays moral responsibility as a scrupulously rational system, when in fact it is a system based on strike-back emotions. And the fact that there is an *inverse* relationship between belief in moral responsibility and protection of the innocent makes clear the actual nature of the emotional belief in just deserts and moral responsibility.

When moral responsibility beliefs are powerful, concern for protecting the innocent becomes a low priority. This is a mystery if moral responsibility is a rational process; it is quite understandable when we recognize that moral responsibility provides cover—and justification and comfort—for the powerful strike-back emotions: emotions that are, after all, rather careless about their targets. The primitive desire to pass the pain along remains at the base, and though—through the system of moral responsibility—we assure ourselves that we are punishing only those who justly deserve it, we don't much worry if we happen to pass the pain along to someone who is innocent. The stronger the commitment to moral responsibility, as in the neo-liberal United States, the less concern with targeting exclusively the guilty. "Just deserts" provides a patina of respectability for the darker emotional core.

When we understand that just deserts and moral responsibility are built on a foundation of strike-back emotions (rather than on reason), then the true nature of the moral responsibility system becomes clear. As psychologist Mark Alicke notes:

> Whereas normative models based on jurisprudence and moral philosophy specify rational criteria for responsibility, blame is an inherently psychological construct. Predisposing biases, which represent departures from normative responsibility models, are endemic to ordinary blame ascription. For this reason, the psychological processes manifested in cognitive and motivational biases are central rather than peripheral to the psychology of blame.
>
> (Alicke 2000, 556)

In practice, belief in moral responsibility *distorts* and twists not only our reasoning but also the *content* from which we draw our conclusions concerning who justly deserves blame and punishment: "cognitive shortcomings and motivational biases are endemic to blame" (Alicke 2000, 557). When something harmful happens, we want to *blame*—and punish—someone for the harm caused. To *justify* such blame and punishment, we attribute negative characteristics to the person blamed. When a person harms another, we are more likely to conclude that the person causing the harm foresaw the harmful consequences; if no harm occurred, the assumption that the danger was foreseen is less likely (Alicke, Weigold, and Rogers 1990). When subjects consider the case of a homeowner who shoots a burglar (an action that is considered justifiable), they conclude that the fact that the homeowner had earlier consumed two beers and was in a bad mood had no effect on his action; but when the shooting victim is instead the boyfriend of the homeowner's daughter (who was collecting clothes for his daughter's beach trip, at his daughter's request), then the two beers and the bad mood are judged to be factors in the wrongful shooting, providing more grounds for blaming the shooter (Alicke, Davis, and Pezzo 1994). In another study subjects were asked to judge a psychiatrist's decision to release a patient who had been hospitalized by a court order. After reading the evidence that the psychiatrist considered, one group was told that the released patient subsequently caused no harm, while a second group—reading the same evidence—was informed that the patient had assaulted a woman shortly after his release. Based on the same evidence, the first group considered the psychiatrist's decision to be justified; but the second group not only blamed the psychiatrist but also concluded that evidence against the release was *stronger*: learning of a negative outcome changed the perception of the strength of the evidence they had considered (Alicke, Davis, and Pezzo 1994).

The moral responsibility system is not the rationally grounded protector of innocence that it is represented to be; rather, it is the system employed to justify the infliction of punishment that the strike-back desire demands. We cannot eliminate the deeply ingrained strike-back desire, and it would probably be a bad idea even if it were possible (Waller 2015a, 45–49), causing serious damage to our emotion-based ethical judgments (Damasio 1994). But rather than *celebrating* the strike-back desire as the basis of righteous retribution, and affirming it through a system of moral responsibility, we should recognize it as an essential but dangerous desire that should be treated with caution. Blaming contributes to false beliefs concerning the character and emotions of those blamed, and it blocks deeper understanding of the actual causes of behavior. We will not eliminate—and probably should not wish to eliminate—the spontaneous but distorting blaming reaction. But strong belief in the moral responsibility system exacerbates those problems, while taking a more skeptical and inquiring and deeper perspective ameliorates them (Indermaur et al. 2012).

## Celebrating Strike-Back Emotions

There is a simple retributive justification for punishment: it is justly deserved. The strike-back passion at the foundation of retributivism is not merely acknowledged by retributivists, but celebrated. Michael S. Moore offers the example from Dostoyevsky's *Brothers Karamazov*, in which a cruel nobleman turns his vicious dogs loose on a small child, while the child's mother is forced to watch the child's murder. For Moore, the obvious moral of the story is that the nobleman:

> should suffer for his gratuitous and unjustified perpetration of a terrible wrong to both his young serf and that youth's mother. As even the gentle Aloysha murmurs in Dostoyevsky's novel, in answer to the question of what you do with the nobleman: you shoot him. You inflict such punishment even though no other good will be achieved thereby, but simply because the nobleman deserves it. The only general principle that makes sense of the mass of particular judgments like that of

Aloysha is the retributive principle that culpable wrongdoers must be punished. This, by my lights, is enough to justify retributivism.

(1997, 188)

Robert C. Solomon states:

Sometimes vengeance is wholly called for, even obligatory, and revenge is both legitimate and justified. Sometimes it is not, notably when one is mistaken about the offender or the offense. But to seek vengeance for a grievous wrong, to revenge oneself against evil—that seems to lie at the very foundation of our sense of justice, indeed, of our very sense of ourselves, our dignity, and our sense of right and wrong.

(2004, 37)

And while it may not be "justified" to seek vengeance "when one is mistaken about the offender or the offense," such mistakes are of much less concern than the desire to satisfy the strike-back motive. Solomon is right about "the very foundation of our sense of justice"; the legitimacy of that foundation and the retributive justice system built upon it is another matter.

The basic *primitive* emotional foundation is not retribution, but the strike-back emotion; and even deeper and more basic than *strike-back* at the *source* of our pain is the desire to "pass the pain along." When we finally reach retributive emotions, we are no longer operating with some basic "intuition," but with a combination of deep emotionally based motives. Retribution is based in the strike-back emotion, and it channels wrath in the general direction of the apparent cause of the suffering. This is a refinement of the generalized emotional desire to inflict pain on *whatever* is handy. But the basic desire to pass the pain along remains, and remains fundamental, and as a result we are unlikely to be scrupulous in selecting the target of our attack. Another element of retributivism is the belief in a just world (discussed in the following chapter), that reassures us that since we must strike-back (the desire to pass the pain along is powerful) we are morally justified in doing so: in a *just* world, unjust acts cannot be required of us. This is no longer a basic desire to strike-back at *something*, but a sense of *righteous retribution* that aims suffering at someone who justly deserves to suffer.

We want and need to strike back, or pass the pain along; and when we combine that with a just world belief then retribution becomes righteous, and approved by God. When we recognize that we must punish, it comes full circle: we must, so it must be just (in our just world). Belief in moral responsibility and just deserts and "righteous retribution" seems an obvious and almost indubitable belief. Peter van Inwagen makes the depth and certainty of that belief evident: "To deny the free-will thesis is to deny the existence of moral responsibility, which would be absurd" (1983, 223). That is hardly surprising. The belief is locked in place by a pair of deep and powerful motives: the strike-back motive, and the deeply comforting belief in a just world. Of course, the strike-back desire is grossly inaccurate, and belief in a just world is obviously false; but they are strong emotional commitments, often operating nonconsciously (especially our belief in a just world), so they are seldom subjected to careful scrutiny.

As Frans De Waal notes, we should not reject an emotion because of its history of development:

> Even if a diamond owes its beauty to millions of years of crushing pressure, we rarely think of this fact when admiring the gem. So why should we let the ruthlessness of natural selection distract from the wonders it has produced? Humans and other animals have been endowed with a capacity for genuine love, sympathy, and care—a fact that can and will one day be fully reconciled with the idea that genetic self-promotion drives the evolutionary process.
>
> (De Waal 1996, 16–17)

Natural selection also produced a powerful strike-back motive; but primitive emotions don't always result in diamonds. If we need any reminder of that fact, racism and tribalism are always handy.

The retributive "intuition" is a primitive emotion combined with a false belief: strike-back emotion combined with belief in just world. It is a deep and strong emotion; but that is reason to fear and control it, not grounds to celebrate it. We should not judge it negatively because it grew up on the wrong side of the tracks; rather, judge it on its own merits. Its merits are few, if any (it is not a protector of innocents); and its faults are many (the blocking of deeper inquiry being the most basic). There is no doubt that we feel strike-back desire, and it may well be that we do not wish to stop feeling it (the way we wish we *could* stop feeling racist or sexist or tribalist emotions). It may be an essential emotional force, but it is not essential that we honor it as righteous retribution.

# 5 A Just World, Moral Responsibility, and the Justice of Punishment

Ah, love, could you and I with him conspire,
To grasp this sorry scheme of things entire,
Would not we shatter it to bits?
And then remold it nearer to the heart's desire?
>                    The Rubáiyát of Omar Khayyám, trans. Edward Fitzgerald

Malt does more than Milton can,
To justify God's ways to man.
>                                                                       A. E. Housman

Adina Roskies (2014, 121) opts for compatibilism because it "preserves perhaps the most vivid of our intuitions about human behavior: that, given certain circumstances, we are responsible for our choices and actions." Vivid it certainly is, but the vividness of this "intuition" carries no justificatory weight. "Vivid intuitions"—from belief in God to belief in evil spirits, from certainty that the Earth is stationary to the certainty of fixed species, from the evil of homosexuality to the superiority of my ethnic group—do not have a strong track record. Our strike-back desire meshes with our deep belief in a just world to form a powerful moral responsibility "intuition"; but that does not enhance its plausibility.

## Belief in a Just World

The "vivid intuition" of moral responsibility is the combined result of two deep impulses. The essential deep foundation for belief in retributivism and the moral responsibility system is the strike-back desire. But in order for that desire to grow into the vivid "intuition" of retributive moral responsibility, it required an additional element: belief in a just world. The pioneer researcher into just world beliefs, Melvin Lerner, called belief in a just world a "fundamental delusion" (1980). Adrian Furnham gives this brief account of the basic belief in a just world (BJW): "The BJW asserts that, quite justly, good things tend to happen to good people and bad things to bad people despite the fact that this is patently not the case" (2003, 795). The belief is widely—though usually nonconsciously—held, though the grounds for that belief have long since disappeared (disappeared, at least, from the naturalistic world view championed by most contemporary philosophers).

Determining the origins of belief in a just world is probably impossible. Did belief in a just world convince humans that the god who directs that world must be orderly and just? Or did belief in a just god motivate belief in a just world? Probably belief in a just and orderly world promoted belief in a just god governing and ordering that world. In any case, it is worth noting that in his comparative youth, the Hebraic god was hardly a paragon of justice, and in fact not even consistent or orderly. To the contrary, he was a rather capricious god, who acted without thinking, changed his mind, lost his temper, and seemed arbitrary in his allegiances and enemies. This youthful god had little interest in justice; his motto seemed to be something like: "If you have as much power as I have, you need not worry about justice." Job was—as God acknowledged—"a perfect and an upright man, one that feareth God, and escheweth evil" (Job 1:8); but on a silly dare with Satan, God allowed the death of all Job's children and the destruction of all his property, and then Job was smitten "with sore boils from the sole of his foot unto his crown" (Job 2:7) Not surprisingly, Job expressed his disappointment with this treatment. God swiftly put Job in his place but said nothing about why his treatment of Job is just, instead giving a harsh lecture on his awesome power and the comparative insignificance of puny humans:

> Where wast thou when I laid the foundations of the earth? declare, if thou hast understanding. . . . Whereupon are the foundations thereof fastened? Or who laid the corner stone thereof; When the morning stars sang together, and all the sons of God shouted for joy? Or who shut up the sea with doors?. . . . Canst thou draw out leviathan with an hook?
>
> (Job 38:4 and 6–8; 41:1)

Furthermore, if Job complains that he is a just man who received unjust treatment from God, that implies God is unjust; an outcome that God makes clear is an unacceptable alternative:

> Then answered the Lord unto Job out of the whirlwind, and said, Gird up thy loins now like a man: I will demand of thee, and declare thou unto me. Wilt thou also disannul my judgment? Wilt thou condemn me, that thou mayest be righteous? Hast thou an arm like God? Or canst thou thunder with a voice like him?
>
> (Job 40:7–9)

Or in short, who are *you* to question God? *Whatever* I do to you *must* be just, and you are not to question God's judgments and ways.

One might well fear this tempestuous god, but it would be hard to consider him just, and implausible to suppose that such a deity would fashion and govern a just world. For a tribe of nomadic warriors, the world is a dangerous and disorderly place, and the god in charge of it is known by the disorderly world he manages. But eventually—as settled farmers watch closely the signs and the seasons—God becomes more orderly, more concerned with justice, and begins to take an active interest in running a just world.

Once the Hebrew god grows up and becomes steady and orderly and just—and particularly when this god takes on omniscient and omnipotent characteristics and becomes the Christian god—some serious problems emerge. There are the obvious problems of how a passionate personal creator god who constantly intervenes in his creation can merge with the impersonal Aristotelian god that is not a creator, never intervenes, and has no emotions whatsoever: problems that have perplexed Christian theologians for centuries. But there is another problem, more immediate and disturbing than the esoteric questions debated in the monasteries and universities: how can a *just* god knowingly and purposefully create millions of humans who are hopelessly fated for eternal torture? Since all power—including all power of choice—belongs to *omni*potent god, these unfortunate hell-destined creatures can do nothing to avoid their cruel fates. The nature of the trinity is one thing, and the Franciscans and Jesuits and Dominicans can debate that from morning to night; but this idea that I will be tortured for all eternity, that I was destined for such damnation long before I was born, and there is nothing I can do to avoid this horrific destiny: that is a serious and troubling problem, whether priest, prince or peasant. How could an omnipotent god construct me in such a form that I am inescapably evil, *know* (as an omniscient god) that I am necessarily corrupt (and that I will not be one of the lucky few who receive the gift of grace), and then *justly* condemn this helpless creature to eternal torment?

Christian theologians from Augustine to Aquinas struggled with the problem, but with little success. Finally they gave up, threw in the towel, decided that the problem was beyond human understanding, and insisted we must accept on faith the justice of eternally torturing multitudes who have no power to avoid such torture. The great humanist scholar of the fifteenth century, Lorenzo Valla, concluded that the problem was beyond human understanding, and that we must accept by faith that God is just:

> Indeed the most worthy reason may be adduced as to why He hardens this one and shows mercy to that, namely, that He is most wise and good. For it is impious to believe otherwise than that, being absolutely good, He does rightly.
>
> (1443/1948, 176–177)

Therefore the understanding of God's justice is something we should not seek, much less question:

> Let us therefore shun greedy knowledge of high things. . . . I will no longer be anxious about this question lest by investigating the majesty of God I might be blinded by his light.
>
> (1443/1948, 181)

And in the next century Martin Luther would champion the same conclusion:

> This is the highest degree of faith—to believe that He is merciful, who saves so few and damns so many; to believe Him just, who according to His own will makes us necessarily damnable. . . . If, therefore, I could by any means comprehend how that same God can be merciful and just who carries the appearance of so much wrath and iniquity, there would be no need of faith. But now, since that cannot be comprehended, there is room for exercising faith.
>
> (1525/1823, section 24)

Apparently Luther had sufficient faith to believe that God's punishment is just when he burns multitudes of sinners in eternal fire for the way this same omnipotent God made them. Paul the Apostle also regarded such treatment of the damned as just:

> Therefore hath he mercy on whom he will have mercy, and whom he will he hardeneth. Thou wilt say then unto me, Why doth he yet find fault? For who hath resisted his will? Nay but, O man, who art thou that repliest against God? Shall the thing formed say to him that formed it, Why hast thou made me thus? Hath not the potter power over the clay, of the same lump to make one vessel unto honor, and another unto dishonor?
>
> (Romans 9:18–21)

But few people can muster that level of faith. Try as you will, this appears to be a god of "wrath and iniquity" rather than a god of mercy and justice.

This was a desperate problem, and desperate problems prompt desperate measures: in this case, the desperate solution that humans have godlike *causa sui* powers as "unmoved movers." This was a solution congenial to the human ego: we are very special, and God gives us a special gift of free will that breaks the causal chain; we are like gods, we are capable of being first causes. This was the "solution" offered by Pico della Mirandola in the late fifteenth century—a solution to Valla's problem that was very different from the "solution" of abject faith favored by Luther a few years later. Pico's solution was quite radical: God grants to humans (God's last and favorite creation) godlike powers of first cause self-making:

> The nature of all other beings is limited and constrained within the bounds of laws prescribed by Us. Thou, constrained by no limits, in accordance with thine own free will, in whose hand We have placed thee, shalt ordain for thyself the limits of thy nature. We have set thee at the world's center that thou mayest from thence more easily observe whatever is in the world. We have made thee neither of heaven nor of earth, neither mortal nor immortal, so that with freedom of choice and

with honor, as though the maker and molder of thyself, thou mayest fashion thyself in whatever shape thou shalt prefer. Thou shalt have the power to degenerate into the lower forms of life, which are brutish. Thou shalt have the power, out of thy soul's judgment, to be reborn into the higher forms, which are divine.

(1486/1948, 225)

That "solution" was heretical, of course. After all, if humans have godlike powers—even if those powers are a gift from God—then God may now be quite powerful, but he no longer has *all* power, he is no longer *omni*potent but only very potent. John Calvin might be outraged by any reduction in God's majestic power, but most of the faithful found it perfectly acceptable: much better to have a god with less power and more justice than a god with total power and no justice. Heretical though it was, this solution was too attractive to resist (though both Catholics and early Protestants struggled to suppress it), and—though rejected by the theological hierarchy—it eventually became the dominant view of the faithful (both Catholic and Protestant), and remains so to this day. God's punishments and rewards are *just*, because each of us has the special power of choice to embrace or reject salvation, and each of us could literally go *either way*, and nothing determines which path we take save our own undetermined free choice.

So how does this work? God—and God's Earthly authorities—mete out harsh punishments; such punishments *must* be just (because they come directly or indirectly from a just god); so we must justly deserve such punishment (we must be morally responsible). And that requires that we have godlike powers. Of course, most philosophers no longer believe in a just god (or any god), or in miracles by either gods or godlike humans, or—consciously— in a just world. Nonetheless, many still hold the deep belief in moral responsibility together with the *deeper* nonconscious belief in a just world, though the foundation for those beliefs has long since disappeared.

## Stubborn Belief in a Just World

Once the idea of a just world—governed by a just god, or by just cosmic forces—takes hold, it becomes deeply entrenched. When the grounds for that belief are destroyed, the belief remains strong—perhaps even stronger, since its powerful influence now operates nonconsciously. It is a widespread belief, both in Western and Asiatic cultures: what goes around comes around, justice will be served, "Everything happens for a reason," "All things happen for good, for those who love God and keep his commandments"; or as Alexander Pope famously declared in *An Essay on Man*:

> All nature is but art, unknown to thee;
> All chance, direction, which thou canst not see.
> All discord, harmony, not understood;
> All partial evil, universal good:

> And, spite of pride, in erring reason's spite,
> One truth is clear, Whatever is, is right.

Sharon Salzberg (a best-selling self-improvement author and teacher of Buddhist meditation practices) insists: "Things don't just happen in this world of arising and passing away. We don't live in some kind of crazy, accidental universe. Things happen according to certain laws, laws of nature. Laws such as the law of karma, which teaches us that as a certain seed gets planted, so will that fruit be" (Salzberg 2010). In our just world we get what we justly deserve—even if justice requires additional life cycles.

Belief in a just world is comforting, it may be inspiring, and it is certainly in some respects a beneficial belief. As Lerner and Miller point out, the belief in a just world may motivate positive behavior and combat the sense of helplessness:

> Individuals have a need to believe that they live in a world where people generally get what they deserve. The belief that the world is just enables the individual to confront his physical and social environments as though they were stable and orderly. Without such a belief it would be difficult for the individual to commit himself to the pursuit of long range goals or even to the socially regulated behaviour of day to day life.
>
> (1978, 1030–31)

Belief in a just world is not a human universal, and clearly there have been cultures that were skeptical of any claim that we live in a just world. The god of Adam and Abraham and Moses seemed more capricious and arbitrary than just; and the ancient Greeks during the period of the great Greek dramatists clearly recognized that the world is not a just world: some people exert heroic efforts to live virtuously and avoid evil and still—like the unfortunate Oedipus, who strives to live a life of honor and virtue but commits the horrific double crime of patricide and marrying his mother—come to a very bad end indeed; others—such as Agamemnon (as described by Bernard Williams 1993, 132–133)—face forced choices between terrible wrongs, and live in a world in which acting justly is impossible.

Like the ancient Greek dramatists, Jesus of Nazareth recognized that the world is unjust. One of his most famous—and most often misrepresented—parables makes precisely that point. The parable of the talents (found in the Gospels of Matthew and Luke) tells of a wealthy man who must travel to a far country, and who assigns three of his servants to manage his affairs while he is away. To one servant he gave five talents (measures) of gold, to another two, and to a third only one. The servant who received five talents "went and traded with the same, and made them other five talents" (Matt. 25:16), and the servant with two talents also doubled the master's money. When the master returns he is well pleased with those two servants, and makes each a "ruler over many things." But the servant with one talent was not so fortunate:

> Then he which had received the one talent came and said, Lord, I knew thee that thou art an hard man, reaping where thou hast not sown, and gathering where thou hast not strawed: And I was afraid, and went and hid thy talent in the earth: lo, there thou hast that is thine.
>
> His lord answered and said unto him, Thou wicked and slothful servant, thou knewest that I reap where I sowed not, and gather where I have not strawed: Thou oughtest therefore to have put my money to the exchangers, and then at my coming I should have received mine own with usury. Take therefore the talent from him, and give it unto him which hath ten talents. For unto every one that hath shall be given, and he shall have abundance: but from him that hath not shall be taken away even that which he hath.
>
> (Matt. 25: 24–29)

Who is this wealthy man who praises the servants who doubled his money and condemns the servant who simply returned to the master that and only that which is rightfully his? Contemporary Christians typically imagine that this wealthy master represents God, who is well-pleased by those who accumulate more wealth and "get ahead." He obviously does not (Herzog 1994). To the contrary, this master is a "hard man, reaping where thou hast not sown, and gathering where thou hast not strawed." He demands that his servants lend out his money at high interest to those who are in need—the exploitative practice of *usury*, which was universally condemned among the Jewish people. In the very similar version told in the Gospel of Luke, the character of this powerful and wealthy but cruel and unscrupulous man is made clear: "But his citizens hated him, and sent a message after him, saying, We will not have this man to reign over us" (Luke 19:14). Cruel, avaricious, and unscrupulous: in the parable of the talents, this master does not represent God; rather, he represents those who hold power in this *unjust* world. And those who "get ahead" in this unjust world—like the master's two servants who are made "rulers over many things"—are likely to be those who join in the unjust treatment of those who are weaker, "reaping where they do not sow" and taking from the poor by exploitative practices such as usury. The hero of the story is the servant who returns to the master only what is rightly his, and refuses to oppress and exploit others to satisfy the master's greed. He is *not* the servant who is rewarded in this unjust world, but instead the one who is treated harshly. Jesus makes the moral of the story plain:

> For unto every one that hath shall be given, and he shall have abundance: but from him that hath not shall be taken away even that which he hath.
>
> (Matthew 26:29)

The rich get richer and have more than they need, and the poor get exploited. That's the way of the world, as Jesus makes brutally clear; but it is not the way of a just world.

Contemporary Christians typically interpret this parable to mean precisely the *opposite* of what Jesus taught (even when they realize that the "talents" of the story are measures of gold, rather than special abilities). That is not surprising; after all, the belief in a just world runs deep, it is solidified by the Christian belief in a just and omnipotent God who governs the cosmos, and it is hard for Christians to imagine that Jesus is teaching something entirely different. So most Christians take the moral of the story to be that if you work hard and use your "talents" well, you will be rewarded; but if you are lethargic or waste your talents and do not use them wisely, then you will be justly punished.

Like most contemporary Christians, Paul of Tarsus believed in a just world: "Be not deceived; God is not mocked: for whatsoever a man soweth, that shall he also reap" (Galatians 6:7). A similar idea is found in the Hindu tradition: "As a man himself sows, so he himself reaps; no man inherits the good or evil act of another man. The fruit is of the same quality as the action" (Mahabharata, xii.291.22). But Jesus knew that there are many who "reap where they did not sow," and that those who do the hard work of sowing often are deprived of any benefits, and exploited by those who practice usury. Jesus knew that Roman might does not equal right; and like all Jews, he was painfully aware that in contests between virtue and Roman might, virtue had suffered a sad string of defeats. The world in which Jesus lived was not just, and he recognized the injustice: neither the prosperous nor the impoverished are receiving their just deserts.

The implausible just world belief is so strong that rather than abandon it in the face of compelling counter evidence, believers invent even more implausible metaphysical machinery to preserve the otherwise falsified belief in a just world. It is true that in all our worldly experience, the wicked prosper while the virtuous suffer; but in the afterlife, we virtuous ones will be rewarded and the wicked will get theirs. One of the most difficult challenges for belief in a just world is the suffering of small children: how can the suffering of innocent children be squared with belief in a just world? A striking example of the extraordinary measures taken to defend the comfortable belief in a just world can be found in the writings of Eileen Gardner, whose written work came to light after she was appointed by William Bennett (Ronald Reagan's Secretary of Education) as special assistant in the Office of Educational Philosophy and Practice. Gardner had written that children with severe disabilities should not receive special aid, because they justly deserve their suffering. Their vile behavior in a previous life resulted in an inferior "level of inner spiritual development" which brought justified suffering upon themselves: "They falsely assume that the lottery of life has penalized them at random. This is not so. Nothing comes to an individual that he has not, at some point in his development, summoned" (quoted in McCombs 1985). Outrageous and ugly as this view may be when stated baldly, it is in fact a powerful and widespread belief: often at the nonconscious level, but openly affirmed in the doctrine of karma. If belief in a just world requires an afterlife of pearly gates and streets of gold, then such a place *must* exist. If belief in a just world requires believing that the child who is suffering is somehow the reembodiment of some evil person (never mind how we can make any sense whatsoever of an identity between myself and some person in an earlier age about whom I remember nothing and with whom I have almost nothing in common save an inscrutable soul) then somehow souls must go through bodily cycles. This is a classic case of explaining the implausible by appeal to the absurd.

We might be tempted to suppose that the "folk" are inveigled by belief in a just world, while philosophers rise above it. But in fact the history of Western philosophy is permeated with belief in a just world. Bernard Williams (1993) gives a brilliant account of the deep philosophical influence of belief in a just world. Plato is the exemplar of a philosopher motivated by belief in a just world; and perhaps it is clearest in Plato because he is operating in the context of a culture—as manifested in Greek drama—that *rejects* belief in a just world. Plato's great work, *The Republic*, is designed to answer Glaucon's challenge, and prove that the world *is* just (appearances to the contrary), and that the virtuous person will always live better than the vicious person (even if the latter holds the ring of Gyges and a position of power and has a wonderful—but false—reputation for virtue).

Plato is by no means the only philosophical defender of belief in a just world. Aristotle builds his ethical theory on that belief: the world is such that the virtuous person will (usually) flourish and find genuine happiness; indeed, such flourishing is the mark of genuine virtue. In Kant, belief in a just world probably achieves its philosophical apex: the world *must* be such that we can have free will and practice virtue, and the world must be such that whenever we have an obligation we have the means of fulfilling that obligation: *ought* implies *can*. Not surprisingly, natural law theorists build their views on belief in a just world; but at least they are entitled to do so, since they can build on a foundation of belief in a just and omnipotent Creator who imposes a just order on his creation.

Bernard Williams describes a key element of philosophical history:

> Plato, Aristotle, Kant, Hegel are all on the same side, all believing in one way or another that the universe or history or the structure of human reason can, when properly understood, yield a pattern that makes sense of human life and human aspirations.
>
> (1993, 163)

Justice is built into the world order, on their view. Contemporary philosophers, Williams notes, no longer claim that the world is just, and contemporary philosophical work shares this basic perspective with the ancient Greek dramatists:

> We are in an ethical condition that lies not only beyond Christianity, but beyond its Kantian and its Heglian legacies. . . . We know that the world was not made for us, or we for the world, that our history tells no purposive story, and that there is no position outside the world or outside history from which we might hope to authenticate our activities. We have to acknowledge the hideous costs of many human achievements that we value, including this reflective sense itself, and recognise that there is no redemptive Hegelian history or universal Leibnizian cost-benefit analysis to show that it will come out well enough in the end. . . . We are like those who, from the fifth century and earlier, have left us traces of a consciousness that had not yet been touched by Plato's and Aristotle's attempts to make our ethical relations to the world fully intelligible.
>
> (1993, 166)

Williams is obviously correct that most contemporary philosophers do not consciously believe in a just world, but that is hardly surprising. Could any minimally reflective and observant person imagine that we live in a just world? We live in a world in which ethnic groups suffer discrimination and even genocide, in which children die from drought and starvation and painful diseases, a world in which innocent people are caught up in warfare, in which tens of thousands are displaced from their homes and live in the desperation of refugee camps (or die in vain efforts to reach such camps). Using the methods of science we have discovered a great deal about the natural order; but careful scrutiny does not reveal any *just* moral order. If there is any moral order to our observable world, it is the same order that Jesus observed many centuries ago: to him that hath shall be given, and he shall have abundance: but from him that hath not shall be taken away even that which he hath. A *just* moral order is not a feature of our world. But *belief* in a just world has not disappeared; rather, it has gone underground, and lodged deep in our nonconscious belief system.

Contemporary philosophers—who generally reject miracles and mysteries and cycles of life in which *ultimately* the good will triumph—know that the world is not fair and just, and we do not reap what we sow (and even when we do reap what we sow, we are sowing different qualities of seed over different qualities of soil with widely divergent agricultural skills and knowledge); or at least they know it when they consciously scrutinize the belief. But belief in a just world usually operates nonconsciously, and exerts its subtle influence on not only the folk, but also on philosophers, including many of the most impressive members of the philosophical tribe.

Daniel Dennett and George Sher are rigorous and insightful philosophers who are well-informed concerning contemporary research in the sciences (including psychology and biology) as well as being wise in the ways of the world. Neither clings to any conscious belief in a just world in which the virtuous and the vicious reap what they sow, nor do they believe that the world is inherently fair and that we all enjoy essentially equal opportunity. But their *non*conscious belief in a just world exerts a powerful influence on their ideas and arguments; and the fact that both are well aware of the force exerted by nonconscious cognitive operations does not shield them from that influence. Consider one of the many inventive arguments Dennett offers in favor of the moral legitimacy of holding people morally responsible:

> Suppose—what certainly seems to be true—that people are born with noticeably different cognitive endowments and propensities to develop character traits. . . . Is this 'hideously unfair' . . . or is this bound to lead to something hideously unfair? Not necessarily.
>
> Imagine a footrace in which the starting line was staggered: those with birthdays in January start a yard ahead of those born in February, and eleven yards ahead of those born in December. Surely no one can help being born in one month rather than another. Isn't this markedly unfair? Yes, if the race is a hundred yard dash. No, if it's a marathon. In a marathon such a relatively small initial advantage would count for nothing, since one can reliably expect other fortuitous breaks to have even greater effects. . . . Is it fair enough not to be worth worrying about? Of course. After all, luck averages out in the long run.
>
> (1984, 95)

Dennett is thoroughly familiar with the relevant psychological research and he is an astute observer, and he certainly knows—when he is not under the powerful nonconscious influence of belief in a just world—that it is *not* the case that "luck averages out in the long run." Initial advantages are more likely to be augmented by additional advantages, while initial disadvantages typically result in greater long term handicaps. In our society, the cumulative advantages of being born into affluence are too obvious to require comment; but staying with sports metaphors, the subsequent cumulative dramatic differences that typically result from small initial differences in starting points are easy to track. Emma and Isabella are youthful soccer players of somewhat similar abilities, though Emma has a slight edge (Emma had a luckier starting point, since her mother played soccer and they often kicked a soccer ball together at the park). When the two wind up on the same youth team, Emma gets a bit more attention and encouragement from her coach, somewhat more playing time, and she plays positions that require more ball handling—and Emma's skills, stamina, and confidence gradually distance themselves from Isabella's. At the end of the season, Emma is picked for the all-star team (Isabella is not), and plays more games against better competition and with better coaching. The next year, Isabella remains in the recreational league, while Emma is selected for a traveling team that plays many more games and has intensive practices run by a professional coach with a well-designed workout schedule: within a very few years, the small gap between Emma and Isabella becomes a chasm. A similar process could be outlined for small initial differences in schoolwork that ultimately result in enormous differences in educational accomplishments (and career prospects). The cumulative effect of initial differences in malnutrition, lead-poisoning, and childhood abuse are painfully obvious. This does not imply that the respective "fates" of Emma and Isabella are fixed and finalized at a tender age. But deep belief in a just world motivates belief in "equal opportunity" and "roughly equal chances"—so that everyone "justly deserves" what they wind up with; and that insidious but comfortable belief is a pernicious myth.

I do not mean to suggest that Dennett is unaware of the problem of unequal opportunity, or that he does not take it seriously; to the contrary, he is and he does. But deep nonconscious belief in a just world inclines us to think that the world is fairer than it is, and particularly that the system in which we live—and in which we enjoy privileged positions (as everyone who reads this book does)—is fair, or at least fair enough.

George Sher is a philosopher who is both well-informed and quite concerned about the many subtle psychological processes that shape our behavior (Sher 2009); but that knowledge does not immunize him against the nonconscious influence of belief in a just world, as evidenced by his account of the fair opportunity afforded by the distribution of talents and abilities:

> Even if M is initially stronger or more intelligent than N, this difference will only entail that M does not deserve what he has achieved relative to N if the difference between them has made it impossible for N to achieve as much as M. However, differences in strength, intelligence, and other native gifts are rarely so pronounced as to have this effect. The far more common effect of such differences is merely to make it more *difficult* for the less talented person to reach a given level of attainment. He must work harder, husband his resources more carefully, plan more shrewdly, and so on.
>
> (1987, 31–32)

The story of Emma and Isabella—and their distinctly different trajectories—will also serve to illustrate the problems in Sher's model of how differences in talents can be overcome by superior effort and planning. By comparison to Emma, Isabella is "the less talented person"; but it is not the case that Isabella's capacity to work harder and plan more shrewdly offsets Emma's talent advantage; to the contrary, Emma is also likely to gain the cumulative advantages of greater fortitude and shrewder planning (the invaluable "court savvy" she gains by additional play against better opponents). As Emma plays more and gains better coaching and superior conditioning, she develops greater endurance and fortitude. Her self-confidence (her sense of self-efficacy) is enhanced. Greater fortitude, superior self-confidence, enhanced ability to plan shrewdly: these are not passed out in a natural lottery governed by principles of fairness; rather, they tend to cluster with other advantages. Once again, this is not a matter of Isabella's inferior prospects being governed by implacable fate; but it is a much more realistic picture than the just and equitable world imagined by Sher.

Sher's story of N—who overcomes the disadvantage of being weaker or less intelligent by working harder—is charming and inspiring, and stories of that type are perenially popular: the Forrest Gump movie, the story of Dick Whittington ("Turn again, Whittington, Lord Mayor of London"), Oliver Twist, Cinderella, Horatio Alger, the Little Engine That Could. The Little Engine That Could didn't have the power of the big locomotives, but nonetheless made it to the top of the mountain through fortitude and determination. We love these stories: the resolute tortoise outraces the lethargic hare, the little engine scales the great mountain, Ragged Dick (one of Horatio Alger's heroes) starts as a homeless boot-black on the New York City streets but—thanks to his energy, industriousness, honesty, and optimistic attitude—achieves success and security. Perhaps it is good to tell such stories to our children: you *can* succeed, you *can* overcome obstacles and disadvantages. When children hear such stories, that may encourage their efforts. Still, the stories are typically fiction. Some people do rise from poverty to riches by great luck, special abilities, or brutal ruthlessness, but they are rare exceptions; and those few help to perpetuate the myth, especially in the United States, where upward social mobility is in fact rare—even less common than in most of Europe. Sometimes attributes balance out, and superior fortitude makes up for superior skill. But that's rare: More commonly the fortitude and skill are joined, as inferior skill results in lethargy.

## The Harmful Effects of Belief in a Just World

Our children need to know that they can overcome obstacles, and they should be encouraged to do so. But the children whose loving elders read to them the story of The Little Engine That Could are already the lucky ones. They grow up believing they can overcome obstacles, they develop fortitude as the adults around them give them tasks at which they can succeed when they try, and they develop both their self-confidence and their powers of making sustained efforts; and those who care for them make sure that the children do not gain success with no efforts of their own, and take care that the tasks set for them are not so difficult that their efforts will result in repeated failures (results that shape lethargy and a weakened sense of self-efficacy). But the other edge of that sword is the harmful conviction that since I succeeded through effort and pluck, so can *anyone*; and anyone who does not succeed justly deserves to suffer deprivation, while I justly deserve the fruits of my labor. The Little Engine That Could climbed the mountain, the persistent tortoise won the race, and I achieved success through my own individual efforts, and those who fail have no one to blame but themselves. It is easy to believe that the world is just and everyone had equal opportunities from a perch on top of the mountain; sadly, even those who are far down in the valley often absorb the same lesson, and add bitter self-recrimination to their cumulative disadvantages.

As already noted, there are benefits to belief in a just world: it gives us a sense of order, and hopefulness, and at least some sense of control. If the world is *just*, then my good honest efforts should be rewarded, and I have greater motivation to make such efforts. But it is a deeply entrenched, largely nonconscious belief that also results in great harms (Furnham 2003; Hafer and Bègue 2005). While it may have been more beneficial than detrimental in earlier centuries—at a time when our resources for exploring causes and conditions were quite limited—we have long since reached the point at which the enormous harms of belief in a just world far outweigh the limited advantages. The basic harm that results from (nonconscious) belief in a just world—and the harm most extensively studied by researchers on belief in a just world—is the harm of *blaming the victim*.

Belief in a just world provides a sense of comfort and order and reassurance: if I behave well in this just world, then I will be safe and secure. But that belief is under constant threat, as we observe innocent children afflicted with terrible diseases, innocent people who are killed (or lose their families) in earthquakes, tsunamis, ethnic purges; innocent people who are victims of brutal and traumatizing violent rape. How can the comforting belief in a just world be preserved in the face of such suffering visited upon innocents? The solution is easy: the "victims" must not have been so innocent after all. The impoverished person who cannot find work is not really trying, or is improvident, or in any case brought this misfortune on himself. The tsunami victims did not take adequate precautions—or perhaps they offended God by rejecting the true religion. The victim of rape—the most extensively studied example—did something to invite the attack: she "led him on," she "dressed provocatively," she drank too much, she is a promiscuous person, she acted recklessly in accepting a ride. She *must* have done; otherwise I and my loved ones—who are good people—could be subject to the same sort of brutal attack, and the comfort of living in a just world is shattered. Those with the strongest belief in a just world are also those most inclined to blame victims for their misfortune (Wagstaff 1983; Furnham and Gunter 1984; Harper and Manasse1992; Dalbert and Yamauchi 1994; and Montada 1998). Belief in a just world exacerbates the pain suffered by victims, as they are not only blamed by others but also blame themselves (Lerner 1980, 123–125). This is deeply entrenched, and is manifest even in small children: if I had been a better child, Mommy and Daddy would not have divorced; if I were good, I would not suffer such abuse.

## A Just World Requires Moral Responsibility

There are other harms—deeper and more systemic—that flow from belief in a just world. Belief in a just world joins with strike-back emotions to form the foundation for the moral responsibility system: the system of blame and just deserts and righteous retribution. Belief in a just world motivates belief in moral responsibility because moral responsibility is required to make punitive measures *just*. Start from the recognition that punishment cannot be avoided. We may try to keep it to a minimum and struggle to reduce the harshness and cruelty and degradation that is often involved in punishment, but no society has been able to eliminate punishment.

So long as the world is not just, there is no problem of justifying punishment. The Hebrew god might visit his wrath on the adversaries of the Israelites, and might allow Job to be treated very harshly indeed by Satan; and in Greek drama, a character might be placed in a situation in which wrongdoing is inevitable and is still severely punished; but the *justice* of such punishment was not a question of great interest. Why should we expect justice in a cosmos of arbitrary gods and general disorder? But when the world and its gods became just, and punishment remained necessary, then the punishment itself had to be *just*. In a just world, anything you *must* do (including the infliction of punishment) cannot be unjust. So we must punish, and therefore punishing must be just; but what can make punishment just? Punishment is just if the person punished *justly deserves* to be punished: it is just if the person punished is *morally responsible* for the act that is punished. Once the world (and its gods) becomes just, then *moral responsibility* is needed to keep the world and its essential punitive activities just. Belief in moral responsibility is the harsh companion of the cruel belief in a just world.

Belief in a just world seeps deep into both the folk and the philosophical nonconscious belief systems, and yields a widely accepted but profoundly implausible philosophical shibboleth: the principle that *ought implies can*. For Kant, "ought implies can" is legitimate; Kant's ontology contains a just god, and that god maintains a just order; and this just god would not play such vile tricks as *forcing* us to commit a wrong that we *ought* not do. But contemporary naturalistic philosophers have no such godly assurance. This is not a just world created and directed by a just god. Rather (as Darwin observed) it is a world to inspire a devil's chaplain. But while the foundation and plausibility of a just world has long since crumbled away, the deep nonconscious belief in a just world endures, and assures us that anything we *ought* to do is something we *can* do. And that belief pushes even deeper. Since ought implies can, it follows that *must implies just*, when dealing with punishment: If we ought not-punish, then we can not-punish; but it is not the case that we can not-punish (punishment is unavoidable); so—by *modus tollens*—it is *not* the case that we ought not-punish. We must punish, so punishment must be *justly* deserved; and because moral responsibility is essential for just deserts, we know that moral responsibility exists.

*Must* does not imply *just*. When we consider the violent character of Robert Harris, we know that we must lock him up; but when we consider the life of Robert Harris, we know that such treatment is not justly deserved, however *necessary* it may be. Why does it *seem obvious* that such incarceration is just? Only because we have a deeply entrenched belief in a just world, and ought implies can. We *must* do it, so it must be just. The ancient Greeks would have been perplexed at that inference; and so would we, were we not deeply immersed in the belief that the world is just. Robert Harris was a brutal person who did terrible things, and he's a lot like you: had you had the same background, with the same brutalizing history, you would also have become a moral monster (unless you contain some "divine spark" that Robert lacked—and if you do, it was a gift of grace, not of works). In that case, you would have done terrible things, just as Robert did; and you would have caused many innocent people great suffering, just as Robert did. But you would not justly deserve to suffer punishment; rather, your necessary "coerced seclusion" would be—as Levy (2011) says—the second of a set of double wrongs: the wrong of punishment which follows the initial wrong of your harsh early environment. At this point it may be a *necessary* wrong (we cannot turn back the clock and take the steps we should have taken to prevent the cruel treatment Robert received in childhood) but that does not make the punishment *just*.

It is comforting to imagine that we live in a just world, in which we justly deserve our comfortable station in that world and those who suffer are not innocent victims but are instead receiving justly deserved punishment. It is comforting to believe that there will never be a hopeless conflict between what we ought to do and our agential capacities, and comforting to believe that whatever is necessary for us to do must also be just. And it is comforting to believe that the punishment we strongly desire to inflict—the strike-back motive is powerful—is also *just*. It is hard to acknowledge that the world is not just, that we must sometimes impose punishments that are not just, and that we cannot avoid being active participants in unjust acts. We contrive elaborate schemes of moral responsibility and just deserts to avoid facing the deeply disturbing nature of our world and our unjust but unavoidable acts in that world. Such false comforts impose high costs on others, and ultimately high costs on ourselves. Examining the failure of efforts to make our punishment system fit into a just world is the task of the following chapters; examining the benefits of facing up to the inevitability of that failure is the work of the final chapters.

# 6 Does Denying Moral Responsibility Threaten Dignity, Rights, and Innocence?

The goal is to *eliminate* moral responsibility and just deserts, and replace the moral responsibility system entirely. But the denial of basic moral responsibility—the moral responsibility that supports just deserts—triggers fervent opposition and deep fears. One of the deepest fears is that without belief in moral responsibility and just deserts we would lose the foundation for personal dignity and individual rights and protection of the innocent. Justly deserved punishment counts everyone as a member of the kingdom of ends, as autonomous self-governed law givers. Anyone who does wrong is making a *choice* to do wrong, and that autonomous choice must be honored (rather than excused or explained away). It must be honored by punishing the person who freely chose wrong over right. It is only as autonomous morally responsible *persons*—Herbert Morris insists—that we have basic rights:

> First, that we have a right to punishment; second, that this right derives from a fundamental human right to be treated as a person; third, that this fundamental right is a natural, inalienable, and absolute right; and, fourth, that the denial of this right implies the denial of all moral rights and duties.
>
> (1968, 476)

For Morris, to be a "person" involves being morally responsible, because the only humans who are not persons are those who are deeply incompetent. Therefore, if we deny that an individual is morally responsible (and justly deserving of punishment for his or her misdeeds), then we must be classifying that individual as a nonperson who is incapable of making competent choices and decisions.

Treating everyone as incompetent to make decisions and choices would indeed be destructive of rights and dignity. But that is *not* the appropriate grounds for denying moral responsibility and just deserts.

## Fearing the Loss of Human Dignity

The belief that moral responsibility protects freedom and dignity is so strong that even those who are richly aware of the powerful case against moral responsibility are reluctant to completely relinquish it. Thomas W. Clark insists that we can and must keep the belief that we are justified in holding people morally responsible (on pragmatic grounds), and thus reassure everyone that the denial of libertarian free will "is no threat to responsibility, morality, or the social order" (1999, 282); and the implication appears to be that if we dropped moral responsibility altogether, then morality and the social order might well be imperiled. Galen Strawson gives a brilliant account of the "basic argument" against moral responsibility, but still insists that we can and should preserve belief in moral responsibility "in ordinary circumstances":

> One cannot institute oneself in such a way that one can take over true or assume moral responsibility for how one is in such a way that one can be truly morally responsible for what one does. This fact is not changed by the fact that we may be unable not to think of ourselves as truly morally responsible in ordinary circumstances. Nor is it changed by the fact that it may be a very good thing that we have this inability—so that we might wish to take steps to preserve it, if it looked to be in danger of fading.
>
> (2008, 335)

Derk Pereboom and Gregg Caruso (2016)—valiant leaders in the attack on moral responsibility—insist that although we cannot make sense of *basic* moral responsibility and just deserts (in the sense of truly deserving reward or punishment for one's acts), it remains vitally important that we maintain a system of forward-looking moral responsibility (in contrast to the abandoned retrospective version of moral responsibility that justifies retributivism).

The brilliant and resourceful champion of the effort to preserve belief in moral responsibility—the ultimate implausibility of that belief notwithstanding—is Saul Smilansky, who proposes an *illusionist* defense of moral responsibility. Smilansky has no illusions about the *implausibility* of basic moral responsibility and just deserts. He characterizes libertarian free will—which he claims is essential for genuine moral responsibility—as a fairy-tale, even while insisting we must cling to that fairy-tale because the "basic tenet of our view of ourselves and others which is the fairy-tale of libertarian free will is indispensable" (2000, 246).

Smilansky is committed to preserving the illusion of libertarian free will and moral responsibility, and his motives are pure. He is convinced that widespread belief in moral responsibility is essential for sustaining a substantive moral order: "We cannot envisage a civilized moral order bypassing individual agency and responsibility. . . . The idea of giving up blame is merely fanciful, but to give up on deep blame-*worthiness* is momentous and destructive of deep moral feeling, appreciation, and justification" (2000, 162–163). The moral responsibility that libertarian free will supports is vital, and belief in libertarian free will itself is a basic condition of a rich genuine ethical life:

> The very absence of libertarian free will . . . is shattering to those who realize it and have ethical and personal depth. The grounding for matters such as self-respect, deep ethical appreciation, justifying social practices on the basis of desert, true internal acceptance of responsibility and remorse, and even our view of our loved ones, is *diluted*.
>
> (2000, 190)

I do not believe in libertarian free will, and the experience has not been shattering; to the contrary it opens the way to inquiries that are not blocked by gods, miracles, mysteries, or the principled myopia of compatibilism. The possibility of learning without limits about the natural world and the human animals that inhabit it more than compensates any supposed loss. This might seem to confirm what some have long suspected: that I lack "ethical and personal depth." But of course Smilansky himself does not really believe in libertarian free will; and he is certainly a person of ethical and personal depth, who is by no means *shattered* by that absence of belief. So perhaps the rejection of libertarian free will and just deserts and moral responsibility is not quite so vital for our ethical lives as Smilansky suggests. The supposed perils of abandoning belief in moral responsibility are serious perils indeed, according to Smilansky:

> One can let oneself be somewhat influenced by hard determinism, as a cure for an over-expanded ego, or as a means of shedding some of the burden of remorse. . . . But it is hard to see a serious experimental attempt at internalizing the truth about the free will problem [that there is no libertarian free will and thus no basic moral responsibility] as ending in happiness. To attempt to disengage from the 'quasi-compatibilist' 'form of life' [which embraces belief in moral responsibility] is to risk one's social integration, reactive feelings, self-respect, and perhaps personal integration. It is to risk one's mental health.
>
> (2000, 255)

If the denial of moral responsibility carried such risks, it would be rash indeed to reject belief in moral responsibility, and we would be well-advised to maintain any illusion that could preserve that belief. These dangers have been warned of so often by philosophers that they seem like common knowledge; in fact, they are common beliefs the plausibility of which rests on false assumptions, mistaken beliefs about the grounds for denying moral responsibility, and the numbing power of repetition.

It is false that the rejection of moral responsibility poses risks to "one's social integration, reactive feelings, self-respect, and perhaps personal integration." To the contrary, it is the commitment to moral responsibility that threatens social integration and self-respect and personal dignity. Close examination of some easily observed facts makes that clear, but the contrary belief is so widespread that it blocks the examination and obscures the observation. So prior to examining why belief in moral responsibility *threatens*—rather than protects—personal dignity, it is essential to see why the opposite is the orthodox doctrine of philosophical faith.

Consider the first reason for the fear that the demise of moral responsibility destroys personal dignity: without moral responsibility (and the special power of libertarian free will that props it up) we would lose our special human status and our special human dignity. The "folk" may worry that without moral responsibility we are no longer made in the image of God, but this concern will not bother most contemporary philosophers, who are quite comfortable with atheistic naturalism; but it is part of the case that C. S. Lewis makes in favor of moral responsibility and capital punishment: "To be punished, however severely, because we have deserved it, because we "ought to have known better," is to be treated as a human person made in God's image" (1971, 246). When behavioral scientists argued that their research left no room for libertarian free will and moral responsibility, Joseph Wood Krutch expressed the disgusted reaction felt by many people:

> Perhaps Hamlet was nearer right than Pavlov. Perhaps the exclamation 'How like a god!' is actually more appropriate than 'How like a dog! How like a rat! How like a machine!'
>
> (Krutch 1954, 32–33)

The common concern that denying moral responsibility (and the special power of libertarian free will) would deprive us of our special "godlike" status is one more act in a long-running play. When Copernicus removed the Earth from the center of the cosmos and sent it careening around the Sun, he deprived humans of our special center stage status. As John Donne expressed the sense of confusion and demotion: "New philosophy calls all in doubt, The element of fire is quite put out." But worse was yet to come. Copernicus might have hurled us off center stage, but we were still God's unique and favorite creation, in a distinctly different category from all other species. Darwin changed all that. Rather than being God's special creation, closely related to the angels, we learned that our closest relatives were chimpanzees.

We are not the center of the cosmos, we are not God's special and favorite creation, we are not made in the image of a (nonexistent) god; so—the story goes, in each act—humans will be devoid of any special dignity. Our uniquely human moral responsibility was the last straw to which we could cling, and now that is lost. So once again is heard the old lament: when the moral responsibility that made humans special and unique is lost, then respect for personal human dignity and individual rights will be lost as well.

In comparison to "the folk," contemporary philosophers are less likely to worry that denial of moral responsibility will destroy some special human uniqueness: a uniqueness that forms the foundation for human dignity and human rights. Few contemporary philosophers suppose that we are radically different from other animals, that God created us as his special favorites, and that we alone are "made in the image of God." Still, some very insightful naturalistic philosophers regard moral responsibility (even without libertarian free will) as something that makes humans very special (if not quite godlike) and sets us apart from the "lower animals." Harry Frankfurt states:

> We do in fact assume . . . that no member of another species is a person. Accordingly, there is a presumption that what is essential to persons is a set of characteristics that we generally suppose—whether rightly or wrongly—to be uniquely human.
>
> It is my view that one essential difference between persons and other creatures is to be found in the structure of a person's will.
>
> (Frankfurt 1971, 6)

And John Martin Fischer makes a similar assertion, insisting that if he were convinced of the truth of determinism:

> I feel confident that this would not, nor should it, change my view of myself and others as (sometimes) free and robustly morally responsible agents—deeply different from other animals.
>
> (2007, 44)

## The Excuse-Extensionist Strawman

For some the desire for human uniqueness—a uniqueness built on free will and moral responsibility—may motivate the concern that loss of moral responsibility would erode commitment to human dignity and rights. Certainly, it is a factor in the "folk" concern about rejection of moral responsibility. But in the post-Darwinian naturalistic nonmiraculous world inhabited by most philosophers, there is a different source for the fear that denial of moral responsibility would erode respect for rights and dignity. That source involves a natural but deeply mistaken view of the rejection of moral responsibility: the *excuse-extensionist* account of the denial of moral responsibility.

Excuse-extensionism is an easy mistake to make, because it follows from the deep assumptions of the moral responsibility system. Belief in moral responsibility is strong and widespread, and so pervasive that it seems the default situation: unless there is some special circumstance or condition, then people are assumed to be *morally responsible* for their acts. Under the moral responsibility system, when do we *not* hold someone morally responsible? As P. F. Strawson (1962) makes clear, people are not held morally responsible when they are *excused* or *exempted*. That is, people are not morally responsible when they are temporarily or permanently *flawed* or *incompetent* or *deranged*: when they suffer from flaws which *excuse* their behavior. If there is a *universal* denial of moral responsibility—as the moral responsibility skeptics propose—then it is natural to suppose that this universal denial of moral responsibility must be based on *universal* incompetence; that is, the universal denial of moral responsibility must be based on an excuse-extensionist model that *extends* the range of incompetence until it covers everyone and all behavior. That is the model of moral responsibility skepticism that P. F. Strawson has in mind, as seen in this passage:

> For it is not a consequence of any general thesis of determinism which might be true that nobody knows what he's doing or that everybody's behavior is unintelligible in terms of conscious purposes or that everybody lives in a world of delusion or that nobody has a moral sense, i.e. is susceptible of self-reactive attitudes, etc.
>
> (1962, 74)

So powerful is the grip of the moral responsibility belief system that one of the best known mid-twentieth century moral responsibility opponents—John Hospers (1952, 1958)—bases his own rejection of moral responsibility on excuse-extensionism. Starting with cases of neurotic compulsion, Hospers then *extends* and enlarges such compulsion until it covers everyone: "psychiatrists began to realize, though philosophers did not, that the domination of the conscious by the unconscious extended, not merely to a few exceptional individuals, but to all human beings." (Hospers 1952, 572). Tyrannical unconscious compulsion ultimately erodes the intelligent control at the foundation of moral responsibility.

Hospers denies moral responsibility because we are all the helpless puppets of the deep irrational forces of our unconscious psyches, and P. F. Strawson draws the opposite conclusion: we are *not* all manipulated by deep delusions, and so we *are* morally responsible. Though they ultimately go in opposite directions, they start from a deep common assumption. This is Strawson's description of the conditions for denying moral responsibility (and adopting the objective attitude):

> Seeing someone, then, as warped or deranged or compulsive in behaviour or peculiarly unfortunate in his formative circumstances—seeing someone so tends, at least to some extent, to set him apart from normal participant reactive attitudes on the part of one who sees him, tends to promote, at least in the civilized, objective attitudes.
>
> (1962, 66)

For Strawson, the condition for being exempted from moral responsibility (and regarded with "objective attitudes") requires that one be classified as "warped or deranged or compulsive." Thus, for both Strawson and Hospers, *universal* exemption from moral responsibility requires that *everyone* be "warped or deranged or compulsive." From that common assumption, they draw very different conclusions; but the important and too easily accepted assumption is that the universal denial of moral responsibility must be based on universal derangement. This conclusion is echoed by Herbert Morris:

> When we treat a human being merely as an animal or some inanimate object our responses to the human being are determined, not by his choices, but ours in disregard of or with indifference to his. And when we "look upon" a person as less than a person or not a person, we consider the person as incapable of rational choice.
>
> (Morris 1968, 490)

This deep assumption—universal denial of moral responsibility implies universal derangement—is not surprising. The moral responsibility system exerts a powerful hold, and its basic assumption is that *everyone* is morally responsible unless there is some special excusing or exempting condition. From that perspective, it follows that universal denial of moral responsibility must be based on universal derangement or rational dysfunction. That assumption is difficult to avoid when operating deep within the moral responsibility system.

With the exception of Hospers, those who reject moral responsibility do not do so on the basis of excuse-extensionism; that is, they do not start from the assumption—basic to the moral responsibility system—that other than exceptions for *special* cases, *everyone* is morally responsible. To the contrary, most who deny moral responsibility maintain that when scrutinized carefully, holding *anyone* morally responsible—no matter how rational, reasons-responsive, well-adjusted, self-aware, and resourceful—*cannot* be justified. Whether good, bad, or indifferent, our characters and capacities were shaped by factors that were ultimately beyond our control. We do in some ways "make ourselves," but such self-making is the product of different levels of initial skill, widely varying self-making abilities, dramatically different workshop situations, and significantly different raw material, none of which resulted from our choices or efforts. Obviously, that case against moral responsibility remains controversial, and both libertarians and compatibilists have made vigorous attacks on it. But the present point is that it is *not* the excuse-extensionist position that critics often assume it to be. It is not the view that no one is morally responsible because no one is rational, skilled, self-controlled, or competent.

The excuse-extensionist mistake is at the foundation of the common claim that denying moral responsibility threatens personal dignity. From the perspective of excuse-extensionism—that is, from the perspective *within* the moral responsibility system—the universal denial of moral responsibility must imply universal derangement. While we may be concerned about such sadly demented individuals—concerned for their own welfare, as well as concerned that they do not harm us—we can hardly treat them with the *respect* to which we believe competent people are entitled. They cannot make reflective decisions based on their own values, they cannot exercise informed consent, they cannot make intelligent choices for themselves; and supposing they can would not respect their rights and their integrity, but instead place them in great peril: if people lack the capacity for effective choice, then *forcing* them to make choices (respecting their "right" of self-determination) is a cruel substitute for the protection they actually need. If that were the situation of us all—were we all demented, all incapable of making informed decisions for ourselves—then respect for individual rights and personal dignity would have no basis.

This distortion is the product of a moral responsibility system in which moral responsibility is taken as obvious, and exceptions require special grounds. The universal *rejection* of moral responsibility does not start from that assumption. Moral responsibility is universally rejected not because everyone is infirm; rather, *no* one is morally responsible because the conditions for moral responsibility are impossible to meet. Many people are rational (at least some of the time), moderately reasons-responsive, self-controlled, deliberative. But *all* of us were shaped by critical developmental factors we did not choose or control. Therefore, it is unfair to hold people morally responsible for their characters or behavior. Whatever the plausibility or implausibility of that universal denial of moral responsibility, it is clear that it is *not* based on universal incompetence or derangement. We are not forced into the false dilemma of choosing between moral responsibility and the denial of all competence or deliberation, because there is another alternative: we do not meet the impossible demands of moral responsibility, but we are still competent, self-controlled, reasons-responsive, self-directed individuals who are worthy of individual respect and whose right to make choices and exercise control remains valuable and must be protected.

The claim that denial of moral responsibility is based on universal derangement is a distortion. When that distortion joins forces with the false dilemma fallacy, the result is a dangerous and destructive challenge: *either* you acknowledge the legitimacy of moral responsibility or you are claiming that everyone is so flawed that they are incompetent to make their own decisions, and are fit only for paternalistic treatment. Or on a more personal level: either acknowledge your own moral responsibility for your acts (and accept your just deserts) or be repudiated as a deranged and irrational "non-person" and ostracized from the community of human persons enjoying human rights.

When we understand the terrible threat of being effectively banished from the human community, then it is less shocking that many of those who have suffered the harshest treatment and the greatest disadvantages still clutch at the straw of moral responsibility. When all else is lost they are desperate to retain some shred of human dignity and social inclusion, even in the form of capital punishment. In 1979 the state of Florida electrocuted

John Arthur Spenkelink, the first person executed in Florida following the re-introduction of the death penalty in the United States. Spenkelink was a drifter, a heavy drinker, and had compiled an extensive criminal record before murdering a fellow drifter in their shared motel room. The problems for Spenkelink started early. At age 12 his alcoholic father committed suicide, and returning from school John discovered his father's body in the garage. Two years later he was arrested for driving a stolen car, and the rest of his short life was spent in and out of juvenile facilities and adult prisons. One might suppose that having spent his childhood with an alcoholic father, discovering his father's corpse at age 12, suffering his own serious problems with alcohol, and experiencing the tender care of juvenile detention facilities and prisons for much of his life would lead Spenkelink to doubt that he had enjoyed much opportunity for exercising free will, and certainly to doubt that he had sufficient control to qualify for moral responsibility. Instead, one of his last comments insisted on his own moral responsibility: "Man is what he chooses to be. He chooses that for himself" (Curry 1979, 14).

Consider the case of Robert Harris, made philosophically famous by Gary Watson's (1987) superb article. Harris was a brutal and callous man, who murdered two young men seemingly for the fun of it, and later laughed and boasted about what he had done. When Watson recounts in detail the almost unimaginable horrors of Robert's life, it becomes difficult for even the most dedicated believer in moral responsibility to count Harris as morally responsible: Harris was repeatedly beaten by his alcoholic father, rejected and despised by his severely abused mother, teased constantly for his speech impediment, raped and brutalized at a federal detention center at age 14. But Watson notes that "Harris himself seems to accept responsibility for his life," quoting someone who had interviewed Harris shortly before his execution: "He told me he had his chance, he took the road to hell and there's nothing more to say" (1987, 281n.). If the "choice" is between accepting moral responsibility and horrible punishment, or on the other hand *not* being morally responsible and thus counted as demented or even subhuman and banished from the human community, then it is not surprising that desperate persons will insist they *are* part of the morally responsible human family. That may be particularly true of those who have suffered such severe mistreatment that they may wonder if they are valued as real members of the human community. Better to be killed by your "fellow humans" than ostracized from the human community altogether.

Under the excuse-extensionist distortion of the universal rejection of moral responsibility, it may seem that moral responsibility is the only possibility for preserving personal dignity and human rights: whatever its problems, at least the recognition of moral responsibility can allow competent people to manage their own lives and make their own decisions and intelligently consider their own values, while the denial of moral responsibility destroys those possibilities. When we are no longer looking through the darkened lens of excuse-extensionism, it is clear that moral responsibility does not protect against the erosion of personal dignity and human freedom and human rights, but has the opposite effect.

## Preserving Take-Charge Responsibility

Denial of moral responsibility is not based on incompetence or derangement. But there is another potential confusion behind the common belief that denial of moral responsibility threatens personal dignity and individual rights. Personal dignity and the exercise of individual rights and control and choices flourish in the absence of *moral* responsibility; but if no one could have what H.L.A. Hart calls *role* responsibility, and I have expanded and called *take-charge* responsibility, then our right to exercise control and make decisions—and the personal dignity and rights bound up in such control and decision-making—would indeed be threatened, or even destroyed. Hart gives this account of *role* responsibility:

> Whenever a person occupies a distinctive place or office in a social organization, to which specific duties are attached to provide for the welfare of others or to advance in some specific way the aims or purposes of the organization, he is properly said to be responsible for the performance of these duties. . . . If two friends, out on a mountaineering expedition, agree that the one shall look after the food and the other the maps, then the one is correctly said to be responsible for the food, and the other for the maps, and I would classify this as a case of role-responsibility.
>
> (1968, 212)

If the Pittsburgh Pirates should make the remarkably stupid decision to play me in center field, then it would be my role responsibility to catch fly balls hit into that vicinity. Given the fact that I am a slow runner with weak eyesight and lousy hand-eye coordination, it is unlikely that I would fulfill that role responsibility well. But being role responsible for playing center field is very different from being *morally* responsible. One might well say: Bruce had role responsibility for center field, and he did an awful job of it; but we should not blame him—hold him morally responsible—for his role ineptitude; after all, his eyesight is so bad that he has trouble distinguishing a fly ball from a pigeon. I have *role* responsibility for teaching my intro to philosophy course. If you muscle in on my role responsibility for my class, I will resent it, and will regard it as an assault on my rights and my dignity. Of course, I might welcome your friendly *suggestions*: "You should use the trolley problem when discussing utilitarianism, my students loved it." But the *decision* about how to teach the course is *my* role responsibility. If you propose to deprive me of that role responsibility, the most likely grounds would be that you regard me as incompetent to perform that role effectively.

Expanding upon Hart's role responsibility, consider my larger *role* responsibility for managing my life and making my own choices and living by my own values: what we might call my *take-charge* responsibility. I may tolerate or even welcome your *advice* on how I should live my life: "You should get some more exercise, and actually finish that article on Schopenhauer you keep meaning to write." But if you try to tell me what I *must* do with my life—what political party I must support, what career I must follow, what friends I can and cannot have—then I will deeply resent your interference, and conclude that you consider me incompetent to make my own decisions.

This valuable and dignity-preserving *take-charge* responsibility is very different from *moral* responsibility. You might well conclude that I have and *should* have take-charge responsibility for my own life (I am not deranged or incompetent) but that I am not *morally* responsible for handling that responsibility well or ill (because in the latter case I failed to develop strong powers of self-control at an early age, or in the former because I started with the tremendous advantages of a loving and supportive family and a great education). Denying my moral responsibility for my life and my important decisions does not threaten my dignity or my control or my rights; depriving me of take-charge responsibility certainly would. If we could not exercise take-charge responsibility—especially take-charge responsibility for ourselves—that would undermine personal dignity and rights, and license unacceptable interference in our lives. But (as discussed in more detail in Chapter 13) once we recognize that the denial of moral responsibility does not deny self-control, genuine choice, and deliberative preferences, then there is no reason to suppose that it denies take-charge responsibility.

There is another reason why denial of moral responsibility is commonly considered a grave threat to individual rights and dignity. As discussed in Chapter 2, it is widely assumed that moral responsibility and free will are inseparable. As a result, the denial of moral responsibility is automatically taken to imply the denial of free will (including *compatibilist* free will with its emphasis on free choice and exercise of control and following one's own deep values). If the grounds for compatibilist free will were denied, that would indeed threaten personal dignity and individual rights. But (as will be discussed further in the final chapter) there is no inconsistency in affirming an enriched compatibilist free will (Waller 2015b), while denying that this vital form of free will can support just deserts and moral responsibility (Waller 1990).

When the denial of moral responsibility is distinguished from the excuse-extensionist distortion of that view (which assumes the denial to be based on claims of universal infirmity), and it is understood that natural free will and take-charge responsibility flourish in the absence of moral responsibility, then no reasons remain for supposing that denial of moral responsibility threatens rights and liberties and respect for persons. But that is only the beginning of the story. The denial of moral responsibility *enhances* respect for and support of personal rights (as discussed in Chapter 13), while the moral responsibility system is a *threat* to personal dignity and individual rights.

The main problem with the "orthodox" view—denial of moral responsibility threatens human dignity and individual rights—is not that it is false (though it certainly is). The more severe problem is that this widely held belief has blinded us to the real threat to individual dignity and rights. It is not *loss* of moral responsibility that threatens such rights; rather, the threat comes from the stubborn *commitment* to moral responsibility. That is not to deny that at one time the moral responsibility system had positive effects: it protected the children and siblings and friends of a murderer or miscreant from honor attacks; and it provided a range of excuses that offered some degree of protection to those who—by accident, insanity, or overwhelming situational factors—caused harms. But the time is long past when the benefits of the moral responsibility system outweighed its flaws. When we look at it closely without the distorting lens of the moral responsibility system, it is clear that moral responsibility undermines individual dignity rather than protecting it. The next chapter offers empirical evidence for that claim, while Chapter 8 describes *why* belief in moral responsibility threatens rather than protects personal dignity and individual rights.

# 7 Empirical Examination of Moral Responsibility

The goal of this chapter, the previous chapter, and the next chapter is to weaken and ultimately undermine the deep commitment to the moral responsibility system, and prepare the way for acceptance of an emerging new system: a system that offers a better way of dealing with the inescapable problem of punishment (along with other benefits). The previous chapter examined and rejected the claim that denial of moral responsibility undercuts personal dignity and weakens individual rights. This chapter moves beyond that defensive position to a stronger claim: belief in moral responsibility and just deserts *threatens* rather than preserves personal dignity and individual rights. It is not easy to challenge philosophical orthodoxy, and belief in moral responsibility as a guardian for individual dignity is an article of philosophical faith. The basic challenge to that belief requires examining some plain but painful facts: Western cultures with the strongest commitment to individual moral responsibility typically have the worst records of protecting individual dignity; as commitment to moral responsibility waxes, commitment to the protection and promotion of personal dignity wanes; and as the commitment to moral responsibility weakens, the commitment to individual rights and dignity flourishes.

What is the empirical evidence showing that belief in moral responsibility threatens rather than protects personal dignity and individual rights? Anecdotal "evidence" will have no more value here than in other contexts. Justice Antonin Scalia was a fervent champion of moral responsibility, who embraced the miraculous powers that support it:

> The doctrine of free will—the ability of man to resist temptations to evil, which God will not permit beyond man's capacity to resist—is central to the Christian doctrine of salvation and damnation, heaven and hell. The post-Freudian secularist, on the other hand, is more inclined to think that people are what their history and circumstances have made them, and there is little sense in assigning blame.
>
> (Scalia 2002, 19)

Scalia was also a stubborn advocate of denying rights to homosexuals, allowing torture in prisons, denying the right of privacy, limiting appeals of those who have been wrongly convicted, and rejecting both Miranda warnings and right to counsel. But exhibiting a person who champions moral responsibility while opposing basic individual rights is no more convincing than the usual anecdotal "evidence": "My cousin Joe was on the banana diet, and he lost 30 pounds." "Uncle Bill smoked three packs a day for 60 years, and he died at age 80 with never a trace of cancer." But of course the anecdotal evidence in the other direction is equally weak. It is true, and certainly worth nothing, that there are strong advocates of moral responsibility—such as John Martin Fischer and Daniel Dennett—who are ardent critics of the cruel dignity-destroying punitive practices (capital punishment, Supermax prisons, extremely harsh conditions and lengths of imprisonment) found in the United States; but that does not show that belief in moral responsibility enhances support for human dignity. If it shows anything, it shows that thoughtful and observant persons like Fischer and Dennett cannot avoid recognizing the brutal excesses of the U.S. justice system.

## Cultural Comparison of Commitment to Moral Responsibility

Extensive cultural comparisons carried out by sociologists and criminologists offer the best evidence concerning the actual effects of belief in moral responsibility. In those studies we can observe the effects of stronger and weaker commitments to moral responsibility, and see them writ large in cultural practices and perspectives. That is not to say we can find two identical cultures, in one of which belief in moral responsibility is strong while in the other culture belief in moral responsibility does not exist. First, while there are certainly cultures where robust belief in moral responsibility flourishes, there is no Western culture in which moral responsibility has been entirely eliminated. However, it is possible to compare cultures in which belief in individual moral responsibility is much *weaker* than in cultures which place great emphasis on moral responsibility. Other cultural differences will remain, of course, ranging from homogeneity or diversity of the population, degree of urbanization, level of wealth, and many other factors; so this will hardly provide a conclusive empirical proof of the effects of differing degrees of moral responsibility belief. However, there is enough evidence to cast serious doubts on the common claim that belief in moral responsibility promotes individual dignity and rights.

When comparing strength of belief in moral responsibility, the greatest contrast among Western cultures is between social democratic corporatist cultures and neo-liberal cultures. The most prominent example of a neo-liberal culture is the United States, with England close behind. Neo-liberal cultures celebrate free-market capitalism (with minimal regulation), have extreme income differentials, place strong emphasis on individualism, and practice social exclusion of less favored groups (especially the economically disadvantaged). They also have strong law and order orientations and high imprisonment rates. In stark contrast are social democratic corporatist cultures, exemplified by Sweden, Finland, and Norway. Social policy is more corporate than individualistic and the orientation is more egalitarian, with generous universal welfare support and particular care for the sick and young. In social democratic corporatist cultures the penal system emphasizes the retention of rights by offenders. In contrast to neo-liberal cultures, the operation of prisons and other correctional processes is viewed as strictly a function of the state: allowing a private market in such processes poses the threat of profit-driven expansion as well as unacceptable methods of cost-cutting. In the United States, the private prison industry is enormous and very profitable, and its economic and political power is a major factor in the catastrophic surge in imprisonment rates (Schlosser 1998; Selman and Leighton 2010; Harcourt 2012; Isaacs 2014).

As sociologists Cavadino and Dignan draw the contrast, in neo-liberal societies:

> Economic failure is seen as being the fault of the atomized, free-willed individual, not any responsibility of society. . . . Crime is likewise seen as entirely the responsibility of the offending individual. . . . And as neo-liberal societies have become even more neo-liberal in recent decades, so they have become more punitive. . . . [In] the United States . . . the toughening of criminal justice and penal policies under the Reagan and Bush (senior) presidencies . . . accompanied a systematic reversal of various "incorporative" social policy initiatives in other spheres . . .
>
> On the other hand, corporatist societies like Germany—and to an even greater extent, social democratic ones, like Sweden . . . tend to pursue more inclusionary economic and social policies that offer their citizens a far greater degree of protection against the vicissitudes of market forces, binding citizens to the state via national interest groups and ensuring the provision of welfare benefits and care of various kinds to ensure that all citizens are looked after. The communitarian ethos which gives rise to these policies—and which is in return shaped by them—also finds expression in a less individualistic attitude toward the offender, who is regarded not as an isolated culpable individual who must be rejected and excluded from law-abiding society, but as a social being who should still be included in society but who needs rehabilitation and *resocialization*, which is the responsibility of the community as a whole. The corporate citizen, unlike the neo-liberal, is much more his brother's keeper—even if he has done wrong—with a stronger sense that "there but for the grace of God go I"—in terms of both economic failure and criminal activity.
>
> (2006a, 448)

Comparisons between neo-liberal societies (with strong commitment to moral responsibility) and social democratic corporatist societies (in which belief in moral responsibility is much weaker) can be made along three dimensions. First, the general comparison of larger cultures (such as the neo-liberal United States) in comparison with social democratic corporatist cultures (such as Sweden and Norway). Second, the comparison within predominantly neo-liberal cultures of those areas where neo-liberal/individual moral responsibility beliefs are strongest (such as Texas) with areas where they are weakest (such as Vermont). Third, comparative changes as countries (such as the United States and England) become more intensely neo-liberal. One might expect an intensely individualistic neo-liberal society to exhibit a powerful commitment to individual rights and dignity. That expectation is plainly false.

Consider first the basic respect for the dignity and rights and opportunity of ordinary law-abiding citizens. In an affluent society, respect for their dignity and rights must involve at least the prospect for a decent life with genuine opportunities to pursue their own goals, and the essential support to live in modest physical and material comfort. That right is taken very seriously by social democratic corporatist societies; in contrast, while neo-liberal societies may celebrate their commitment to "equal opportunity for all," the reality is a very different story. As Cavadino and Dignan point out:

> The neo-liberal society tends to exclude both those who fail in the economic marketplace and those who fail to abide by the law—in the latter case by means of imprisonment, or even more radically by execution. This is no coincidence. Both types of exclusion are associated with a highly *individualistic* social ethos. This individualistic ethos leads a society to adopt a neo-liberal economy in the first place, but conversely the existence of such an economy in return fosters the social belief that individuals are solely responsible for looking after themselves. In neo-liberal society, economic failure is seen as being the fault of the atomized, free-willed individual, not any responsibility of society—hence the minimal, safety-net welfare state. Crime is likewise seen as entirely the responsibility of the offending individual. The social soil is fertile ground for a harsh 'law and order ideology'.
>
> (2006a, 448)

The verbal insistence on "equal opportunity" is overwhelmed by the powerful belief that each individual is basically deserving of what he or she gets: we live in a *just* world, so those who *have* are being justly rewarded, and those who have *not* must likewise justly deserve their deprivations. That includes the benefits and deprivations that children receive from the just deserts of their parents: the wealthy suburban child justly deserves outstanding health care, a healthy environment, the best schools, and special consideration at the most prestigious colleges and universities; and the poor child—living in rundown buildings with peeling lead paint, suffering the effects of air and water pollution, attending substandard and even dangerous schools, and having limited or no access to decent health care—is also living in a *just* world.

A student who struggled against enormous disadvantages and managed against all odds to compile an academic record comparable to that of the richly advantaged suburban students is admitted to a highly competitive university through a small boost from "affirmative action." That is widely condemned in neo-liberal societies (and the more neo-liberal the society, the stronger the condemnation) as giving "unfair advantage" to the child who overcame enormous unfair *dis*advantages. But when many wealthy children who have enjoyed all the advantages receive preferential treatment through "legacy" admission practices, there are few complaints. Harvard, for example, accepts a token number of disadvantaged affirmative action students, while over a third of its admitted students received substantial legacy preference.

To those who have shall be given, and it must be just and fair, because the world is just and therefore they justly deserve their special advantages. After all, each of us "makes it—or fails to make it—on his own"; so the poor kid from the slums obviously has as much opportunity as the wealthy kid; and denying that would call into question the whole moral responsibility system. Compare the "opportunity" of impoverished lead-poisoned children in the neo-liberal United States with the opportunity of the least advantaged children in Sweden, and decide whether a commitment to individual moral responsibility actually fosters a commitment to the right of genuine opportunity. Compare the poorest homeless person in the United States with the relatively poor person in Scandinavia who receives—as a matter of basic *right*, with no stigma attached—decent housing and adequate economic support to live a dignified life, and consider whether strong belief in moral responsibility really supports individual dignity.

## Criminal Justice in Neo-Liberal Culture

The contrast becomes even more marked as we consider the treatment of criminal suspects in the neo-liberal environment with their treatment in other cultures, as well as the changes in treatment and weakened respect for the rights of suspects as the culture becomes more deeply neo-liberal and stronger in its commitment to moral responsibility. The United States is the model for a strongly neo-liberal culture, and has also been the major force in exporting neo-liberal views to other countries; and the United States is all but unique in its system of bail bonds as a means of assuring that those who have been indicted—but not yet tried and found guilty—appear for trial (only the Philippines, a former U.S. commonwealth, uses anything like the U.S. system). In the United States the bail bond system has become so deeply entrenched that it is difficult to recognize what a strange and perverse system it is. Under the bail system, the poor person who cannot afford to pay his or her bail remains in jail awaiting trial, often for an extended period: awaiting trial for more than a year is not rare. Then before the trial, the prosecutor offers the defendant a "plea bargain": plead guilty to this reduced charge, and we'll let you out with time served (or in any case considerably less time than if you go to trial and are found guilty). Your overworked lawyer—a public defender who has scores of cases, and has very little time to work on any individual defense—offers this apt advice: you would be a fool not to take that deal. They're not going to give you the time back, and if you demand a trial they will tack on a hefty "trial tax": the criminal courts do not like being burdened with actually allowing defendants their supposed right to a trial by jury, so if a defendant demands a trial and is found guilty (and with an overburdened public defender against all the resources of the police and the prosecutor's office, that guilty verdict is very likely) then the penalty for insisting on your "right" to a jury trial will be a substantially harsher sentence than the sentence being offered in the plea deal. So the poor defendant spends his time in jail awaiting "trial," takes a plea bargain, and is released with "time served" (along with a felony record). Like Alice in Wonderland: sentence first, trial later.

This is not a rare event in the United States. In 2013, the Drug Policy Alliance released a report on the situation in New Jersey, which found that on a typical day there were more than ten thousand people in New Jersey jails who were awaiting trial (and had not been found guilty of anything); and the average length of time in jail awaiting trial was ten months. Of those, some 40 per cent had the option of posting bail, but could not obtain the funds (in more than 10 per cent of those cases, the bail was at $2500 or less); and more than half of those awaiting trial were charged with non-violent offenses. The profound injustice is obvious, and the attack on the defendant's basic rights is blatant; but this has gone on for decades jointly with the United States' deep commitment to moral responsibility, and few seem to care (though a few states have recently made reforms, they are exceptions).

The defendant, whether guilty or innocent, is already under enormous pressure to accept a "plea"—especially those defendants who are in jail while awaiting trial. That pressure is increased by deceitful interrogation practices that are not only standard procedure in the United States, but openly taught in criminal justice classes and textbooks on the subject of police interrogation. If we sincerely believe in the *dignity* of a person, one basic element of respecting that person's dignity is dealing with the person *honestly*, and not lying to or deceiving the person. But in the neo-liberal United States, lying to suspects is routine and systematic. Suspects are told that their finger prints have been found at the crime scene, told that if they will confess then the interrogator will make sure nothing bad happens to them, told that they have already been identified by eyewitnesses, told that a friend—who was picked up at the same time, and is being interrogated separately—has admitted to being present at the crime, but is insisting that all the planning and violence was the work of the person now being inter-rogated (and "if you don't tell your side of the story, your friend is gonna get a deal from the D.A. and you will be the one doing serious time while he walks out clear and free"). As Margaret Paris (1997) points out, it less-ens the dignity of the police to operate like sleazy used car salesmen; even more clearly, it means that the person being interrogated—who is suppos-edly presumed to be innocent, and may well be innocent—is being treated as someone who is not entitled to the basic dignity of being dealt with *truthfully*.

If a defendant is so rash as to exercise his or her "right" to a jury trial—the severe penalty for claiming that right notwithstanding—then unscrupulous prosecutors may and do use "jailhouse informants" to make up for the lack of incriminating evidence. A prisoner who is in jail awaiting trial, or awaiting sentencing, or already convicted and serving a sentence, contacts (or is contacted by) the prosecutor. This prisoner-informant offers to testify under oath that the jailed suspect confessed or bragged to the informant that the suspect actually committed the serious crime with which he is charged; and the informant is willing to testify to that conversation, under oath, at the suspect's trial—*if* the prosecutor is willing to let the informant plead to lesser charges, or is willing to drop the charges against the informant, or can pull strings to get the informant special treatment while serving his sentence (such as early release to a half-way house). Everyone involved in this ugly process—except the jury—knows that the informant is lying (such informants are typically repeat performers), and lying in exchange for a very substantial bribe: the bribe of a "get out of jail free" card.

As Brandon L. Garrett (2011, 124) notes: "Informants who are already in jail and testify against cellmates have long been considered notoriously unreliable sources." And Myrna S. Raeder (2007, 1438) makes the ques-tion painfully clear: "Is it really arguable that prosecutors do not know that jailhouse informants who repeatedly claim they obtained confessions are likely to be fabricating?" Justice Stephen Trott (of the 9th Circuit) stated in open forceful language what everyone dealing with the corrupt system of jailhouse informants cannot avoid knowing:

> Because of the perverse and mercurial nature of the devils with whom the criminal justice system has chosen to deal, each contract for testi-mony is fraught with the real peril that the proffered testimony will not be truthful, but simply factually contrived to "get" a target of sufficient interest to induce concessions from the government. Defendants or sus-pects with nothing to sell sometimes embark on a methodical journey to manufacture evidence and to create something of value, setting up and betraying friends, relatives, and cellmates alike.
>
> (Northern Mariana Islands v. Bowie, 243 F.3d at 1124,
> 9th Circuit 2001; quoted in Raeder 2007)

In Canada, outrage at the wrongful conviction of Thomas Sophonow (that resulted in an innocent man spending years in prison) led to a major investigation revealing that important "evidence" in the trial was provided by lying jailhouse informants (Wolson and London 2004). As a result, Canada basically banned all use of jailhouse informants. In the neo-liberal United States, there have now been dozens of cases—many involving death row inmates, and many others involving innocent people who spent years in prison—in which DNA evidence has established the innocence of the person wrongfully convicted; and in a *majority* of those cases, an important part of the "evidence" against the wrongfully convicted defendant was the purchased perjured testimony of a jailhouse informant. But the use of jailhouse informants continues unabated, and with few restrictions. Indeed, the U.S. Supreme Court—stacked with neo-liberal appointees—has ruled that offering reduced or dropped charges in exchange for jailhouse informant testimony is perfectly legitimate. Prosecutors are not allowed to offer jailhouse informants money in exchange for their testimony; but apparently a get out of jail free card has no monetary value.

In the neo-liberal United States many defendants plead guilty to crimes they did not commit; and in many cases that is certainly the prudent course, when they face a draconian sentence with few resources for their defense in a contest against all the powers of the state. Faced with coercive "plea bargains" (enforced by the threat of harsh sentences for those who refuse), lies by interrogators, falsified evidence, inadequate counsel, and jailhouse informants eager to gain a reduced sentence through their perjured testimony, innocent defendants plead guilty and take the best deal they can get. This is an everyday occurrence in the United States, with its deep commitment to moral responsibility, and with a pretense of protecting the rights of the innocent.

One might suppose that a country deeply committed to moral responsibility and just deserts would make great efforts to prevent the punishment of those who are actually innocent. The neo-liberal system and its devotion to individual moral responsibility doesn't work that way. False forensics evidence—some accidental and some purposeful—has been found in city crime labs in Chicago, Cleveland, Detroit, Houston, Oklahoma City, Omaha, San Francisco, and Washington; state crime labs in California, Illinois, Maryland, Mississippi, North Carolina, Virginia, and West Virginia; the FBI crime lab; and the crime lab of the U.S. Army (Balko 2011). A National Academy of Sciences report (2009) noted that crime lab work in the United States often employs investigative techniques with no scientific validity. These problems are widely known, but the lack of effort at fixing them belies claims that commitment to moral responsibility fosters commitment to protecting the innocent. Even when the forensics errors and wrongful convictions are discovered, often little or no effort is made to free those who are incarcerated. The *Washington Post* reported that in the District of Columbia, Justice Department officials "had known for years that flawed forensic testimony and false matches might have led to the convictions of hundreds of potentially innocent people," but the Justice Department generally did not inquire further, and "in many cases that the agency did review and found problems with, prosecutors never notified defendants or their attorneys of the issues uncovered" (Hsu 2012). This is the ultimate lack of concern for protecting the innocent: even when we *know* defendants have been wrongly convicted, there is little interest in releasing them. It might seem that when mistakes are made and an innocent person is imprisoned, a culture devoted to moral responsibility would make great efforts to free those who have been wrongly convicted. Though philosophically plausible, it is empirically false.

It is not just that flawed forensic "evidence" is widespread, but the problem is exacerbated by the fact that prosecutors often knowingly present such evidence in their efforts to "win" a conviction at any cost. As Bennett Gershman (2003, 26–27) points out: "Documented cases of open and notorious misconduct by forensic laboratories and of rogue experts giving fraudulent testimony strongly suggest that many prosecutors are fully aware that the laboratory and the expert have been engaging in a long-standing practice and pattern of misconduct." Not only is flawed forensic "evidence" presented as legitimate, but prosecutors not infrequently withhold evidence (in violation of discovery and disclosure rights) that would support the innocence of the accused. Gershman (2003, 21n) notes a 1999 study reporting that "convictions in 381 homicide cases nationwide have been reversed because prosecutors concealed evidence suggesting the defendants' innocence or presented evidence they knew to be false." Prosecutors have abundant resources to bring forward impressive forensic evidence backed by the testimony of highly-credentialed experts; but the great majority of defendants have no resources for challenging such evidence, no matter how flawed it may be.

When the neo-liberal devotion to moral responsibility took root in the UK—after the seeds blew over from the United States—the effects were not an enhancement of respect for dignity and individual rights, but precisely the opposite. John Mortimer (the distinguished British barrister famous for his delightful stories of "Rumpole of the Bailey") celebrated the right to silence as "the golden thread of British justice"; but the powerful desire to hold *someone* morally responsible and punish criminal acts soon tarnished that golden thread. Too many people were "hiding behind" the right to silence, and no one was being punished, so the basic right to silence was eliminated. If you are suspected of or charged with a crime in the UK, then if you cannot or will not give answers that support your claim of innocence, that counts as evidence of guilt (O'Reilly 1994). That shifts the burden of proof, commits the fallacy of appeal to ignorance, and undermines the right to privacy and the assumption that you are innocent until proven guilty. But the desire to "prove" moral responsibility and guilt and eligibility for punishment was stronger than the commitment to basic individual rights. Under neo-liberal influence, Britain also adopted the notorious IPP program: Imprisonment for Public Protection. Under that "tough on crime" policy persons convicted of two "serious" crimes (and who a judge *suspects* might commit another crime) are sentenced to life imprisonment. (Jacobson and Hough 2010)

With the increasing influence of neo-liberalism, promising programs to find the causes of juvenile crime and help those adolescents being drawn or pushed into criminal behavior were deemed counterproductive. Efforts to understand the causes of crime and the problems faced by those with difficult childhood histories were ridiculed and rejected by the neo-liberal forces of law and order and individual moral responsibility, with a call by Prime Minister John Major for harsh punishment of juvenile crime: "Society needs to condemn a little more and understand a little less" (1993, 8). After all, there really was not much need for deeper inquiry into social causes and societal problems, as Major asserted in a speech at the 1992 Conservative Party Conference: "Crime wrecks lives, spreads fear, corrupts society. It is the fault of the individual, and no one else." As so often happens, this invasive neo-liberal species spread rapidly and soon destroyed much of the native flora and fauna, including some hard-won and long-cherished basic individual rights.

Belief in moral responsibility confers moral legitimacy on the powerful desire to strike back when one is harmed, and to strike back when we observe others being harmed. The strike-back desire is not very selective, striking out at the source of harm if that is easily available but otherwise at any convenient target. And belief in moral responsibility requires that we not look in depth at the causes and circumstances of the harms, which in turn contributes to an absence of careful scrutiny of what happened and whether the accused is actually the perpetrator or is instead innocent. Appealing to moral responsibility for protection of the innocent is like using gasoline to put out fires.

## Moral Responsibility and Criminal Rights

When a defendant is found guilty—whether actually guilty or not—does strong belief in moral responsibility protect the dignity of those who are subjected to criminal punishment? The two most radically neo-liberal Supreme Court Justices, Scalia and Thomas, would allow prisons to torture inmates (on constitutional grounds, they claim) [Hudson v. McMillian, 503 U.S. 1 (1992)]; and the United States places many inmates in total isolation in Supermax prisons (a practice condemned as torture by the European Union). But there are some improvements: the U.S. Supreme Court recently banned capital punishment for children [Roper v. Simmons, 543 U.S. 551 (2005)] (though true to form, the staunchly neo-liberal justices—Scalia and Thomas and Rehnquist—dissented); and President Obama has now blocked solitary confinement for juveniles in federal prisons (though it continues in state and local facilities), following extensive studies documenting the profound and permanent psychological damage such confinement causes juveniles (Mitchell and Varley 1990; Simkins, Beyer, and Geis 2012; Castillo 2015).

When someone—whether guilty or innocent—is convicted of a crime, the same pattern holds: those countries with the greatest devotion to moral responsibility show the least concern for protecting (much less promoting) the dignity of the convicted individual. The neo-liberal United States, with its singular commitment to moral responsibility and just deserts, is the only Western country that practices capital punishment. A terrified prisoner is taken from his or her cell—where he or she has been hopelessly counting the hours and minutes until execution—and the prisoner is rendered totally helpless by being strapped to a gurney or into a chair to await the precisely scheduled moment of death. The condemned Roman citizen was offered a dagger; slaves were not allowed such a choice. When condemned to death, Gary Gilmore sought to preserve some modicum of individual dignity by using drugs to take his own life; he was rushed to a hospital and his stomach pumped, so that the state could deprive him of any control whatsoever over his rigidly planned execution.

Advocates of capital punishment are at the extreme edge of belief in moral responsibility and righteous retribution; but their concern for imposing such punishment solely on those who are actually guilty is much weaker than their concern for striking back when a terrible crime occurs. Ernest van den Haag was a leading advocate of capital punishment, and in 1985—before DNA evidence had demonstrated the fearful regularity of false convictions—he argued that we should not abandon capital punishment merely because mistaken convictions result in "the loss of innocent lives through miscarriages" of justice:

> Miscarriages of justice are rare, but do occur. Over a long enough time they lead to execution of some innocents. Does this make irrevocable punishments morally wrong? Hardly. Our government employs trucks. They run over innocent bystanders more frequently than courts sentence innocents to death. We do not give up trucks because the benefits they produce outweigh the harm, including the death of innocents. Many human activities, even quite trivial ones, foreseeably cause wrongful deaths. Courts may cause fewer wrongful deaths than golf. Whether one sees the benefit of doing justice by imposing capital punishment as moral, or as material, or both, it outweighs the loss of innocent lives through miscarriages, which are as unintended as traffic accidents.
>
> (1985, 967)

The cavalier attitude toward erroneously executing the innocent is rarely expressed so openly, but it is obviously not uncommon among supporters of capital punishment. In some 25 years of use of DNA evidence, there have been 20 Death Row prisoners exonerated through DNA tests, and no doubt there are many more where no DNA evidence was available to prove their innocence; and many prisoners have been exonerated through evidence other than DNA testing. But evidence of wrongful convictions and the likelihood of innocent persons being executed have not resulted in a demand for the end of capital punishment, which continues to be favored by a majority of Americans. If moral responsibility and just deserts were rational processes designed to protect the innocent and punish only the guilty, the fact that innocent persons are sent to execution would be a powerful reason for rejecting capital punishment. If instead moral responsibility functions to provide ethical "justification" for our strike-back desires—desires that are not so discriminating about their targets—then the absence of concern over mistaken executions is not surprising. But it is not just a lack of real concern that an innocent person might face the ultimate in "just deserts"; in many cases there is vigorous opposition to any review process that would reverse a mistaken conviction, and that opposition is strongest in places—like Florida—with the deepest commitment to just deserts, especially just deserts in the form of capital punishment. As noted in a 1999 article in the *St. Petersburg Times*, Florida prosecutors sometimes seem more interested in carrying out punishment than in making sure the punished person is actually guilty:

> Although DNA has helped free dozens of prisoners in other states, several Florida prosecutors are blocking—mostly on procedural grounds—DNA test requests by inmates who claim they are innocent, including three on death row. "We've had unprecedented resistance in Florida, with prosecutors citing a procedural rule to bar DNA testing instead of going along with tests in the interest of justice," says former O. J. Simpson lawyer Barry Scheck.
>
> (Freedberg 1999)

No country has a stronger cultural commitment to individual moral responsibility than the United States, and in no place is that commitment stronger than in Texas. But that intense commitment to moral responsibility does not result in an intense commitment to avoiding wrongful convictions. In 1992, Cameron Todd Willingham was charged with a terrible crime: murdering his three young children by intentionally setting a fire that burned his home. The case against Willingham was ridiculously flawed. Not only did it feature a jailhouse informant (who has since admitted lying in exchange for reduced charges in another case) but the forensics investigation was so bad that a review of the case led the Texas Forensic Science Commission to recommend major changes in the training and procedures of fire investigators. Leading forensics investigators from around the country examined the evidence and concluded that the fire had been started by accident: there was no arson, and hence no murder. Governor Rick Perry received a report reviewing the strong evidence that the fire had been a terrible accident rather than a crime, but refused a stay of execution and Willingham was killed by lethal injection. In an intensive culture of moral responsibility and righteous retribution, making sure the right person is punished for the crime—even making sure that there was a crime at all—is less important than being sure that *someone* receives his or her "just deserts." Though the Willingham case is notorious, it fits the pattern in a state where commitment to individual moral responsibility is strongest. Texas has a long and disturbing record of assigning flawed defense attorneys to defendants charged with capital crimes: attorneys who have major alcohol addiction problems, and who have been known to sleep through much of the trial.

Consider the prison system in the neo-liberal United States. The imprisonment rate in the United States is approximately 700 people for every 100,000; most European countries are well under 100. When we focus in on the imprisonment rate for blacks in the United States, the numbers are even more shocking; as William Stuntz (2011, 48) notes, the incarceration rate for blacks in the United States is 80 percent higher than the rate at which Stalin sent Russians to the Gulag. Not only does the United States imprison more people for longer periods—in some cases (using "three strikes" legislation) imposing a life sentence for three felony convictions—but also imprisons them in much harsher conditions than are found in social democratic corporatist Europe. The most horrific example is the widespread use of Supermax prisons, in which many prisoners are kept for long periods in total isolation: a practice that often causes severe psychological damage to the prisoner (Grassian 2006; Arrigo and Bullock 2008; Casella and Ridgeway 2016), and which the European Court of Human Rights condemned as a form of torture that violates basic human rights. Amnesty International (2012) reached the same conclusion concerning Arizona's maximum security prisons, and the New York Bar Association (2011) condemned conditions in U.S. Supermax prisons as violations of the constitutional protection against cruel and unusual punishment.

It is not only Supermax prisons that assault the dignity of prisoners in the United States. Among those most committed to moral responsibility and just deserts are the strong advocates of *shaming* those who justly deserve such punishment. That "justly deserved" punishment should involve shaming and degradation is a widespread belief in neo-liberal cultures, but few express that belief as openly as does Dan M. Kahan, a contemporary supporter of "shaming" practices who regards shaming as an inherently desirable element of criminal punishment:

> Prison . . . does unequivocally evince disgust. . . . By stripping individuals of liberty—a venerated symbol of individual worth in our culture—and by inflicting countless other indignities—from exposure to the view of others when urinating and defecating to rape at the hand of other inmates—prison unambiguously marks the lowness of those we consign to it.
>
> (1998, 1642)

Many in neo-liberal cultures believe that prisoners should not only suffer, but should also be shamed and demeaned; and that view is strongest in areas where the neo-liberal culture and "rugged individualism" and the commitment to moral responsibility and just deserts are most intense: chain gangs were revived in Alabama and Arizona, with the shackled prisoners placed in highly public areas in order to maximize the shaming effect. Kahan affirms prison rape as a practice that "unambiguously marks the lowness" of the incarcerated, and regards marking that lowness as a positive outcome. Even in neo-liberal cultures, few would voice support for such a brutal policy; but the well-known rampant violence and sexual abuse in U.S. prisons (Sigler 2006) causes little concern among most of the neo-liberal citizens.

Prison conditions are perhaps the clearest contrast between the "human dignity preserving" policies of cultures that are most and least committed to moral responsibility. In the former category the poster child is the United States, with the psychologically devastating long-term isolation of its Supermax prisons, the endemic violence and abuse throughout its prison system, and the dearth of rehabilitation and education programs within its prisons. At the other end of the scale is the social democratic corporatist culture of Norway, which minimizes imprisonment by seeking effective alternatives. When imprisonment cannot be avoided, prisons in Norway emphasize respect for prisoners, programs that aid in their rehabilitation, and a constant goal of effectively reintegrating prisoners into society. Dan Kahan—an advocate of U.S. prison shaming practices—regards the isolation of vile prisoners away from good people like ourselves as one of the great advantages of mass imprisonment: "imprisonment removes offenders from our midst, shielding us from their contaminating influence" (Kahan 1998, 1642). Norwegian prisoners are not regarded as vile sources of contamination, but as fellow citizens who remain a part of society, and must be reintegrated into the larger society as swiftly and effectively as possible. Rather than making prisons fortress-like facilities emphasizing control and containment of prisoners, Norwegian prisons involve as little as possible of the "lockdown" model, striving instead to make prisons resemble residential colleges or other relatively comfortable living spaces.

Bastoy Island is the largest of Norway's five low-security prisons. Its inmates include drug smugglers, murderers, and persons guilty of various violent crimes. In the United States, some of these prisoners would probably be serving long terms in Supermax prisons, perhaps in solitary confinement. In contrast, inmates at Bastoy have jobs, including cooking, mechanics, farming, fishing, forestry, and operating the ferry to the island. The inmates plan their work, manage their schedules, learn important skills, and are treated with respect. In contrast to the U.S. recidivism rate of 60 percent, the rate in Norway is 20 percent. Arne Kvernvik Nilsen, the governor of Bastoy Island prison, believes in the work at Bastoy:

> I believe that we as human beings, if we are prepared to make fundamental changes in the way we regard crime and punishment, can

dramatically improve the rehabilitation of prisoners and thereby reduce the reoffending rates. . . . I believe the UK is going in the wrong direction—down a completely mad and hopeless path, because you still insist on revenge by putting people in harsh prison conditions which harm them mentally and they leave a worse threat to society than when they entered.

(Hernu 2011)

When James Conway, former superintendent at Attica Correctional Facility in New York, visited Halden (one of Norway's maximum security prisons), he was amazed at the contrast. During his visit, he stated that he had never worried about the well-being of Attica inmates: "It was your actions that put yourself here; who cares how they feel?" (Quoted in McCormack 2014). The prisoners at Attica made their own choices, and bear total moral responsibility for the punishment they are justly suffering. Conway was uncomfortable with the respectful treatment accorded prisoners at Halden, drawing a stark contrast with the way prisoners were treated at Halden and the way Conway believed they justly deserved to be treated:

Prison is not supposed to be comfortable. Prison is not a comfortable situation. Society is supposed to be comfortable, the inmate has given up his right to be in society by violating laws, by violent crimes, by committing murder, by committing rape. That person shouldn't be coddled, shouldn't be given a situation where we're concerned about how they should feel if someone should walk by their cell and see them on the toilet. Who cares how they feel?

(Quoted in Francis 2014)

That such dedication to shaming and degrading prisoners is counterproductive and promotes violence and a higher recidivism rate is obvious. What is even more obvious is that the harsh "just deserts" model is the opposite of any system that fosters human dignity. In social democratic corporatist Norway there is deeper examination of the causes of criminal behavior and serious consideration of how to help prisoners prepare for successful life outside prison. Such deep examination is blocked in the United States by fierce commitment to moral responsibility and just deserts, and the result is harsh assault on the personal dignity and basic human rights of U.S. inmates.

In the United States' struggle for civil rights for blacks, one of the key goals of that struggle was securing the right to vote. The right to vote is a basic individual right that is fundamental to one's self-respect and sense of self-determination. In the neo-liberal United States—with its obsessive commitment to moral responsibility—the right to vote is routinely denied to those who are incarcerated. The only exceptions are Vermont (the state closest in its culture to social democratic corporatism) and its neighbor, Maine. The states where neo-liberal beliefs are most dominant—states such as Florida, Alabama, Mississippi, Arizona, and Virginia—continue to deny the right to vote even to those who have served their prison terms. In contrast, no Western European democracy deprives prisoners of their voting rights: the European Court of Human Rights ruled that the European Union's Charter of Fundamental Rights protects the voting rights of prisoners. But there is one exception: the most neo-liberal European country, Britain, where there is a total ban on voting by prisoners. A spokesperson for its neo-liberal Prime Minister, David Cameron, stated that:

> David Cameron has made clear that prisoners will not get the vote as long as he is Prime Minister. Nothing is going to change. He has made clear that the idea of them getting the vote makes him physically sick.

If the right to vote is a basic right and a basic element of human dignity—as civil rights champions have long insisted—then the neo-liberal culture, with its central element of moral responsibility, is on the wrong side of the struggle for human dignity. Empirically, the results are painful and plain: devotion to moral responsibility threatens rather than protects individual dignity and rights.

Norwegian prisons more closely resemble the dormitory facilities at U.S. public universities than any five-star resort: reasonably comfortable, but far from luxurious. Of course, by comparison to the extremely harsh conditions of U.S. prisons, Norwegian prisons are indeed luxurious. They are, after all, designed to promote the rehabilitation of prisoners, rather than designed to inflict suffering on those who justly deserve to suffer. Still, even the modest comforts of Norway's prisons are often better than the conditions under which poor people in the United States must live. Nikola Milanovic—in "Norway's New Prisons: Could They Work Here?"—describes the enormous differences between Norway's modestly comfortable prison facilities and harsh U.S. prisons. She concludes that Norwegian prisons probably would *not* work here, and one of the reasons she gives (a reason she does not endorse) is that in the United States, many poor people live in harsher conditions than do prisoners in Norway's maximum security prisons:

> In the United States, high levels of poverty and underdevelopment in many areas (especially rural areas, where prisons are usually located) would cause massive backlash against the installation of a prison like Norway's. It would be impossible for public officials to justify creating a detention facility for those members of society who had violated their duties to the law that would create arguably better living conditions than exist for those who didn't break the law. The social safety net in Norway guarantees basic minimums for members of society that might make people more complacent with such a luxurious facility. Americans, by contrast, are more culturally adapted to the ideology of rugged individualism and reaping deserved reward: people only deserve what they can afford, the American mindset implies, and they can afford

what they earn. Convicted felons, in the United States, would not merit a very high standard of treatment.

(Milanovic 2010)

What's the moral of the story? The United States has very harsh conditions for the law-abiding poor, so it would be politically impossible to provide better conditions for those who break the law. That marks quite clearly the systemic nature of the problem. The "ideology of rugged individualism and reaping deserved reward" is based on a deep commitment to individual moral responsibility; and that is the source for the absence of concern for the human dignity of both prisoners and the poor. Everyone is morally responsible, everyone is "self-made" and the product of their own choices, and everyone justly deserves what they get—whether poverty or punishment—so we need not be concerned that they are demeaned. To the contrary, they justly deserve the treatment they are receiving, and intervening to protect dignity or prevent suffering would violate the just order. Both the degradation of prisoners and the neglect of the poor are fruits of the same moral responsibility tree.

When discussing prisons in Norway, and even acknowledging how far superior they are—in respect for human dignity, lower recidivism rates, and more effective programs of rehabilitation—some commentators still insist they would not work in the United States. We might learn something from them, but "there are a number of reasons why recreating Norwegian prison systems in America is a bad idea" (Sharma 2015). The Norwegian prison system would not work in the United States—according to Rakesh Sharma—because while Norway has an extensive and generous social welfare system, the United States provides very restricted social welfare resources to its citizens. In addition, Norway has "a much lower rate of [economic] inequality," while the United States has extreme differences of wealth. Sharma is quite correct: the Norwegian prison system—a system that is clearly far superior in respecting the human dignity of prisoners—would not fit into the U.S. culture; but that is because the U.S. neo-liberal culture promotes a *system*—a system based on individual moral responsibility—that threatens human dignity at many levels. The harsh and degrading treatment of prisoners is one part of a system that also metes out harsh treatment to the poor and promotes grossly unfair distribution of wealth. Norwegian prisons provide basic levels of comfort, and it is true that they are considerably better than the situations of many poor people in the United States. But the complaints should be against an enormously wealthy country in which many of its citizens live in desperate poverty, not against a country which provides decent conditions for its prison population. It is also true, of course, that in the United States there is much greater demand for harsh punitive measures against those who are convicted of committing criminal acts, and so a more humane prison system would not gain favor. But again, this is a function of the deep commitment to moral responsibility and just deserts. Rather than concluding that we should reject a prison system that is more effective in rehabilitation, less cruel, and promotes rather than assaults the human dignity of prisoners, perhaps we should consider rejecting the moral responsibility system that produces a culture hostile to a more humane prison system.

## Moral Responsibility Extremes

Though there are many people who are committed to moral responsibility and who abhor the cruel and degrading conditions of U.S. prisons, those who are most enthusiastic in support of complete individual moral responsibility are typically in favor of the harshest and most degrading punitive measures. Rather than extreme commitment to moral responsibility fostering deeper commitment to human dignity, the opposite is more commonly the case. A clear illustration of this trend can be found in an essay by Jeffrey Tuomela, a professor at Liberty University: an institution where the belief in absolute individual free will and complete individual moral responsibility—a moral responsibility that can justify eternal divine torture of those who freely choose wickedness—is a foundational principle. Tuomela insists that "punishment, properly understood, is an essential moral value of a justice system." (1995, 14) Indeed, Tuomela waxes quite eloquent concerning the moral and spiritual value of punishment:

> We should respond with satisfaction in seeing wickedness punished, not out of vengeance, but out of respect for justice.
>    Punishment of sin is a necessary condition of Christian salvation. If that requirement is rooted in the very nature of a righteous, just and holy God, punishment should be viewed as a positive moral value.
>
> (1995, 22)

Thus, desire for severe punishment is not based in a primitive strike-back desire shared by rats, chimpanzees, and humans; rather, it is a defining characteristic of a "just and holy God." Some might imagine this to be an extreme and even desperate effort to find a moral justification for punishment—severe retributive punishment is just, because it is approved by a severely retributive God, and whatever God approves must be just—but that is another question. In any case, the real causes of crime cannot be social problems—such as "illiteracy, poverty, inadequate housing, unemployment, malnutrition, substance abuse, or broken homes" (1995, 24)—because the real cause of criminal behavior is "the sinful nature of man" and the free choice to reject the path of righteousness and salvation. According to Tuomala:

> Scripture makes it clear that punishment is valuable and that it contributes to rehabilitation and public safety. When law-abiding people see justice done they should rejoice, and the wicked should be terrified.
>
> (1995, 27)

Scripture may indeed make clear that severe punishment "is valuable and that it contributes to rehabilitation and public safety," but the empirical study of the conditions that cause crime and recidivism reaches a very different conclusion.

Tuomala, however, is certain that severe punishment is justly deserved. After all, God approves it, so it must be justly deserved by morally responsible wrongdoers, and criminological studies are irrelevant. But the main point of his essay is to promote the use of corporal punishment such as flogging or caning, as a replacement or supplement to prison sentences. And aside from the Scriptural approval of severe corporal punishment—Tuomela notes that according to Scripture, "The benefits of corporal punishment are that it drives out foolishness, imparts wisdom, cleanses evil from the inmost being and saves the soul from death" (1995, 29)—his main argument in favor of corporal punishment is that it is really no worse than sending the convicted person to prison, in which:

> There are all sorts of dangers to his person—beatings, homosexual rape, increased risk of disease, and even death. There is a loss of privacy and dignity and perhaps the mental torture of an indefinite sentence.
>
> (1995, 28)

On that point, Tuomala may well be correct: in many cases, incarceration in a U.S. prison may be as bad or worse than being cruelly flogged. But the conclusion he draws from that fact is perverse: our prison system is so cruel, dangerous, and demeaning that it is comparable to the torture of flogging; therefore, flogging must be morally acceptable. But without the deep assumption that cruel treatment of prisoners is morally justified, another possibility might be considered: that because our prison system is comparable in its cruelty and degradation to flogging, we should radically reform both our prison system and the culture that produces such prisons.

In countries with genuine respect for human dignity, flogging has long since been abolished. It was a punitive measure not only designed to inflict severe suffering, but also intended to emphasize the lowness of the person flogged—a status not much different from beasts. Enlisted men and common sailors were flogged, but never officers; slaves were flogged, but never masters; barbarians were flogged, but not citizens of Rome. Commitment to justly deserved retributive punishment is supposed to provide special protection of the personhood of the individual punished. One of the protections—according to Berman (2008, 280n.)—is against torture, which is "person-disrespecting"; but as the essay by Tuomala makes clear, the strong insistence on punitive just deserts is at least as likely to encourage torture as to protect against it. The real lesson to be drawn from the essay by Tuomala: the more extreme the belief in moral responsibility and just deserts, the greater the willingness to embrace extreme and degrading punitive measures that are the opposite of policies aimed at promoting human dignity.

## Moral Responsibility and Economic Stigmatization

Strong belief in moral responsibility does not protect the rights of those accused of crimes, nor does it protect—much less promote—the human dignity of those convicted and imprisoned. The same conclusion follows if the focus is on those who face economic hardships in a culture with a strong commitment to moral responsibility and just deserts. Tom Clark notes that:

> moral responsibility does nothing to even the playing field of life, rather quite the opposite. It says that winners and losers in life essentially deserve what they get, so inequality is fair—don't look too hard at the system or at what caused a loser to end up that way.
>
> (Clark, Dennett, and Waller 2012, 5)

In countries with the strongest commitment to moral responsibility, accepting aid is stigmatized as the mark of personal failure. In contrast, in countries with the weakest regard for moral responsibility aid is considered a basic human right that offers everyone the opportunity to live a life of dignity and development. As Cavadino and Dignan note, the contrast between neo-liberal cultures (with deep commitment to individual moral responsibility) and social democratic corporatist cultures (where belief in moral responsibility is much weaker) is clearly seen in their treatment of those suffering economic hardship. In neo-liberal societies:

> The general ethos is one of *individualism* rather than communitarianism or collectivism. Under neo-liberalism the welfare state is minimalist and residual, consisting mainly of means-tested welfare benefits, entitlement to which is often heavily stigmatized. Consequently the status and economic well-being of citizens is heavily dependent on how well they can succeed in the (free) marketplace of the economy.
>
> Although social relationships in neo-liberal societies are formally egalitarian, this economic system results in extremely marked (and currently still widening) income differentials. This material inequality, combined with a lack of social entitlements afforded to individuals as of right, results in the *social exclusion* of many who find themselves marginalized by the markets in which they cannot compete effectively or afford to operate, particularly the labour and housing markets. . . . The term 'social exclusion' is not merely a synonym for poverty, but is used to refer to the denial of full *effective* rights of citizenship and participation in civil, political, and social life.
>
> (Cavadino and Dignan 2006a, 440, 442)

The more extreme the dedication to moral responsibility and rugged individualism and the self-made man, the harsher the attitude toward the impoverished—extending even to children. Daniel Payne—a senior contributor to *The Federalist*, a publication that promotes extreme policies of rugged individualism and individual moral responsibility—condemned the Richmond, Virginia, school system for offering free lunch to *all* children. One reason for the policy was to promote better health and nutrition, but what Payne objected to was what Dana Bedden, Superintendent of Richmond Public Schools, noted as a special advantage of the program: "I like it for the health and nutrition aspect, but this also removes the stigma of free lunch." According to Payne, the Richmond Public Schools "are doing a grave disservice by attempting to remove the 'stigma' associated with free government handouts. . . . There *should* be a stigma surrounding government dependency." (Payne 2014) For Payne, stigmatizing children for receiving a free lunch is morally good: they are receiving a handout they do not justly deserve, and therefore should suffer stigma and ridicule and loss of dignity.

While Payne regards it as inherently desirable for the poor—including poor children—to be stigmatized for their moral failure of being poor, he offers another justification as well; we should:

> avoid making needy people feel comfortable being dependent upon the government. To do so would not be merely bad public policy—it would be disingenuous and harmful to poor people, who more than anything need the mental and emotional drive to be free from government dependence.
>
> (Payne 2014)

So if people are shamed and stigmatized by receiving government assistance, that will motivate them to achieve economic success and become self-sufficient. If people feel shamed and degraded, that will give them the self-confidence and the education and the opportunities and the motivation to improve. Aside from the fact that many people who need government help—in the form of food stamps and perhaps other forms of assistance—are already working very hard indeed at jobs (such as those at Wal-Mart) that pay so little they remain deeply mired in poverty, it is also ludicrous to suppose that shaming is an effective way of motivating people to work harder. And when applied to children, it is perverse to suppose that stigmatizing children is an effective way to encourage their success. It is true, of course, that a substantial percentage of U.S. children who grow up in homes that receive government assistance will need such assistance in adulthood. But it is not because they have become happy and satisfied with the generous government benefits they receive (benefits that are minimal at best, and leave families in poverty and often hungry); but rather because they have been stigmatized by the culture that regards them and their families as unworthy failures, and their self-confidence is severely damaged. And to add the obvious, these are children who grow up with the worst schools, inadequate housing, marginal health care, and the greatest likelihood of suffering lead poisoning. Insisting that children justly deserve to be stigmatized by their classmates is appalling. That such an attitude is found among those on the extreme edge of strongest belief in individual moral responsibility is not surprising.

## Why Moral Responsibility Threatens Rights

It is difficult to escape the empirical conclusion that contrary to philosophical myth, as moral responsibility waxes the commitment to individual rights and human dignity wanes. But *why* does stronger belief in moral responsibility weaken respect for human dignity and basic human rights? The myth, of course, is that regarding every human as godlike—as an "autonomous law-giver" and member of the Kantian kingdom of ends, or as a miracle-working first cause that can make or choose its own character—promotes special respect for the extraordinary semi-divine members of the human species. In fact, the belief in moral responsibility has the opposite effect. To understand why requires looking carefully at the larger belief system in which moral responsibility functions and prospers.

The fundamental problem with the moral responsibility system—the basic reason why belief in moral responsibility erodes rather than supports respect for individual dignity and rights—is that the functioning of the moral responsibility system *requires* limits and restrictions on our inquiries and our understanding. The former mayor of New York, Ed Koch, and the former Prime Minister of Britain, John Major, are hardly reliable sources of moral wisdom; but on one point they are precisely right. When a young woman was brutally attacked while jogging in Central Park, Mayor Koch eagerly joined the media and the politicians (Donald Trump purchased a full-page advertisement calling for the death penalty) in demanding swift and severe punishment of the "Central Park Five" (a group of minority youths who were accused and convicted of the crime, and after many years in prison were found—through DNA evidence and the confession of the actual perpetrator—to have been innocent): "To understand is to forgive. I don't want to understand what motivates someone to engage in this kind of horror, I want, rather than to understand them, I want them punished." When there was an increase in juvenile crime in the UK (probably as a result of the reduction in social programs by John Major's party since the election of neo-liberal Margaret Thatcher), Prime Minister Major championed exactly the same policy that Koch had endorsed: "Society needs to condemn a little more and understand a little less" (Major 1993, 8). Koch and Major were right: understanding gets in the way of holding people morally responsible and demanding their "just deserts" of severe punishment. The price for condemning more—the price for stronger commitment to moral responsibility—is paid in reduced understanding of the causes of behavior. Their attachment to retributivism and moral responsibility caused them to favor ignorance over understanding, but at least they recognized the price that must be paid for belief in moral responsibility. Perhaps among neo-liberal politicians, the choice of ignorance over understanding is not surprising: if the deeper causes of the increase in violent behavior are the social policies you have promoted, then ignorance is bliss.

The brutality of our prisons, the neglect of our social welfare system, the neglect of real opportunities and care for many of our children, and the gross inequities in distribution of wealth: these are not accidental correlations with strong belief in moral responsibility, but part of an interlocking system with moral responsibility squarely in the middle. If one is trying to design a system that will undercut respect for personal dignity, start with a deep commitment to moral responsibility. The more moral responsibility, the less understanding; and the less understanding, the more retributive impulses; and the greater the retributive impulses, the more injustice; and coming full circle, belief in moral responsibility blinds us to the injustice. This is a solid flesh and blood problem that is played out both individually and in societies. Individual self-making, myopia, and belief in a just world combine in an unholy trinity that causes deep misery and does enormous harm to individual dignity: not just in philosophical theory, but in harsh observable reality.

# 8 *How* Does Belief in Moral Responsibility Undermine Personal Dignity?

There is a clear correlation between stronger belief in moral responsibility and weaker commitment to individual rights. Any causal claim drawn from such correlational evidence would be strengthened by specifying a causal factor that might account for that correlation. What is it about the moral responsibility belief system that *weakens* support and protection of personal dignity? First and foremost, it is the emphasis on *individual self-making*. The basic problem with the "self-made man"—other than its utter implausibility—is that it blocks better understanding of how to enhance individual powers and dignity while justifying both benign neglect and harsh demeaning judgments. Understanding why belief in self-making has those unfortunate effects requires careful examination. It might seem plausible that if each of us is *self-made*—a characteristic that is remarkable indeed, even godlike—then we should receive special recognition and respect for our self-generation. Unfortunately, the actual result is the opposite. Before digging deeper into why that is so, the self-making process itself must be examined.

## Self-Making and its Limits

Its flaws notwithstanding, the charm and appeal of the self-made man make it a favorite with supporters of moral responsibility, and it is offered by everyone from Renaissance mystics to tough-minded contemporary empiricists. Even Plato (in *The Republic*) offered an account of disembodied souls *choosing* their next life cycle. The reason for its perennial popularity among moral responsibility advocates is not far to seek. If moral responsibility is to be plausible, then some variety of special self-making is the most obvious grounds for supporting it: you are morally responsible for yourself because you *made* or *chose* yourself, and no deeper inquiry into the causes of your behavior and character is relevant. The crucial causal steps *end* in *you*, and no deeper causal inquiry—deeper inquiry that would reveal fatal problems for claims of moral responsibility—is possible.

The most dramatic self-making account was developed by Pico della Mirandola in the late fifteenth century, with God granting to humans—His favorite creation—the unique capacity to create themselves in whatever forms they choose: "We have made thee neither of heaven nor of earth, neither mortal nor immortal, so that with freedom of choice and with honor, as though the maker and molder of thyself, thou mayest fashion thyself in whatever shape thou shalt prefer" (1486/1948, 225). Jean-Paul Sartre (1946/1989) secularized the model, but retained the basic idea that somehow you exist and then *you* (in a way that defies explanation) must create your own essence and nature as a self-created "being-for-itself."

But it is not only existentialists and Renaissance mystics who promote self-making as the path to moral responsibility. Compatibilists—such as the fiercely naturalistic and empirically-minded Daniel Dennett—also appeal to self-making as grounds for moral responsibility:

> I take responsibility for any thing I make and then inflict upon the general public; if my soup causes food poisoning, or my automobile causes air pollution, or my robot runs amok and kills someone, I, the manufacturer, am to blame. And although I may manage to get my suppliers and subcontractors to share the liability somewhat, I am held responsible for releasing the product to the public with whatever flaws it has. Common wisdom has it that much the same rationale grounds personal responsibility; I have created and unleashed an agent who is myself; if its acts produce harm, the manufacturer is held responsible. I think this common wisdom is indeed wisdom.
>
> (1984, 85)

Adina Roskies (2012) proposes an account of self-making (self-authorship, she calls it) which is one of the best when it comes to explaining how self-making is possible in a deterministic and naturalistic universe, and thus one of the best for avoiding fears of fatalism and hopelessness and for promoting the possibility of optimistic improvement. But as a naturalistic account of self-making that can support moral responsibility it is a failure.

The Roskies account of moral responsibility has a special virtue: it recognizes and openly acknowledges that any plausible account of moral responsibility must find a way of halting deeper inquiry into the causes of our behavior. She insists that the choices and behavior of a morally responsible *agent* must call a halt to further explanation. The *agent* made the choice or performed the act, and no earlier causal factors are relevant: "When we look backwards to attribute responsibility, we are looking for a certain *kind* of explanation, a reason to say, 'The buck stops here.'"(2012, 333) If we continue the causal quest—Roskies is particularly concerned that the causal investigation might proceed back to neuropsychological causes—then moral responsibility is undermined, and the *agent* seems to disappear. If we are to have a morally responsible agent, then there must be good reasons to halt the inquiry with the decision of the agent. *That* decision or choice is the cause of the act, and no deeper causes matter:

Although all physical events can be traced backward to prior causes, not all causes have equal status in explaining a phenomenon. For example, we might explain the trajectory of a ball by citing the force with which it was thrown, its mass, and the acceleration due to gravity. But prior causes are responsible for those causes, including the birth of the person that threw it, her conception, the meeting of her parents, the coalescing of the rock and gas that now make up our planet, and the fabrication of the ball. Nonetheless, those causes are simply not relevant to an explanation of the ball's trajectory, not even that particular ball's trajectory, once the relevant physical parameters are specified. There are reasons, pragmatic and otherwise, to limit the backward progression in the causal chain when giving an account of events, even when giving a purely causal account. Similarly, there are reasons to pick out some causes as the relevant ones when giving an account of an agent's choice or action.

(2012, 333)

That is quite true, if our concern is simply describing what happened: why did the ball land here? Because Rachel threw it. Why did Sarah go to the latest Star Wars movie? Because she chose to do so, it was her own choice. But when we are concerned with moral responsibility, the *relevant* causes become much deeper and more complex.

Suppose that our department softball team is locked in a fierce contest with our despised rivals from the comparative literature department. Adina is playing right field, while Zoe plays left field. The struggle goes into extra innings, and in the tenth inning comparative lit has a runner on third base with one out. The batter hits a fly ball to left which Zoe snags; the runner on third tags up and heads for home with the winning run, but Zoe throws a strike to the catcher and the runner is out, and Zoe receives congratulations for saving the team from defeat. Then the eleventh inning, and the same scenario: comp lit has a runner on third with one out. This time the batter hits a fly ball to right—exactly the same distance from home plate—which Adina catches. The runner tags, but Adina's throw is shorter and slower, and the runner scores the winning run. The philosophers crowd around Adina, berating her for losing the game with her lousy throw. "It was the same situation as in the previous inning," complains the department's bioethicist. "Zoe made a good throw and got the runner out, while in the same situation you made a lousy throw and lost the game. Zoe deserves our praise; but you justly deserve departmental opprobrium." Surely one of Adina's colleagues would come to her rescue: "It's not fair to blame Adina. The situations and circumstances were in fact very different. Adina's throw was made later in the day, and the Sun was lower, and directly in her eyes. Also, that was the only hard throw Zoe made all day: her arm was fresh and rested. Adina, on the other hand, had made six or seven very hard throws in the course of the game, and her arm was tired. Besides, Zoe happens to have a stronger arm than Adina: Adina is simply not capable of throwing as fast and far as Zoe. So it is not fair to blame Adina for that bad throw." It is perfectly true that if we are giving an explanation of why the ball went from the outfield to the infield, a simple and shallow explanation will do: Adina threw it. But if we are considering moral responsibility and just deserts, examination of causes must go deeper. We could insist on stopping with the bad throw—"Adina made the bad throw, so she deserves blame for the loss"—but that would be an arbitrary stopping point. (It is true that the criminal courts typically make such an arbitrary halt to inquiries when they discover *who* did the criminal act, treating the forces that shaped the criminal actor's character and behavior as irrelevant; but that only shows that the criminal courts are often as shallow and arbitrary as Adina's nasty teammates.)

When we turn to moral responsibility for a choice or action, the relevant causal factors are significantly richer than Roskies allows, just as they are if we are evaluating moral responsibility for a physical success or failure. Adina and Diana are in similar situations. Both have promised to return the draft of a dissertation to a student, with extensive comments, early tomorrow morning. Both Adina and Diana are eager to see the new Star Wars movie, and both would love to go out for an evening of dinner and drinks and the movie with their friends; while reading and commenting on the dissertation—on a topic both find rather dull, and by a student whose work is not very good and who will need lots of comments and recommendations—is regarded by both as an unpleasant if not an odious obligation. Adina, nose to the grindstone and with two pots of coffee, gets through the dissertation and the comments, and returns them to the student bright and early the next morning; Diana, in contrast, blows off the obligation and the promise, and spends the evening enjoying her friends, her drinks, her dinner, and her movie. Adina was virtuous, Diana was naughty; Adina made a good decision and acted virtuously, while Diana made a bad choice and acted badly. But before we pass judgment on their moral responsibility for their very different choices, we must—just as in the case of the good and bad throws—inquire more deeply.

Diana does not think as carefully—she is a cognitive miser, in contrast to Adina, who is a chronic cognizer (Cacioppo and Petty 1982)—and fails to consider that after a long night of drinking and dining and an exciting movie, she will be in no condition to read a dissertation, much less provide helpful comments. Diana has already made six difficult decisions today, and she is in a state of severe ego depletion (Baumeister et al. 1998) that makes it more difficult for her to sustain hard deliberation (comparable to Adina's six throws that left her arm tired). Perhaps Diana also has a weaker sense of cognitive self-efficacy (Bandura 1997), and fails to deliberate carefully about her choice because she lacks confidence in her deliberative abilities. Diana has recently had few opportunities for pleasant social occasions with friends, while Adina is very popular and often dines out with her friends, and so Diana is significantly more tempted than is Adina. And we might add: Diana simply doesn't have as much fortitude as Adina has, or as great a degree of self-control—and research indicates that powers of self-control are strongly shaped at a very early age (Mischel and Ebbesen 1970; Mischel, Shoda, and Peake 1988).

Roskies seems to believe that when we have noted the agent's deliberative choice, there may remain further physical (neurological) factors that are *irrelevant* in this context; but while irrelevant neuropsychological causes may remain, there are—according to Roskies—no relevant *psychological* factors:

> I am not denying that there will always be some kind of non-reason, physical explanation for the presence of a reason, but what I am suggesting is that that is not the place to look. Certainly, our reasons may be elements of us that are in some sense given. But they are not unchangeable. The agent, in appreciating the content of a reason, can intervene in the way in which that reason operates in his deliberation, in loops of agential control. If he or she did not, and by not doing so the agent accepted and endorsed that reason and its role in his deliberation, then . . . that is the appropriate place to stop. Agents control themselves via conscious access to mental content. We therefore have a convenient way of locating the source of the control: at the agentive, aware level.
>
> (2012, 334–335)

But why does one agent "intervene" in one manner, and another agent in a different manner? Why does one "accept and endorse that reason" while another continues to reflect and ultimately rejects it? Unless that process of intervention is a first and final cause, then we soon find psychological factors that account for such differences, and that do not support claims of moral responsibility. No matter how many "loops of agential control," those loops involve *psychological* factors (without any appeal to neurological causes); and those deeper psychological factors undercut claims of moral responsibility. Unless, that is, reason is a magical process that transcends all psychological influences, and we reason in a bubble insulated from situational and developmental influences.

When we scrutinize the grubby details of the deliberative process, the soaring "loops of agential control" are soon brought down to Earth. Rather than a deliberative process that soars above individual limitations, we find dramatic differences in need for cognition, ego depletion, cognitive self-efficacy and subtle situational factors. Perhaps Roskies is right that in examining moral responsibility we need not trace the causes all the way to the brain activity (though that does not seem nearly as obvious to me as it does to her); but this is not a case of bringing in neuropsychological considerations and causes. The causal factors noted here remain firmly on the psychological plane, and their relevance to the moral responsibility of the actors is clear. If they are ruled irrelevant, there must be stronger reasons to exclude them than merely the desire to find a stopping point that preserves moral responsibility.

Refusal to investigate those deeper psychological factors may indeed match (what Roskies calls) "the folk metaphysics of agency" (2012, 335), and that may explain why it seems legitimate to call a halt to the causal inquiry when moral responsibility is at stake. But the folk metaphysics of agency is false. Appeals to the folk metaphysics of agency are no more convincing than saying that the only way to alleviate the worries of those disturbed by evolutionary natural selection is to retain the folk metaphysics of species fixity. Roskies appeals to the common belief that: "Agents control themselves via conscious access to mental content. We therefore have a convenient way of locating the source of the control: at the agentive, aware level." The notion that our deliberation is open and transparent may fit the folk model, but the folk model is false, and a satisfactory account of moral responsibility cannot be constructed on that false foundation. A more empirically accurate model of our deliberative processes is provided by Jonathan Haidt:

> Automatic processes run the human mind, just as they have been running animal minds for 500 million years, so they're very good at what they do, like software that has been improved through thousands of product cycles. When human beings evolved the capacity for language and reasoning at some point in the last million years, the brain did not rewire itself to hand over the reins to a new and inexperienced charioteer. Rather, the rider (language-based reasoning) evolved because it did something useful for the elephant.
>
> The rider can do several useful things. It can see further into the future (because we can examine alternative scenarios in our heads) and therefore can help the elephant make better decisions in the present. It can learn new skills and master new technologies, which can help the elephant reach its goals and sidestep disasters. And, most important, the rider acts as the spokesman for the elephant, even though it doesn't necessarily know what the elephant is really thinking. The rider is skilled at fabricating post hoc explanations for whatever the elephant has just done, and it is good at finding reasons to justify what the elephant wants to do next. Once human beings developed language and began to use it to gossip about each other, it became extremely valuable for elephants to carry on their backs a full-time public relations firm.
>
> (2012, 45–46)

Deliberation may be special, and it may—at least sometimes—enhance our control and our sense of control; but it is not miraculous. While acknowledging the benefits of deliberation, philosophers must stop treating deliberation in the manner of Aristotle and Descartes and Kant, and instead examine psychological research into what really happens. If we adopt Roskies' view, we ignore most of the real problems that inhibit deliberation, and forgo all the ways that we might enhance deliberative powers. Most of our deliberation is not transparent: generally we are deliberating to defend a position we already favor, not to determine the correct choice, though it certainly seems to us that we are being perfectly "objective." As Haidt notes, the conscious "rider" typically is unaware of "what the elephant is really thinking." We conclude that the rape victim must have "led him on," unaware that the deep nonconscious belief in a just world (Lerner 1980) is shaping our "deliberation." We deliberate and decide to help pick up papers, unaware that finding a dime left in a phone booth (Isen and Levin 1972) has decisively influenced our deliberation. And rather than deliberation being primarily a procedure of evaluating and then choosing among various options, it is more often a process of rationalization for a choice made for nonconscious motives. Even at the best, with ideal and transparent deliberation, we are fortunate—*lucky*—to have such powers and to be so free from prejudices and nonconscious diversions: the capacity to develop such rare powers and have such deliberative freedom was—at the fundamental level—not of our own making or choosing. Self-making is important, but it does not establish moral responsibility for our characters unless we adamantly refuse to look deeper and more carefully into the total psychological causal history. That process of deeper study does not require any examination of brain processes, and stays—as Roskies insists we should—entirely in the psychological realm.

## Real Control

Roskies fails to find grounds for moral responsibility, but she nonetheless makes valuable points concerning how we can deliberately and effectively change and improve our characters and our behavior. Diana *might* decide that she needs more fortitude and stronger self-control, and make efforts—perhaps even successful efforts—to strengthen her self-control (possibly enlisting the help of a behavioral therapist). But that she is able to recognize that shortcoming, that she has the confidence (and a sufficient degree of fortitude) to engage in working to change that capacity, that she has knowledge of the most promising resources for character improvement (rather than seeking out an astrologer or sending money to a television evangelist): these deeper factors deriving from her fortunate history erode any grounds for moral responsibility.

It is important to note that—when we want to do so—often we *can* change, and Roskies notes at least three processes that can facilitate such change. First, she notes that changing and controlling our environment (our situations) can have an important impact on our behavior. She gives a pedestrian but effective example: to avoid the strong (and sometimes overwhelming) temptation to eat mass quantities of potato chips, make sure you never keep potato chips in the house. John Doris (2002, 147–149) supplies another striking example: if you know that a few glasses of wine, a candlelight dinner, and the close proximity of an attractive colleague may overpower your resolve to avoid adultery while your spouse is away, then refuse the attractive colleague's invitation to dinner. But we can also set up environments that will promote positive behavior: for example, we can develop greater fortitude by setting up stretched interval positive reinforcers.

A second important means of self-improvement noted by Roskies is the use of mental images or frequently rehearsed rules to influence subsequent behavior: I can prime myself to picture myself looking grossly obese whenever I am tempted by junk food, or work to recall the joys of positive responses to a published article when I am tempted to stop writing and turn to the ubiquitous temptations of television.

A third point made by Roskies in this context is that agentive control "is not static control, variables themselves can be learned, adjusted, and deliberately engineered" (2012, 331). Consider Deandra, who is weak in self-control: she has trouble sustaining effort, she finds it difficult to resist immediate temptations, and this is resulting in bad habits and poor work and great frustration. Deandra can take steps to improve her self-control (for example, by arranging with a friend to take her out to a pleasant dinner once she has successfully finished a task on which she usually would have given up). Not only does the external reward strengthen her fragile powers of self-control, but the satisfaction of finishing a challenging project through her own hard work is also a positive reinforcer. Next time Deandra will find it a bit easier to sustain hard efforts, and likely will work harder and even longer (and that will itself be positively reinforcing). Gradually, Deandra can—through her own control—develop greater fortitude and stronger capacity for avoiding immediate gratification in favor of long term goals.

The three suggestions for "self-making" and self-improvement offered by Roskies are perfectly legitimate, if not particularly original or exciting. But rather than writing a self-help book, Roskies is making an important philosophical point: we can indeed exercise control and shape ourselves in important ways, and that is a worthwhile point to emphasize in this context. It avoids the fears of fatalism and lack of control and helplessness. We know the debilitating effects of lack of control, and of a sense of no control: effects which include not only severe depression, but also greater vulnerability to infection and increase in mortality rate. So the control we can effectively exercise—in a deterministic world—is important, and well worth noting; but it does nothing to support claims of moral responsibility. Roskies notes that:

> Through deliberately thinking and acting in strategic ways we can exert control, modulate and intervene in our future states, both physical and mental. It is this that allows us to shape ourselves in ways that make it the case that we are in some very real sense responsible for who we are.
> (2012, 331)

So long as this is the "very real sense" of being *causally* responsible for some aspects of who we are, and for having greater effectiveness in exercising *take-charge* responsibility, this is positive and beneficial; but if the claim is that it provides grounds for *moral responsibility*—the responsibility of just deserts—then it fails.

## Self-Making and Moral Responsibility

Some advocates of self-making (including Roskies) might respond that my harsh attack on self-making attacks a strawman. Renaissance mystics like Pico, and existentialists like Sartre, claim we are totally self-made; but more sophisticated proponents of self-making are more circumspect: we are not totally but only *partially* self-made, but partial self-making suffices for moral responsibility. We are indeed partially "self-made", and that is worth noting. As Roskies states:

> It is not necessary to create oneself out of whole cloth. Continual shaping of the given over time establishes sufficient control of the agent to suffice as a grounding kind of self-causation.
>
> (2012, 338)

Consider the concert violinist who plays with exquisite skill and artistry. Obviously, this level of accomplishment did not just happen, and was not merely a matter of good luck: you cannot hit the lucky violinist lottery ticket and be transformed into a superb violinist. The wonderful violinist devoted countless hours, made many sacrifices, planned carefully and intelligently, and exerted enormous sustained effort in *making herself* into an accomplished violinist. Some very important self-making was involved. But important and genuine as such self-making is, it does not establish moral responsibility: the violinist is a wonderful artist, but she does not justly deserve special reward for her marvelous abilities or her extraordinary performances. It is not unlikely that she was the fortunate possessor of at least some genetic advantages (at the very least the capacity for developing remarkable dexterity). Almost certainly she had the good fortune to show some special musical aptitude (aptitude that was not the product of her own special efforts or planning) that attracted special encouragement and probably better teachers. And she had—probably at age 3 or 4, if psychological research on this subject is to be believed—significant ability to resist tempting distractions and make sustained efforts to improve her musical talents: she was blessed (or shaped) at an early age with substantial powers of self-control. This is not to deprecate the genuine dedicated efforts of this superb violinist, much less the high quality of her art and her accomplishment. But there is little danger of those being deprecated. The real danger is that the fortunate starting points will be ignored. When she gives a wonderful performance, she is not merely *lucky* to play superbly; it was indeed a performance of great skill and artistry, and such artistry requires tremendous effort and dedication. But she was lucky to have the initial advantages that made possible such hard sustained work and the subsequent level of artistic skill.

A quick side note: obviously the violinist will gain pleasure and satisfaction from her playing that most of us will never experience, and she will thereby gain special reward. Some people might suggest that if one rejects all moral responsibility, then her abilities should be undercut until she no longer gains these special satisfactions, since she does not justly deserve them. But that absurd suggestion does not follow from denial of moral responsibility; rather, it follows from the myth that the world is *just*, or *must* be just. Belief in a just world is basic to the origin of the belief in moral responsibility; those who *reject* moral responsibility are under no obligation to accept the deep but obviously false belief that the world is just. If the world is just, then the violinist must justly deserve the special benefits she receives from her marvelous skill and artistry; but when we deny moral responsibility, we need not suppose that we are burdened with the impossible—and profoundly counter-productive and cruel—task of making belief in a just world plausible. It was the obsessive belief in a just world that motivated belief in moral responsibility; when we give up belief in moral responsibility, it becomes easier to look squarely at the fact that this world is not just, and that at least some attempts to *make* it just would cause great harm (and actually increase the injustice). Even if we suppose that there is some degree of injustice in the fact that the violinist has remarkable musical talent while I have none, destroying her talent would be an *additional* injustice, not a reduction of injustice. A world in which children are born with severe birth defects is not a just world; but a "leveling" effort that imposes such maladies on all children would not be a step toward making the world just.

John Martin Fischer insists that we do have enough control to support claims of moral responsibility:

> Just as an astronaut may still control the lift-off of the rocket, even though she did not build the platform that makes the launch possible (or ever have any control over the platform), we can be accountable for playing the cards that are dealt us, even if we did not manufacture the cards, write the rules of the game, and so forth. We can exercise precisely that sort of control of our behavior that moral responsibility requires, without having an inflated or exalted power of self-creation. It is a kind of wisdom . . . to recognize that, when you play the cards that are dealt you (in a certain distinctive way), you can exercise a robust sort of control, even in the absence of the power to make the cards, to own the factory that makes the cards, to make up the rules of the game, and so forth.

(Fischer 2012, 185)

This is a charming but misleading metaphor. Fischer focuses on how *you* play the cards you've been dealt, or how *you* operate the space launch you are piloting (whatever the comparative quality of the cards or space launch); but what is really at issue is the *you* who is playing the cards or piloting the ship. What is your level of self-confidence, fortitude, cognitive self-efficacy, self-control, need for cognition? Precisely the factors that enable *you* to pilot the ship well (or cause you to pilot it badly) are the relevant factors: the factors that shaped your abilities, well or ill. Certainly, we admire the player or pilot who operates with skill, confidence, fortitude, patience, and careful deliberation; but whether that fortunately shaped individual is morally responsible for her splendid behavior is another question altogether. It is also important that the player have an opportunity to exercise control and make choices and "play the cards as she chooses." That capacity to exercise control is vital for her psychological well-being, but it does not follow that she justly deserves reward or punishment (that she is morally responsible) for playing poorly or brilliantly.

We can admire the way someone plays his cards (even if his hand is a poor one) and the skill he subsequently develops at the game. But bad starting hands can also result in poor development of skill: the better starting hand is more likely to experience more early success, develop greater self-confidence, have the opportunity to work with a better coach, hone his skills against superior competition. Whether you play your cards well or ill is not the result of a first-cause choice to be good or bad, there is not some absolute starting point at which one says "evil, be thou my good" while another opts for virtue. The skill and fortitude and optimism and confidence with which you "play the cards that were dealt you" are ultimately *among* the cards that were dealt you (dealt either by one's genetic legacy or one's early conditioning). One who works hard is often positively reinforced by the results, and that strengthens the person's fortitude, and the process can continue until the result is a person who has developed wonderful powers of sustained effort. If we *start* with "the cards that were dealt you," and say that from now on you are responsible for playing them well or ill, then the basic problems concerning the real starting point can be concealed. When we look closer and deeper, the problems are still there. When one player starts with weaker cards, less skill in playing those cards, and less fortitude for sustaining the patience and concentration required to play the cards consistently well, then it is fundamentally unfair to claim that the winner and the loser justly deserve their respective reward and punishment.

Fischer's account of moral responsibility is similar to that of the legal system: when your act is your *own* unimpeded and uncoerced act, caused by your *own* intent, and thus performed by the person you are, then you are morally responsible for that act. But as Focquaert, Glenn, and Raine note:

> The law's view of personhood tells an overly simplistic story, and the current legal system ignores our advancing scientific knowledge when it

holds people, including those with mental disorders, responsible merely on the basis of their intentional acts.

(2013, 253)

## The Starting Point Problem

John Lemos has made the most serious and sustained effort to deal with the problem of a starting point for moral responsibility: a starting point for personal development that will make us morally responsible for our developed character. Like Robert Kane, Lemos rejects all appeals to miraculous first-cause self-creation—and also like Kane, Lemos clearly recognizes the tremendous difficulties involved in giving such a moral responsibility account. By my lights, Lemos does not succeed; but the great virtue of his work is that he recognizes the problem, and that is a big improvement. If you want moral responsibility, you must refuse to look deeper; or appeal to a godlike self-caused first cause (a cause no one can explain: which is not surprising, given that it is miraculous); or find some other plausible launching pad for self-development that will justify claims of moral responsibility.

Robert Kane insists that moral responsibility requires basic "self-forming acts" (SFAs): acts by which we make our own characters. However, Kane firmly rejects any appeal to miraculous first-cause self-forming or self-choosing acts (the easy answer offered by Pico Della Mirandola, C. A. Campbell, Roderick Chisholm, and Jean-Paul Sartre). Instead, Kane's self-forming acts involve simultaneously willing two conflicting acts: on one side, an act that furthers one's personal goal of success and well-being, and on the other side an act one feels morally obligated to perform. Both acts are willed, and the deciding factor is *not* causally determined but instead is the result of quantum indeterminacy amplified by the internal chaos generated by this conflict of willed choices. Since both choices are willed by the agent, whichever choice is made is the agent's *own* choice; and since indeterminacy is the ultimate source of the choice that the agent makes, there is no deeper cause to probe, and the agent's choice is thus an ultimate self-forming act (Kane 1985, 1996, and 2007).

Kane's subtle, fascinating, and nonmiraculous account of libertarian free will has been the subject of extensive debate, but that ongoing debate is not the present subject. Rather, the issue is the problem examined by John Lemos, a dedicated supporter of Kane's position who recognizes a serious problem that *any* effort to justify moral responsibility must confront: no matter how the willed choices are made, how does the buildup of character *originate*? Even if we grant that a person can be morally responsible for a willed choice (such as a business woman's choice to stop and help someone at considerable expense to her own prospects of success, as in Kane's famous story), the question remains of how the character that produced this meritorious choice was formed. Kane describes the woman as willing two conflicting acts: she wills *both* the altruistic act of helping *and* the act of rushing to her important meeting. But for each of those willed acts, what is its source? If the answer is that it was formed by a previous self-forming act, that just pushes the question back one more step. Ultimately, one must give an account of how the whole process of character formation originated.

That is the problem posed in powerful terms by Al Mele (2006, 51–53) and Randolph Clarke (2002, 372; 2003, 88). Kane does not hide from the problem; to the contrary, he struggles with it honestly and openly. His proposed solution is that the very earliest character formation may be compatibilist (not requiring libertarian self-forming acts) but the subsequent self-forming acts (SFAs) account for the further development of individual character. Lemos sees difficulties in Kane's proposed solution:

> As Mele notes, Kane appeals to *compatibilist* criteria of freedom in accounting for how we can be free in and responsible for our SFAs. On the Kanean view, any human being's first free actions should be SFAs, as they provide the basis for all other human freedom and responsibility. However, we are told that to be responsible for SFAs agents must engage in dual willings leading up to choice and that meeting some good compatibilist criteria of freedom suffice for making these dual willings free. The suggestion that meeting such compatibilist criteria suffices for the freedom of the dual willings appears to be inconsistent with the spirit of Kane's overall theory. . . . As Mele notes, the problem here is that if the dual efforts/willings in SFAs are free by meeting good compatibilist criteria, then it is no longer clear why we need to meet any libertarian criteria at all to be free.
>
> (Lemos 2015, 140)

Lemos proposes a libertarian solution to this problem: a solution not identical to Kane's proposal, but a solution that Lemos develops in the spirit of Kane's view. First, he acknowledges that for the earliest SFAs of children, "the agent's contribution to what is done is so minimal that there is very little responsibility for what is done":

> As Kane has said in various writings, children have very little responsibility for their earliest SFAs. This is because in our earliest SFAs only the compatibilist criteria of freedom are met in the formation of the dual willings/efforts in them. In these early SFAs there is no past history of SFAs allowing for the agent herself to contribute to the construction of her character. Instead, in the earliest SFAs, the desires or reasons which motivate the dual willings/efforts involved are only products of genetic and environmental factors. Given this fact about the source of the dual willings/efforts in the earliest SFAs, the agent's contribution to what is done is so minimal that there is very little responsibility for what is done.
>
> (Lemos 2015, 141)

So how do we get from a starting point of little or no moral responsibility to the full rich moral responsibility of adults? That is *the* tough question for any account of moral responsibility (whether compatibilist or libertarian); and Lemos faces it squarely. He gives an account of how a child might move from a very low level of moral responsibility to the higher level of full rich adult moral responsibility:

> The choices made in SFAs contribute to shaping one's character over time. Thus, as she makes more of these undetermined choices over time she will contribute more and more to the shaping of her own character. This will increase her level of responsibility for later SFAs as those later SFAs will become more and more a reflection of a character that she has shaped herself through prior undetermined decisions which she was at least partly responsible for making through her own efforts.
>
> While children have some responsibility for their earliest SFAs, they have very little responsibility due to the fact that the dilemmatic choices young children face are thrust upon them by genetic and environmental factors which are beyond their control. As a child grows older, she becomes more responsible for her character because she has through her previous free choices done more to shape the character which gives rise to the dilemmas she faces in her SFAs.
>
> (2015, 144)

Certainly, we do shape our own characters through free *compatibilistic* choices: the child who exerts some degree of effort and is positively reinforced by the pleasant result gains greater fortitude and perhaps a stronger sense of self-efficacy, and those positive effects can continue to grow as fortitude and self-confidence increase and positive results accrue from the greater prolonged exertion empowered by those character traits. Kane, Lemos, and I *agree* that such compatibilist development of character traits is *not* sufficient for the basic moral responsibility that supports just deserts. So at some point one must make the jump from the inadequate compatibilist basis for moral responsibility to something that will support a richer account of basic moral responsibility.

In order to bridge that gap, Lemos tells the story of "little Rosa"—aged 3 or 4—who wants to sneak a cookie (against her parents' orders), but who also fears being caught and reprimanded, and who is now pulled in opposite directions by willing to sneak a cookie while also willing to follow her parents' orders. Suppose that this is Rosa's very first SFA: she wills both, and the deciding factor is the amplified quantum indeterminacy at the heart of Kane's account. As Lemos describes the result:

> Little Rosa chooses freely but any responsibility she has for her choice to sneak a cookie is grounded solely in the effort she makes in the face of

the temptation to do otherwise—an effort which is rightly said to be hers as she meets compatibilist criteria of free action in exerting that effort.

(2015, 144)

So where do we find the crucial initiating first step in the process of developing full adulthood moral responsibility? Not in Rosa's desire for another cookie, nor in her concern for obeying her parents; as Lemos acknowledges, those are the products of "genetic and environmental factors which are beyond their control." It cannot at this point be found in the indeterminacy that pushes Rosa to one side or the other as she struggles with her difficult choice: that indeterminacy is just as strong for little Rosa as it is for adult Rosa; and as both Kane and Lemos agree, Rosa as a small child has *very* little moral responsibility for her choice, while adult Rosa has full moral responsibility for her choice. If the indeterminacy itself conferred moral responsibility, there would be no difference between the moral responsibility of Rosa as a small child and Rosa as a mature adult. There is only one place left to provide the critical starting point for moral responsibility, and that is precisely where Lemos turns: "any responsibility she has for her choice to sneak a cookie is grounded solely in the effort she makes in the face of the temptation to do otherwise." Rosa's effort is indeed her own. But this takes us back to will power as the initiating source for the buildup of moral responsibility; and popular as will power is as grounds for moral responsibility, it is not grounds that can bear that weight or provide the essential starting point.

   Kant celebrates will power as the power that enables rational humans—and *only* rational humans—to act morally and have total moral responsibility without any tinge of corruption from the emotions we share with other animals; C. A. Campbell bases his classic account of libertarian free will on the special power of the *will* to overcome temptation, and for Campbell (like Kant) the power of the will is "something for which a man is responsible without qualification, something that is not affected by heredity and environment but depends solely upon the self itself" (Campbell 1957, 169). The criminal courts operate on the basic assumption that all competent persons have the will power to avoid criminal behavior, and all can make the special free choice to exercise that remarkable power; as described by Sanford Kadish, former dean of the University of California Law School:

> While events in the physical world are governed by laws of nature that imply the existence of necessary and sufficient conditions, voluntary decisions are not. They are controlled by the choice of the actor, a "wild card," for whose action no set of conditions is sufficient and no condition is necessary, save the condition of a free act of will. Therefore, though it may be in any particular case that the principal would not have chosen to act without the influence of the accomplice, it is

never so as a matter of necessity, since the principal could have chosen otherwise.

(Kadish 1987, 198)

But when we actually study "will power" and self-control and impulse control and fortitude, we find nothing mysterious or miraculous; rather, such powers are as much a product of one's environmental and genetic (biosocial) influences as are any other psychological features (Mischel and Ebbeson 1970; Raine 2013, 142–147, 269, 310). Will power cannot serve the function that Lemos is seeking: a starting point from a very tender age. For we know that "will power"—the power of fortitude, the power of self-control—is shaped very early in children, and shaped in ways they do not control. Not only are there distinct differences in such powers by the age of four, but subsequent studies indicate that the strength or weakness of such powers at that age have long-term effects that can be measured many years later (Mischel, Shoda, and Peake 1988).

The moral of this story: if you start from a compatibilist version of moral responsibility, you can never get to the *ultimate* moral responsibility that is the goal of Kane's libertarian quest; or more precisely, you can't get there unless you follow the path of *miraculous* will power, a shortcut Kane steadfastly rejects. Kane and Lemos engage in an honest and valiant struggle to solve a problem that most advocates of moral responsibility resolutely avoid (libertarians typically avoid it through appeal to miracles or mysteries, while compatibilists avoid it by declaring the question off-limits). But their quest for the holy grail of moral responsibility resembles the quest by the knights of the round table: the quest is honest and glorious, but doomed to failure.

## How "Self-Making" Threatens Dignity

Self-making is the main road to moral responsibility, but it forks into two distinctly different tracks. One is the traditional appeal to miraculous powers (or some secularized version, as in Sartre's appeal to "being-for-itself" that mysteriously makes its own essence). This is the path of Pico della Mirandola's godlike power of self-forming choice, the first cause of Roderick Chisholm (1982), the "special creativity" of C. A. Campbell (1957), Timothy O'Connor's "ontologically basic" power of conscious willing that shares "a common metaphysical core" with God's miracle-working freedom (O'Connor 2005, 208). The second path is the path of Roskies and Fischer and Dennett, who insist that we must confine ourselves to "how we play the cards we were dealt," while scrutiny of how one's card playing skills were developed, or of why one received one set of cards while another received a very different starting hand, is prohibited and/or ridiculed: Fischer (2012, 21) disparages such inquiries as symptomatic of "metaphysical megalomania," while Dennett (1984, 165) treats them as an obsessive demand for a "total, before-the-eyes-of-God Guilt." When we travel down the path toward moral responsibility, we find a fork that takes us to either miracles or myopia.

Recognizing that we can engage in some degree of self-making and self-improvement is important for a healthy sense of control; but those benefits come from careful examination of what we can do to improve, emphasizing positive steps, and enabling people to effectively and confidently exercise take-charge responsibility. Noting the possibility and methods of change is good; linking them with moral responsibility is not. When our limited powers of self-making are used as grounds for moral responsibility, then those limited benefits become serious detriments. We do "partially make ourselves," and that is worth celebrating; but not if it makes us forget that when Edward (partially) makes a better self than does George, Edward started with better raw materials, more skills, better tools, and better training; and that it is unfair to reward Edward and punish George for the dramatically different end products.

Why, then, does commitment to moral responsibility erode rather than strengthen support of human dignity? The basic reason stems from the commitment to self-making which is at the foundation of belief in moral responsibility. The self-making that justifies belief in moral responsibility is very special indeed: we can somehow "rise above" our mundane history and make ourselves; and this self-making or self-choosing somehow transcends any characteristics that were shaped or given by forces from our very early history. Because we have these remarkable, even miraculous powers of self-making, nothing in our earlier history matters: *everyone* who is morally responsible has the power to make themselves, and therefore our earlier histories become irrelevant. Perhaps you grew up in poverty, suffered abuse, had little or no health care, attended dangerous failing schools, were never encouraged, and were malnourished; or maybe you enjoyed every advantage of top schools, supportive parents and loving grandparents, opportunities for travel, excellent nutrition, and a safe environment that encouraged and rewarded active exploration and promoted sustained effort; but none of that matters because everyone has the special power of self-making, and if you made a lousy self you justly deserve all the blame, while those who fashion more energetic and intelligent and successful selves justly deserve all the credit.

Or suppose we follow the other fork, and refuse to look harder and deeper. That path ultimately arrives at the same destination. In both cases, we count early influences as irrelevant, and insist that it is only what you are and do *now* that really counts. If you are now successful, you justly deserve all the credit; if you are a failure or a criminal, you deserve your punishment and you are receiving your just deserts. From both the libertarian and the compatibilist perspectives you did it all (or at least all that is relevant) yourself, the conditions that shaped you are irrelevant, and so you justly deserve the results. Our deep nonconscious belief in a just world (which motivated the implausible solution of moral responsibility) joins in the account, and provides further justification for our belief that those who suffer deprivation or punishment as well as those who enjoy privilege and reward are being treated justly: since the world is just those on whom fortune smiles must be deserving, and likewise those on whom fortune frowns.

When self-satisfied confidence is combined with our deep strike-back desire—which makes the retributive infliction of pain *feel* righteous—it is hardly surprising that the moral responsibility system metes out harsh punishment, provides little support for the *undeserving* poor, and promotes the firm belief that justice requires that "to him that hath shall be given." In the myopic system of moral responsibility—that blocks the recognition and understanding of the deeper causes contributing to both failure and success—it is *doubly* wrong to expect the wealthy and privileged to aid those who are struggling. Doubly wrong, because first it upsets the just order by taking from those who justly deserve their rewards; and second, it helps those who justly deserve to suffer. When we examine the nature of the moral responsibility system, it is not surprising that the system punishes harshly while also providing meager support to those in need of the help and assistance that would allow them both the material necessities and the genuine opportunity to live lives of human dignity.

Stephen Morse insists that by treating all minimally competent criminals as equal—and studiously ignoring any differences in their histories, conditions, and abilities—we show greater respect for human *dignity*:

> The differences that exist between offenders convicted of the same crime are morally insignificant compared to the similarities. The great value of this position, placing the burden of persuasion on those who believe it is hard to obey the law, is that it treats people with greater respect and dignity than the opposing view, which treats them as helpless puppets buffeted by forces that rob them of responsibility for their deeds.
>
> (1984, 31–32)

But of course those who deny moral responsibility do not regard criminals, law professors, or candlestick makers as "helpless puppets." To the contrary, those who deny moral responsibility recognize that we *do* make decisions and choices and we do have a hand in self-making; but they also recognize the vital importance of the factors that enhance or inhibit effective self-making. Genuine respect for human dignity requires careful examination of the causes that shape our characters and behavior, and using that knowledge to enhance the opportunity of everyone to exercise effective control and live successful satisfying lives. That requires studying the effects of experiencing early childhood violence, a dysfunctional family rather than a loving and supportive family life, lead poisoning, both good and bad educational opportunities, good nutrition compared with malnutrition, excellent prenatal and childhood and adolescent health care compared with substandard or no health care. We *can* through our own efforts—not as puppets—develop talents and abilities and self-confidence and fortitude; but we need support and a positive environment and genuine opportunities to achieve such goals. The dogged refusal to examine closely the deeper causes behind both virtuous and vicious behavior means a refusal to understand and correct the problems that impede and often destroy the hopes, efforts, and opportunities of children in poor environmental surroundings. Refusal to examine those problems and try to fix them does not show respect for the human dignity of those whose lives are damaged. Insisting that those who have suffered such damage are "free and equal" when they are convicted and imprisoned makes a cruel mockery of concern for human dignity.

Rejection of deeper inquiry is inherent in the system of moral responsibility, and that makes an additional contribution to the undermining of respect for individual human dignity. When careful examination of the deeper *causes* of poverty and crime (as well as of fortitude and virtue and success) is blocked by either the miracles or the myopia of the moral responsibility system, then criminals seem strange and alien. You and I would never commit an armed robbery, a brutal assault, a vicious murder; our histories are irrelevant, and in any case they are off-limits when examining such cases; and so the criminal—in dramatic contrast to us—is a strange sort of creature who freely but inexplicably chooses evil. When criminals are inexplicable alien creatures—radically different from good, successful, law-abiding persons like ourselves—then they are perceived as more dangerous and frightening. As Nils Christie (1993) noted, the more unlike us the criminal is imagined to be, the greater the willingness to impose harsh punishment. We fear what we cannot understand, and the moral responsibility system makes the understanding of criminals a near impossibility. It is not surprising that this encourages policies that "lock them away" for long periods in super secure facilities. The problem is further exacerbated by the resulting lack of sympathy, much less empathy, for these dangerous mysterious creatures so different from ourselves.

Giving serious consideration to the deeper causes for criminal behavior has the opposite effect: it significantly reduces the desire for severe punishment (Doob and Roberts 1983; Fishkin 1996; Indermaur et al. 2012). Hanna Pickard (2011) notes that *blaming* patients for their bad behavior is an impediment to a positive therapeutic relationship. She recommends that therapists eliminate that problematic inclination to blame by carefully examining the deeper formative causes that shaped the faulty character of the patient. The process also works in reverse: if we want to blame and condemn and punish severely, we must block deeper consideration of the causes of behavior. That is a fact understood by those politicians who want to exploit harsh law and order rhetoric for political gain. Ronald Reagan, for example, complained that seeking knowledge of the *causes* of crime was getting in the way of harsh punishment of criminals: "Our forebears were never concerned about why a person misbehaves. We are straying from the principle of holding the individual responsible for his action." (Quoted in

Beckett 1997, 66) And John Major rejected deeper understanding of the causes of juvenile crime, recognizing that such understanding mitigates the populist demand for harsh retributive measures against juveniles: "Society needs to condemn a little more and understand a little less" (1993, 8).

## Individualism and Moral Responsibility

One might suppose that it is not the emphasis on *moral responsibility* that is the source of the problem, but the emphasis on *individuality*. It is true, one might argue, that in the United States there is harsher treatment of criminals and less concern for aiding those who face severe economic and social disadvantages, so there is less respect for human dignity in the United States than in moral responsibility-minimizing Scandinavia. But the real source of the difference in respect for human dignity is not a difference in commitment to moral responsibility, but a difference between the intensely *individualistic* orientation in the United States as opposed to the more corporatist or communitarian view prevalent in Scandinavia. But the individualist vs. corporatist contrast between Scandinavia and the United States is not independent of but instead closely linked with belief in moral responsibility. It is tied up with "rugged individualism" and the "self-made man" and individual "free (miraculous) choice." It is part of the belief that each individual—whatever his or her background and starting point—has complete opportunity and so each individual is uniquely and individually responsible for both success and failure, and justly deserves the sweet or bitter fruits of those totally free individual choices. Rugged individualism is an integral element of the moral responsibility system, rather than an independent variable.

Another key element of the moral responsibility system is the belief in a just world. As noted earlier, it is the deep—but typically nonconscious—belief in a just world that provides major motivation for the belief in moral responsibility. Since we *must* punish, and there are obviously those who enjoy great benefits while others suffer severe want, we require some means of squaring those distressing facts with our deep belief in a just world. Moral responsibility provides the analgesic for our discomfort: those who are punished are morally responsible for their bad acts, and receive their *just* deserts; those who are disadvantaged (or severely harmed) must have some flaws (perhaps hidden flaws) for which they are justly suffering; and those who of us who are specially favored with the lion's share of the wealth must likewise be receiving our just deserts for our ingenuity, our diligence, and our virtue. With the secure belief in a just world, it is not only wrong to spare the rod (that would be depriving the wrongdoer of his just deserts, and upsetting the just order); it is also *doubly* wrong to provide significant aid to the severely disadvantaged (they justly deserve the deprivations they suffer) and aiding the disadvantaged would mean depriving those who justly deserve their disproportionate share of the wealth of the full just deserts to which they are entitled.

Among those deeply committed to individual moral responsibility, this slogan seems an obvious and indubitable truth: it is wrong to aid the lazy poor by stealing the bread from the hands of those who have earned it by their own efforts. The idea was expressed clearly by Nathaniel Chipman, an officer in the American Revolutionary War who later became a senator. Chipman was the eighteenth-century version of Ayn Rand, and a fierce advocate of individual moral responsibility:

> Riches are the fruit of industry. Honor the fruit of merit. Both ought, as to their continuance, and the influence which attends them, to be left to the conduct of the possessor. If a man, who, by industry and economy, has acquired riches, become indolent, or profligate, let him sink into poverty. Let those who are still industrious and economical, succeed to his enjoyments, as to their just reward. . . . To exclude the meritorious from riches and honors, and to perpetuate either to the undeserving, are equally injurious to the rights of man in society. In both it is to counteract the laws of nature, which have, by the connection of cause and effect, annexed the proper rewards and punishments to the actions of men. Wealth, or at least, a competency, is the reward, provided by the laws of nature, for prudent industry; want, the punishment of idleness and profligacy.
>
> (Chipman 1793)

So those who are disadvantaged, and those who are punished, are getting their just deserts; and it must be just (otherwise, not only would they not justly deserve their disadvantages and punishments, but I would not justly deserve my special benefits and enjoyments and just rewards). With just deserts and moral responsibility, I *chose* the right path, and the individual malefactor freely chose the wrong, no deeper explanation can be considered, and we both justly deserve the results.

## Conclusion

When we seek a new system to replace the moral responsibility system of just deserts, we are not seeking a substitute for a system that protects individual rights and dignity; rather we are seeking a system that provides the protections that moral responsibility does *not* provide. It should not be surprising that the moral responsibility system endangers rather than protects individual rights, dignity, and opportunity. The moral responsibility system promotes inequality, and hence must promote harshly punitive control measures; it treats wrongdoers as radically different and "choosing evil," and neglects—or scrupulously avoids—careful consideration of the actual causes; and it protects a "just world" view in which wrongs *must* be requited, and the guilty as well as the poor must suffer their just deserts.

Obviously, there are some decent and humane believers in moral responsibility, who deeply regret the vileness of our system of "retributive justice" and the cruelties and indignities it generates. But that does not change the fact that moral responsibility is a force that works against personal dignity. Even through the darkened lens of moral responsibility, the wrongs of the U.S. prison system, the lack of a social support system, and the gross inequities of opportunity shine so brightly that anyone who is perceptive cannot fail to see the abuses. Some philosophical advocates of moral responsibility say, and truthfully, that they hate capital punishment and Supermax prisons and three strikes warehousing and shaming punishments and lack of support for the impoverished; but they fail to recognize that such wrongs are not an aberration but a natural result of the moral responsibility system. Moral responsibility is the driving force and the central belief in the neo-liberal system. As belief in individual moral responsibility becomes stronger, neo-liberalism flourishes. If we want to protect individual dignity and basic rights, the most important step is the utter demolition of moral responsibility, while championing the genuine free will and take-charge responsibility that can flourish when moral responsibility is eliminated.

Losing the moral responsibility system would be our gain, both in improving understanding of human behavior and enhancing respect for human dignity and basic rights. Furthermore, eliminating the moral responsibility system makes room for a better system that facilitates rather than impedes deeper inquiry, and provides better understanding of the unavoidable but unjust role of punishment in society. However, before examining the better system that is now emerging, it is essential to examine some of its competitors as well as some of the challenges the new system must overcome. That is the task of the following chapters.

# 9 Efforts to Make Punishment Just

Those who reject the *basic* moral responsibility of just deserts face a significant challenge: what to do about the criminal justice system and in particular what to do about *punishment*. We cannot base punishment on moral responsibility and just deserts and retribution, but we still have people doing reckless and malicious acts. We must protect ourselves from those who would harm us and our loved ones, but we cannot claim that offenders "justly deserve" to be imprisoned; so what do we do?

The major claim of this book is that punishment *cannot* be just, and we are better off recognizing that disturbing fact and dealing with it: bite the bullet of inescapable unjust punishment, and make the best of it. That is, however, a very bitter bullet, and many efforts have been made to find a system that will make punishment *just*. They range from utilitarian justifications of punishment to punishment as "payment of a debt to society," from imprisonment as a form of "self-defense" to punishment as moral education. All of those solutions fail, in my judgment; but this is not an examination of all the various and sundry attempts at proving punishment is just: their number and variety is ample evidence that there is no account strong enough to withstand criticism and win general acceptance. In any case, an excellent survey of the many proposed accounts and their flaws was recently published by David Boonin (2008), and a briefer survey by Michael Davis (2009). Rather than an exhaustive survey of the legion of attempts to deal with the problem of punishment, this chapter examines only a few that seem most promising. Those few are offered as examples to indicate problems in major attempts to show that punishment is just, to explore those problems, and to argue that we are better off recognizing that punishment is *never* just.

## Self-Defense

The *self-defense* model claims that because we believe we have the right to intentionally harm someone when that is necessary in the course of self-defense, we can extend that right to cases of punishing those who have committed such harms. Boonin notes that while this account might appear attractive, it will not withstand critical examination:

It might seem that a defense of punishment by appeal to the right of self-defense would be a relatively simple matter. But this appearance is deceptive. For there is a crucial difference between harming a person in self-defense and harming a person as punishment. When Moe harms Larry in self-defense, he harms Larry in order to *prevent* Larry from wrongfully harming him. But when the state punishes an offender, it punishes him precisely because he has already *succeeded* in wrongfully harming someone. It is easy to see how the notion of self-defense can justify harm to prevent a particular wrong from taking place. But it is far more difficult to see how an appeal to self-defense could be used to justify inflicting harm in response to a particular wrong when it is already too late to prevent that wrong from taking place and thus too late to provide a defense against it.

(Boonin 2008, 193–194)

Defending ourselves against attack is more like a biological necessity than a right. But even if we grant that one has the *right* to kill or harm an attacker, it is another matter altogether to conclude that doing so was *right*, or that doing so was *just*. To say something is a *right* in this context means only that you are allowed to act in this way or have another act on your behalf; that is the right of self-defense. That does not mean you have done something morally good when you exercise that "right"; clearly there can be times when you exercise that right, but the result is something *wrong*. You kill the old man suffering from dementia who thinks you are an evil space alien and attacks you with a knife (assuming lethal force was your only option in this case). You had the "right" to do so, but no one, surely, thinks that the act of killing the old man was a *just* act or that the demented old man justly deserved to be killed; rather, it was an unjust necessity. So even if we approve of self-defense, and count acts of self-defense as legitimate, it will not establish that the act of self-defense was a just act. If self-defense is then used as a model for making *punishment* just (as opposed to an unjust necessity), it is doubly implausible.

Boonin regards the inflicting of unjust punishment as "morally repugnant" (2008, 213), as indeed it is. As a replacement for punishment, he favors "pure restitution" (2008, 218), a revised version of a position originally proposed by Randy Barnett (1977 and 1980). In pure restitution, punishment is replaced by *compensation* of the victims: compensation that will, ideally, *restore* victims to their previous status. The pure restitution theory has been widely discussed and debated, and adequate examination of that ongoing debate would require an additional volume. But impressive and subtle as Boonin's account of pure restitution is, it seems unlikely to eliminate punishment. As Stephen Kershnar notes, "if an individual refuses to pay compensation, the likely means of ensuring that she does so is to make her suffer" (2012, 73), and that seems to involve punitive measures. Furthermore, Boonin is quite willing to include incarceration—particularly preventive incarceration—as a central element of restitution. Boonin insists that such incarceration is not *punishment*:

> Not every legally imposed restriction on a person's freedom of movement is punishment. It is punishment only if it is done with the aim of making an offender suffer for his offense.
>
> (2008, 233)

But whatever we call such incarceration, it involves the coercive infliction of suffering (and requires neither the consent nor the benefit of the person who suffers).

## The Right to be Punished

Herbert Morris claims we have a *right* to be punished for our transgressions, and that right is based on the "fundamental right to be treated as a person":

> When we treat a human being merely as an animal or some inanimate object our responses to the human being are determined, not by his choices, but ours in disregard of or with indifference to his. And when we "look upon" a person as less than a person or not a person, we consider the person as incapable of rational choice.
>
> (1968, 490)

Exactly what that means—your right to be treated as a *person*—is a matter of considerable dispute. If it means that you have a right to be treated as if you are totally the creator of your self, or that you have some miraculous power of self-making or of first cause choice-making, or that you have a super power of perfect and unlimited reasoning, then it falls into the same category as the king's rule by divine right. But the right to be treated as a person may be very important—and a legitimate matter of concern and protection—when it avoids such supernatural excesses. If it means that we have a right to make choices for ourselves, and—within limits—to decide upon our own values and paths without being manipulated or constrained by others, then it is a right that is both plausible and valuable. Whether that right to be treated as a person somehow makes *punishment* just is a further question, along with the question of whether acknowledging and valuing such a right implies acceptance of moral responsibility.

Suppose you choose to act, in accordance with your own values. If that act violates the laws or rules, does that in itself make punishment just? Does it mean that you have chosen punishment? By no means. If you were shaped to have those values, and your reflective valuing and choosing is a product of that shaping, then it is doubtful that you justly deserve punishment or that you somehow chose punishment. Also, if the laws violated are laws that you consider (and perhaps are) unjust, then it hardly follows that you deserve punishment, much less that you have chosen punishment. You may have chosen to violate those laws, but it does not follow that you chose punishment for violating laws you regard as unjust. If there are laws against hiding escaped slaves, and you violate those laws in accordance with your own deep values, it is implausible to claim that you have chosen to be *punished* for breaking those laws, notwithstanding the fact that you certainly acted as an agent and a person. Consider a different sort of case: there are strong laws against passing a stopped school bus, and you approve of such laws; but one day, while distracted by a philosophical conundrum, you negligently pass a school bus. Have you chosen to be punished? You may accept the punishment, you might even believe you deserve it; but you have hardly chosen it. Suppose no one saw your negligent act, and no one was harmed, and you breathe a sigh of relief as you think of your negligent behavior and the harm it might have caused. If no one punishes you, has your right to punishment been violated?

Consider another possibility, one that is sadly realistic for some people in our society. You grow up in poverty, with little opportunity for a real education in schools that are violent and inferior; you also may have suffered lead poisoning, and possibly other health problems from the toxic wastes that are most likely to wind up in your impoverished community; you have suffered from episodes of malnutrition; and to cap it off, you are also a target of racial discrimination. Finding a minimum wage job—that will leave you living in poverty, with no prospects for a better life—is difficult; finding anything better is all but impossible. You choose instead to pursue a career dealing drugs to affluent suburbanites—certainly a more profitable alternative to minimum wage drudgery, with better hours. When you are caught and imprisoned, does this punishment show respect for your "fundamental right to be treated as a person"? The convicted dealer might well inquire about the status of that fundamental right during the years of his childhood and adolescence, and might also question the value of a right the only benefit of which is a long prison term. In such a case, it is quite implausible to suppose that the person punished has given "implicit consent" to be punished. Michael J. Zimmerman has little patience with the claim of implicit consent to punishment:

> Some philosophers . . . hold that offenders, in committing their offenses, implicitly consent to the punishment that subsequently comes their way. As a general claim, this is of course nonsense.
>
> (Zimmerman 2011, 163)

With Herbert Morris, the only realistic alternative to regarding wrongdoers as morally responsible—and justly deserving of punishment—is to regard them as flawed, as sick, as objects of therapy incapable of making decisions for themselves. But of course there is another alternative: they are healthy agents, but still not morally responsible. They have flaws and virtues, like most of us. The point here is that we can deny moral responsibility and still value agents and actions and take-charge responsibility for oneself. Either morally responsible or deranged is a false dichotomy, the product of an imagination stultified by the constraints of the moral responsibility system. Operating within the assumptions of the moral responsibility system, moral responsibility is the default setting; and (except for children) the only grounds for *totally* denying the moral responsibility of an individual is that the individual is insane, deranged, utterly incapable of intelligent self-governance. But the rejection of the moral responsibility system is not based on the claim that everyone is deranged; rather, the claim is that moral responsibility is fundamentally incompatible with our naturalistic perspective. Moral responsibility requires a world of miracles and deities and self-caused causes; in the natural world, devoid of such miracles and operating entirely by natural causal forces, there is no space for moral responsibility. When we say that someone is *not* morally responsible, we are not failing to show "respect for one as a person"; rather, we are insisting that the person is a human animal and not a deity. Or more precisely, we are rejecting the moral responsibility *system* in which the only alternative to moral responsibility is some form of basic incompetence. We can acknowledge that a cognitively competent person is morally *bad*, and has acted in ways that are morally bad, while *denying* that the person is morally responsible or justly deserves punishment for his or her morally bad acts; because *no one*—no matter what the level of competence—is *ever* morally responsible.

Angela Smith considers the view that Robert Harris—a brutal and callous murderer, who himself suffered terrible abuse as a child and adolescent—might be regarded as morally bad but not morally responsible, and heaps scorn on that approach:

> This distinction itself would require us to regard some agents as the passive victims of their faulty judgments. . . . I think this is a dangerously patronizing and disrespectful stance to take toward another human being, one that we should be very reluctant to resort to in practice.
>
> (2008, 390)

Robert Harris was an active agent who made his own morally bad choices. But like all of us—except those deities who created themselves from scratch—he was shaped in ways that he did not ultimately control, and is (again, like all of us) not morally responsible for his character or acts. Recognizing this does not imply "a dangerously patronizing and disrespectful stance" toward anyone, unless recognizing that humans are mortals rather than deities is disrespectful.

Robert Harris was a coldly rational person, capable of making and carrying out detailed plans; but he was also profoundly flawed, and filled with hate—as most of us would be had we suffered the incessantly cruel and demeaning treatment he endured from infancy into adulthood. A society that ignores the horrific situation of his infancy and childhood, and facilitates the brutal treatment he suffered as a youth in a juvenile detention center, might well be judged a society that takes a "disrespectful stance . . . toward another human being"; but seeking to understand—in hopes of changing—the deep causes that forged the terrible anger and hatred that burned in that unfortunate young man: that is a hopeful and respectful rather than patronizing stance. To study and understand the causes of our behavior, both virtuous and vicious, is a positive and promising step. Disparaging or blocking such study in order to preserve moral responsibility and righteous retribution and strike-back satisfaction is not a means of promoting human dignity.

Michael Moore makes a similar claim. His example is Richard Herrin, a young Hispanic man who grew up in poverty and won a scholarship to Yale, but murdered his wealthy girl friend when she broke off their relationship. According to Moore, when we deny that Herrin is morally responsible and justly deserves punishment for his crime, we are demeaning him as less than human:

> It is a refusal to admit that the rest of humanity shares with us that which makes us most distinctively human, our capacity to will and reason—and thus to be and do evil. Far from evincing fellow-feeling and the allowing of others to participate in our moral life, it excludes them as less than persons.
>
> (1997, 149)

We are not drawing an invidious distinction between Herrin and ourselves, because *no one* is ever morally responsible: the set of morally responsible persons is empty. The category of moral responsibility belongs to a different world and a different outlook—a world of miracles, a just world, and not a world in which either we or Herrin live our lives. We do have will and reason, but these are natural capacities that have limits and causes and degrees, not transcendent powers that rise above our natural world and render our causal histories irrelevant.

## Social Contract Punishment

A social contract model is perhaps the most interesting and innovative effort to establish that punishment is just. Because we *agree* (either explicitly or implicitly) to live within a system in which we can be subjected to punishment for our malfeasance, then we are *justly* punished for our transgressions. Such punishment is simply part of our contract. As is often the case, Daniel Dennett offers a charming version of that model:

People *want* to be held accountable. The benefits that accrue to one who is a citizen in good standing in a free society are so widely and deeply appreciated that there is always a potent presumption in favor of inclusion. Blame is the price we pay for credit, and we pay it gladly under most circumstances. We pay dearly, accepting punishment and public humiliation for a chance to get back in the game after we have been caught out in some transgression. And so the best strategy for holding the line against creeping exculpation is clear: Protect and enhance the value of the game one gets to play if one is a citizen in good standing . . .

   Since there will always be strong temptations to make yourself really small, to externalize the causes of your actions and deny responsibility, the way to counteract these is to make people an offer they can't refuse: If you want to be free, you must *take* responsibility.

(2003, 292)

When the Godfather made his famous "offer he can't refuse," an associate held a pistol in the band leader's ear while the Godfather told him that "either his brains or his signature" would be on that contract. Dennett's offer is not quite so dramatic, but he also offers a very unappealing alternative to accepting the contract (and accepting the legitimacy of being punished): Either accept the rules and order of the society (including the liability to punishment) or be ostracized from the community. As Dennett states:

You don't *have* to play the moral responsibility game; you can be a hermit on an otherwise deserted island, fishing and foraging. But if you want to enjoy the benefits of living in a civilized society, you have to play the game.

(Dennett 2012, 7)

And this is not just living outside a local community, with an option to join another; this is ostracism from the *human social* community. Even worse, as P. F. Strawson describes it (1962) and as it is often viewed: accept the contract, or be counted as so incompetent as to be subhuman. As discussed in Chapter 6, for intensely social human animals such radical ostracism may be worse than execution.

   Dennett is a humane person, and he emphasizes the positive: "Protect and enhance the value of the game one gets to play if one is a citizen in good standing." And there is no doubt that he genuinely desires to make the social community attractive and decent for all its citizens. But given the options on offer, the social community need be neither fair nor decent to make it a more desirable option than total ostracism.

   This coercive offer provides dubious grounds for the legitimacy of punishment. It's not clear that everyone in U.S. society even tacitly "agrees to play" the game as it is currently being played: Jeffrie G. Murphy (1973) argues that our society falls far short of meeting the minimum standards that would justify the claim that everyone can be assumed to consent to the social contract. But even if we agree that in some sense people do "agree to play," it does not follow that the game is fair. Dennett claims that "the fact that almost everybody agrees to play a game means that it is probably as close to a fair game as you could devise" (Dennett 2012, 7). But Dennett himself acknowledges the gross unfairness of the U.S. criminal justice system, and states that "I think the reforms most pressingly needed are obvious: a drastic diminution in the length of sentences, and indeed the elimination of most incarceration in favor of less drastic penalties, much better enforcement of prisoners' rights, and better programs for reintegrating prisoners into society" (Clark, Dennett, and Waller 2012, 9). A system in such glaring need of reform is by no means as "close to a fair game as you could devise," and the fact that profoundly social animals might favor such a system over attempting to live as hermits is no evidence that the system is even minimally fair and just.

John Rawls's "justice as fairness" (Rawls 1971) is an appealing presentation of the social contract model. Step behind the veil of ignorance, so that you have no idea what your starting position will be in the society you will enter (from behind the veil of ignorance you do not know what advantages or disadvantages you will receive from the "genetic lottery" and "initial starting position," nor do you know your gender, race, goals, or interests). But even if gathered behind the veil of ignorance we *agree* on when to impose punishment, it does not follow that the punishment is *just*. Suppose we are a group behind the veil of ignorance, and we believe that harsh punishment of minor crimes is a very effective method of deterring *all* crime (including violent crimes); but we also believe that criminal behavior is largely a product of genetics, and of course one's genetic code is determined by "luck of the draw." We might still punish, but we would not consider it just, much less deserved. We might say: we have to do this; sorry, it's bad luck, you don't deserve this, but we have to do it. We would punish with great sorrow and regret, knowing this person is suffering for our good, and does *not* justly deserve it. We might *justify* it by the larger benefits and the common agreement; but that will not make it *just* punishment.

The liberal justice model—what we would accept behind the veil of ignorance—is procedurally fair, but it has two basic problems. One, if we believed that severely punishing a few minor criminal acts (once we escape the veil of ignorance) would greatly reduce overall suffering, we might agree to do so. But the sacrifice of the individuals drawn by lots—in this case, by the *genetic* lottery—would not be just or fair; or if fair—and it is *procedurally* fair—it would not mean that the persons punished justly deserve severe punishment. When we actually live in the community, we have the unlucky persons who are genetically crime-oriented and who commit crimes. Procedurally, it is fair to punish them; but the whole question of whether they justly *deserve* punishment remains unanswered. Benjamin Vilhauer (2013) develops an impressive system along these lines that gives a nonutilitarian model for the justification of punishment. It might well be successful in *justifying* punishment, and—from a Rawlsian perspective—it might make punishment *fair*. But it does not follow that the punishment meted out to an individual violator is *justly deserved*, or that it is fair in the sense of being fair to the person who ultimately could not avoid such wrongdoing and subsequent punishment. When we look hard at the forces causing such wrongful behavior in that individual, we may realize that the imposed punishment is *unjust*, even though—in our *unjust* world—it is both necessary and as fair as we could make it. Second, this is strictly a procedural process: it makes the individual punished an abstract marker in the procedural system and prevents us from looking at the specific details of that person. When we look in detail and depth at that person, we realize that the punishment is not fair. But it is precisely that deeper detailed inquiry that the procedural process blocks. That may be good for ascertaining as fair a system as we can construct, but it does not mean that implementation of that system will involve no injustice (it only means that we can hide our eyes from the injustice). Ultimately, the problem is that the punished person is *unlucky* in his or her capacities; and that is the person who draws the short straw. That is why our justice system makes it a point not to look too closely at the history of the person: closer scrutiny reveals that it may be procedurally fair, but nonetheless the person punished does not justly deserve punishment.

Punishment cannot be justified in terms of just deserts. We can of course construct a system that specifies the rules under which people will be punished, and then apply the rules of that system in punishing people; but that not only opens the question of whether the system is just, but also the question of whether even a procedurally just system establishes that an individual justly deserves punishment. Examined closely, the social contract model for just punishment fails to prove that punishing in accordance with the rules of a social contract makes that punishment just. After all, did we ever doubt that we could construct a system in which, according to the rules of that system, people "justly deserve" punishment? We might also provide justification for some punishment—at least relatively mild punishment, somewhat similar to quarantine—for "forward looking" reasons, such as protection of people and perhaps deterrence. But again, this will not establish that the person punished justly deserves punishment.

## Restorative Justice

The restorative justice program (Braithwaite 1999; Braithwaite 2002; Johnstone 2003; A. Morris 2002) is a relatively new development that has some positive features. Certainly, it has significant advantages compared to the traditional retributive system. The retributive system focuses on punishing the malefactor, and the punishment often involves *separating* the wrongdoer from the community through imprisonment. As retributive commitments become stronger the prison sentences become longer and the isolation becomes more extreme (culminating in Supermax prisons that lock prisoners in long-term solitary confinement). Rather than focusing on ultimately reintegrating the prisoner into society, the emphasis is more often on marking the prisoner's severe *exclusion* from society: in societies like the United States, with its devotion to retributive punishment, prisoners are almost invariably deprived of the right to vote (signifying extreme separation from participation as a citizen and member of the society); and in the most severely retributive areas of the country, many convicted felons are permanently disenfranchised. Rather than a commitment to reintegrating the wrongdoer, the goal appears to be maximizing and sustaining exclusion. In dramatic contrast, the primary goal of *restorative* justice is restoring the community to wholeness, which includes restoring the offender to full participation in the community. Rather than imposing long prison sentences, under restorative justice every effort is made to avoid employing punitive measures that exclude the wrongdoer from the community. Instead, the focus is on using community resources to bring the offender back into the community and heal the rift caused by the criminal behavior. This alone makes restorative justice a major improvement over the retributive system.

The genuine advantages of the restorative justice system notwithstanding, it also has some serious problems, particularly in its advocacy of *shaming* as an essential element of the larger restorative process. In the classic version of restorative justice, John Braithwaite insists that shaming plays a vital role in restoring the offender to the community and restoring wholeness to the community. The offender must recognize that he or she caused harm and that a victim as well as the community was harmed, the offender must feel shame for the wrong committed, and ultimately the offender should be forgiven and welcomed back into the restored community. Braithwaite repeatedly insists that the essential *shame* is not the destructive shaming that *stigmatizes* the wrongdoer and marks that person as a permanent bad character; rather, the shaming is a *reintegrative* shaming that focuses on the wrongness of the *act* instead of the badness of the person performing the act. Reintegrative shaming is not a *permanent* mark of shame, but instead a temporary shaming process that culminates in forgiving and fully restoring the offender to the community. Reintegrative shaming is considerably better than the destructive stigmatization shaming that permanently attaches shame to the deep character of the offender, and is likely to drive the offender away from the community (and into groups of others who are shamed and marginalized) rather than welcoming the offender back into the community. But it would be better to reject shaming altogether.

Though shaming is regarded as a vital part of the restorative process, Braithewaite insists it must be employed cautiously, with strong family and community support, and in the form of *reintegrative* rather than *stigmatizing* shame. But shaming at its best has great potential for harm, and when a program officially incorporates shaming into its procedures the dangers are exacerbated. There have been cases (Retzinger and Scheff 1996) in which the shaming process has been intense and brutal, including sarcasm and other demeaning elements. Braithwaite acknowledges that even "reintegrative" shaming (which he favors) can be quite harsh: "Reintegrative shaming is not necessarily weak: it can be cruel, even vicious" (Braithwaite 1989, 101). And while the shaming process is supposed to be followed by forgiveness and reconciliation and "decertification," clearly the shaming occurs first and independently of the hoped-for reconciliation and forgiveness. Demeaning and sarcastic shaming processes are a violation of the way restorative justice is supposed to proceed, but once the Pandora's box of shaming is opened it is difficult to control what emerges.

The real danger of even reintegrative shaming is recognized by Braithwaite, who emphasizes that such shaming must be followed by a ritual ceremony that will "decertify deviance" and remove the stain of shame. But if such a decertification ceremony is essential, that in itself is recognition of the serious harm that can be done to those who are shamed; otherwise, why an essential decertification ceremony to remove the damage? And while shaming an offender may be a comparatively easy process, the "decertification" that repairs the harm of shaming may be much more difficult. Because the community may not be quite so eager to carry out the decertification as they were to impose the shame, there is danger that the harm from shaming will not be repaired. Furthermore, there is always the potential—and the temptation—for the reintegrative shaming to escalate into a harsh stigmatization shaming that attacks not only the bad act but also the "bad character"; and since many offenders already have a weakened sense of self-esteem, this may be a profoundly damaging process. As Roger Matthews points out, shaming is a dangerous and often damaging force, and even those in restorative justice who emphasize the importance of following the shaming process with forgiveness and reconciliation and reintegration recognize the destructive power of shaming:

> Shaming clearly carries a strong punitive and exclusionary component. If it were not such a powerful mechanism of disintegration there would be no point in spending so much time and effort in trying to reintegrate those shamed.
>
> (Matthews 2006)

James Q. Whitman is a powerful critic of all varieties of criminal justice—restorative justice included—that incorporate and legitimize shaming processes carried out by the community; and he fears that promoting the legitimacy of shaming processes will encourage a lynch-mob mentality:

> Shame sanctions amount to a kind of posse-raising legal politics, with all of the risks that implies. They are, at base, a form of officially sponsored lynch justice, meted out by courts that have given up on the obligation

of the state both to define what is criminal and to administer criminal sanctions itself.

(1998, 1088–1089)

Allison Morris, in her powerful response to a variety of criticisms of restorative justice, makes this response:

> Restorative justice is sometimes equated with community or popular justice, which is, in turn, equated with vigilatism. It is true that some forms of community justice can be repressive, retributive, hierarchical and patriarchal. But these values are fundamentally at odds with the defining values of restorative justice and cannot, therefore, be part of it.
>
> (Morris 2002, 609)

No doubt Morris is correct concerning the basic values of those advocating restorative justice. But Whitman is concerned about the dangerous forces that can follow from the introduction of shaming policies, and those forces might at times push aside the restraints and restrictions that are supposed to limit the shaming process in restorative justice.

There are special hazards when shame is employed in restorative justice conferences. Often too little attention is given to inequities in power and status among different groups. As Rob White notes in his critique of restorative justice:

> The issue of "power"—who holds it, how it is exercised, how it is manifested in institutional arrangements and interpersonal contact—is especially problematic in the 'shame and reintegration' model. . . . What needs more discussion—and explanation at a theoretical level—are issues such as inequality, class power and the different social interests which are unequally represented in our major institutions. . . . Part of the problem here is a failure or reticence to conceive of society in wider structural terms. Society is seen in terms of "individuals" (rather than classes or other defined social categories), and social activity or action is conceived in terms of the interactions of particular individuals and groups (rather than social forces).
>
> (1994, 183–184)

When we consider the basic *just deserts* framework in which restorative justice processes are employed, there is (as White notes) a danger:

> it opens the door to practical applications which may in fact go against the intentions of the original theorists and practitioners. . . . The translation of . . . "just deserts" ideology into the community justice context will in all probability engender the use of shaming as a punishment (rather than reintegrative) strategy.
>
> (1994, 189–190)

In restorative justice, it is important to condemn the offense rather than the offender. However, the initial focus remains on the individual offender showing remorse. But often the focus should be on the deeper cause, which may lie in the situation, or in the nature of the flawed community itself, rather than in the individual offender. The "place in the community" to which the individual is restored may be a place of unfair treatment, a role with no opportunity or autonomy or control. Juvenile boot camps are designed to "restore" the individual to the community; but the position to which the individual is "restored" is often a subservient position in a profoundly unfair community. Of course, there are those in restorative justice who recognize the need to scrutinize the community itself; but that is basically a secondary issue, with the focus on the individual to "repent" for his wrong, and be restored to the essentially good community. While that is an improvement over the U.S. system, in which wrongdoers are often permanently ostracized, it still may operate as a patch on a system that is deeply flawed.

## Beyond Shame

There are some special dangers in applying shaming in the criminal justice context, when dealing with those who are being shamed in order to change their criminal behavior. Feelings of shame often motivate violent behavior, and shaming practices in prisons are more likely to exacerbate those violent tendencies than rehabilitate the prisoner. When restorative justice promotes shaming (of whatever variety) in its program, it is incorporating a process that can be dangerous and destructive. Psychologist James Gilligan directed the Center for the Study of Violence at Harvard Medical School, and he has made a special study of the relation between emotions of shame and the causes of violent behavior:

> There is a great deal of evidence . . . that shame is spread via the social and economic system. This happens . . . through what we might call the "vertical" division of the population into a hierarchical ranking of upper and lower status groups, chiefly classes, castes, and age groups, but also other means by which people are divided into in-groups and out-groups, the accepted and the rejected, the powerful and the weak, the rich and the poor, the honored and the dishonored. For people are shamed on a systematic, wholesale basis, and their vulnerability to feelings of humiliation is increased when they are assigned an inferior social or economic status; and the more inferior and humble it is, the more frequent and intense the feelings of shame, and the more frequent and intense the acts of violence.
>
> (2001, 38)

Policies that promote shame—and shame is a close companion of moral responsibility—are not just ineffective in reducing violent criminal behavior, but actually exacerbate the problem: a problem which, as Gilligan notes, is already chronic and systemic in the United States:

> In fact, the social and economic system of the United States combines almost every characteristic that maximizes shame and hence violence. First, there is the "Horatio Alger" myth that everyone can get rich if they are smart and work hard (which means that if they are not rich they must be stupid or lazy, or both). Second, we are not only told that we can get rich, we are also stimulated to want to get rich. For the whole economic system of mass production depends on whetting people's appetites to consume the flood of goods that are being produced (hence the flood of advertisements). Third, the social and economic reality is the opposite of the Horatio Alger myth, since social mobility is actually less likely in the U.S. than in the supposedly more rigid social structures of Europe and the U.K. As Mishel, Bernstein, and Schmitt (2001) have noted: "Contrary to widely held perceptions, the U.S. offers less economic mobility than other rich countries . . ." [cf. also Jäntti et al. 2006; Jäntti 2008; Corak 2016; DeParle 2012] Fourth, as they also mention, "the U. S. has the most unequal income distribution and the highest poverty rates among all the advanced economies in the world . . ." The net effect of all these features of U. S. society is to maximize the gap between aspiration and attainment, which maximizes the frequency and intensity of feelings of shame, which maximizes the rates of violent crimes.
>
> (2001, 44–45)

Allison Morris is a resourceful defender of restorative justice, but she recognizes the dangers of incorporating *shaming* into the restorative justice program, and recommends dropping shame in favor of remorse and the development of empathy. As she notes: "Despite our good intentions . . . the shaming we intend to be reintegrative might be taken by the offender to be stigmatic" (Morris 2001, 11). And with an emphasis instead on remorse and empathy, the dangers of stigmatic shaming could be eliminated while any benefits of the restorative justice program are retained:

> research does *not* show that disapproval (shaming) was necessarily the mechanism which invoked the remorse. Another way of interpreting these data is that *empathy* or understanding the effects of offending on victims was the trigger. If this interpretation is right, the practice and policy implications are very different from a continuing emphasis on shaming (disapproval). . . . It is certainly possible that it is empathy which triggers remorse, and not shaming (disapproval). If this is so, it would mean that the emphasis in conferencing (or in other restorative justice processes) should be not on processes of shaming (disapproval) but on processes which focus on the consequences of offending

for others (for families and communities as well as for victims). In the meantime, the use of the words 'shame' and 'shaming' in the development and refinement of reintegrative shaming is best avoided. They are too readily and easily misunderstood and it is not that difficult in practice to slip from the intent of reintegrative shaming to the practice of stigmatic shaming or for intended reintegrative shaming to be perceived as stigmatic.

(Morris 2001, 12)

It is important to recognize my own flaws, and the harm they cause. But we can gain the benefits that supposedly accrue from shaming by instead supporting and nurturing stronger empathy and common commitments among the offender, the victim, and the community; and we gain those benefits while avoiding the grave dangers associated with the shaming process.

My own flaws—such as my weak and acquiescent response to strong authority (Milgram 1063) or group pressure—may not only disgust me, but also surprise me: situations may reveal flaws of which I was blissfully ignorant, flaws I was confident I did not have. Peter's denial of Jesus is a case in point. Peter insists that "I am ready to go with thee, both into prison, and to death" (Luke 22:33). Jesus tells Peter that Peter will deny him not once but three times: "the cock shall not crow this day, before that thou shalt thrice deny that thou knowest me." When faced with a hostile crowd that came to apprehend Jesus, Peter was eager to take up the sword and fight: he seemed quite willing to go with Jesus "both into prison, and to death," and the suggestion that he would deny Jesus seemed highly improbable: certainly it seemed so to Peter himself. But later, sitting quietly by a fire, Peter was asked three times whether he was with Jesus, and each time denied knowing him: "Woman, I know him not" (Luke 22:57). During the third denial, Peter heard the cock crow, and realized his own weakness, "and Peter went out, and wept bitterly" (Luke 22:62).

Peter had a deep weakness of which he was unaware. Like most of us he lacked insight into a deep personal flaw. I may wear my question authority t-shirt proudly, but still cave before authority when it counts (as did *many* who "named names" before the House Un-American Affairs Committee, and *most* of those who were subjects of Milgram's experiment). This is a flaw, and a very common flaw in our deeply hierarchical species, with our built-in deep respect for authority; but still a flaw. We can sincerely regret it, and feel deep remorse when it causes us to act in ways we consider weak or even cowardly, and particularly when it leads us to harm or abandon a friend; but we can feel this deep remorse while recognizing that we do not deserve blame, and should not feel shame. The greater our ability to avoid feeling shame, the greater the likelihood of actually doing something to fix the problem, and also the greater the willingness to make a sincere apology (Waller 2007 and 2011, 191–199). I recognize that I did harm, as a result of my own flawed character, and I am genuinely sorry: sorry both for the harm

I have caused as well as for the flaw deep within myself. But I can better come to terms with that—acknowledge the harm I have caused, sincerely apologize, and take steps toward improvement—if self-blame and myopic shame do not block deeper inquiry into my flaws and their sources.

It is important to feel regret, and even remorse; but that does not require shame in any form. I can recognize my own weaknesses and flaws—that we all have—without feeling deep shame. In the absence of shame I can look harder and with less painful resistance at the deeper causes of the problems, including the deeper causes of my character flaws. I may recognize that the flaws are not as bad as I thought, and the real problem is the larger system. In any case, I can recognize that the flaws were not ultimately of my own making. That facilitates sincere apology, as well as a better understanding of my own character and its development. We do not justly deserve to suffer remorse; but in some cases it may be appropriate, and even essential, when we recognize our own shortcomings and the harms they caused. But remorse is not shame, which is another thing altogether. Remorse can be eye-opening to our own flaws, and facilitate change; shame tends to be eye-closing, and promote helplessness.

Rather than shame, we need to recognize and understand that a wrong was committed, and look at the *causes*: perhaps in one's own character and the way it was shaped but also in the situation and the community and the system. Focus on individual justly deserved shame and individual *repentance* blocks the way to such deeper inquiry. The restorative element in restorative justice is valuable; but with shaming at its center, restorative justice is rotten at the core. Shaming makes it *more* difficult to recognize and acknowledge our flaws, and is more likely to exacerbate than ameliorate them. Rather than a Tychonic restorative justice system that hangs on to pieces of the failed retributive system in the form of justly deserved shame, we should sever all ties with the system of retribution and just deserts and moral responsibility.

# 10 Is Therapy an Alternative?

Of the myriad attempts to deal with the problem of punishment, one is particularly attractive to those who reject moral responsibility and just deserts: the *therapeutic* model. The therapy approach does not make punishment *just*. It dissolves rather than solves the problem of punishment: Punishment disappears and is replaced by therapy.

There are a number of advantages to the therapeutic model. First, it avoids inflicting retributive punishment—that cannot be justified when moral responsibility is denied—and substitutes a system of nonpunitive *therapy*. Second, it provides a policy for protecting society against those who harm others: we do not *punish* them, but we can isolate them from society (and prevent them from causing harm) by *quarantining* them (as we quarantine those who spread sickness to others, though those quarantined obviously are not morally responsible for the harm they cause). Third, we can seek the deeper causes of criminal behavior, just as public health organizations seek the causes of illness patterns. So under the therapeutic model, the problem of punishment disappears, society is protected, deeper causes of crime are addressed, and those who cause harm receive beneficial therapy rather than painful punishment. Small wonder this is an attractive alternative to the retributive punishment model, especially for those who reject the moral responsibility foundation on which retribution is built.

## Unfairly Harsh Criticisms of the Therapeutic Model

The therapeutic approach is a fundamentally decent attempt to develop a more humane way of dealing with wrongdoers. To judge by the criticisms it has provoked, one would suppose it is an attempt to reinstate trial by combat, extract confessions by use of the rack, and promote drawing and quartering for juvenile offenders.

In some ways it is surprising that the therapeutic/quarantine model has been the object of such vitriolic attacks. Whatever its flaws, it is an appeal for treatment that would be much less harsh—and considerably more promising in its benefits—than that demanded by the retributive punishment system. C. S. Lewis was a fervent advocate of retributive "justice" and a fierce supporter of the death penalty (1949), who apparently thought that dragging the condemned to the scaffold and ceremoniously breaking his neck was a celebration of human dignity, while seeking to rehabilitate the person in the gentlest and most humane manner possible manifests contempt. Karl Menninger, a prominent advocate of the rehabilitative model, had a very different view of capital punishment: "To a physician discussing the wiser treatment of our fellow men it seems hardly necessary to add that under no circumstances should we kill them" (1959, 64). Most philosophical critics of the therapeutic model are also opponents of the death penalty and are disgusted by the debilitating conditions of U.S. prisons. So why has the therapeutic system prompted such vehement opposition, even among enlightened philosophers? Whatever its flaws, it is not nearly so awful as the prison and execution system that its proponents hope to replace, and it is not so flawed as to justify the opprobrium heaped upon it, nor the contrived fears that have been used to distort and attack it.

The first reason—at least the first reason that many of its opponents, particularly its philosophical critics—are likely to emphasize is that it "undermines human dignity." Why does it undermine human dignity? Because those advocating the therapeutic approach believe there are *causes* for human behavior, and we can understand those causes and improve character and behavior. But if we can understand the deeper causes, then the special "dignity" of being the ultimate source of oneself is lost.

There is a second reason for the harsh attacks on the therapeutic model. The therapeutic approach looks deeper for causes, and finds them; and in the words of Pogo, "We have met the enemy; and he is us." When we seek the causes of criminal behavior we find causal factors of inequality, toxic wastes, racism, poor schools, lead poisoning, discrimination, inadequate health care: causes that those in positions of power often produced, and in any case did little to fix. *Fixing* these deeper causes—in contrast to simply blaming those who are impaired by them—would require social changes that the powerful do not want to make: changes that would undercut their places of privilege (maintained by racial discrimination, preferential "legacy" admission to elite universities, and powerful networks of influence). Recognizing the need for such changes would reveal the shibboleth of "equal opportunity" to be a blatant lie. The basic fear is not that the therapeutic model would fail, but that it would *work*. If there are real problems that can be fixed, we would have to justify our gross neglect of fixing them. We cannot shape people for brutality and failure all through their formative years, and then conclude that "nothing works" because a cheap quick fix can't correct the damage. It is not surprising that "nothing works" (Martinson 1974) was enthusiastically embraced, the utter implausibility of the nothing works agenda notwithstanding. Forget reform, it's too costly, and doesn't work anyway; just blame, punish, and long-term incarcerate.

Another prominent objection to the therapeutic approach is a strawman: the therapeutic model gives too much power to the medical profession and leaves prisoners too vulnerable. It is ludicrous for those opposing the therapeutic model to claim special concern for the welfare of prisoners—prisoners who are being railroaded by lying jailhouse informants, "defended" by incompetent or overworked counsel, killed either quickly or on the prison installment plan, psychologically damaged by isolation in Supermax prisons (condemned by the European Union as a form of torture), exposed to physical and sexual abuse and the most demeaning of punishments. If this is a genuine concern, rather than a blatant scare tactic, then they strained at a gnat and swallowed a camel. There are plenty of real horrors for those who want to protect prisoners; so why do they invent possible dangers? Because it is cheaper and easier to protect against possible threats rather than fix the real ones.

## Benefits of the Therapeutic Model

There are genuine benefits of the therapeutic model, particularly when it is compared to retributivism: advantages that make retributivism appear atavistic. Those advantages are spelled out clearly by Derk Pereboom, one of the strongest advocates of the therapeutic approach, who notes that it:

> would not justify the sort of criminal punishment whose legitimacy is most dubious, such as death or confinement in the most common kinds of prisons in our society. More than this, it demands a certain level of care and attention to the well-being of criminals which would change much of current policy. The free will critic [moral responsibility skeptic] would also endorse measures for reducing crime that aim at altering social conditions, such as improving education, increasing opportunities for fulfilling employment, and enhancing care for the mentally ill.
>
> (2014, 174)

Those are substantial advantages indeed. If rehabilitation is better than retribution, then the therapeutic model is a major improvement.

Pereboom includes "public health" concerns (including "altering social conditions") in his model, and that is an essential positive element of any therapeutic model. Gregg Caruso (2016) develops the public health model in more detail, focusing on fixing social problems *before* they result in criminal behavior. While (in my judgment) the problems of the therapeutic model outweigh its benefits, that in no way diminishes the importance of the public health emphasis in dealing with violent and criminal behavior. Adrian Raine (2013, 184–191 and 198–231) describes the enormous range and depth of studies showing the destructive and violence-enhancing effects of many prenatal and early childhood environmental factors, including maternal smoking and drinking during pregnancy, childhood malnutrition, and early exposure to lead, cadmium, manganese, and mercury. As Raine argues, recognizing these profoundly destructive environmental forces should lead to a dedicated public health initiative to fix the environment that is the cause of so much crime and violence:

> The question of *whether* brain deficits in individuals contribute to violence is, frankly speaking, no longer a useful one. Since there is no longer any doubt that brain deficits contribute in some way to anti-social and aggressive behavior, we should instead be asking the more important question, What's happening very early on in life to cause the brain abnormalities that we find in adult offenders? Once we can identify these early processes, we are halfway toward new intervention and prevention studies that reshape a child's trajectory away from violent offending. With this knowledge we can begin to reel in the unacceptable level of violence we see not just in the United States, with its high homicide rate, but also everywhere else in the world.
>
> (Raine 2013, 183–184)

There are other advantages of the therapeutic model that are worthy of note. It pushes us to recognize that *many* cases of criminal behavior *are* the result of mental illness (including addiction); that often these are problems that *can* be successfully *treated* by competent therapeutic programs; and that punitive programs often exacerbate rather than resolve the problem. But the genuine virtues of the therapeutic/quarantine/public health model notwithstanding, it also has problems. One of the virtues of the model is that instead of imposing harsh retributive punishment on offenders, it treats offenders as having flaws that should be treated through a rehabilitation process; but on the other side of the same coin, one of the potential *problems* of that model is that it treats offenders as flawed and—often—as sick.

## The Therapeutic Model and Sick Offenders

Fundamental to the therapeutic model is proposed *treatment* for those who commit crimes, on the grounds that they do not justly deserve retributive punishment because they are themselves the victims of psychological disorder. In *Erewhon*, Samuel Butler developed a brilliant satire incorporating a therapeutic model. Butler's Erewhonians regard physical illness in the same manner as our society regards criminal tendencies, and his account of the harsh and futile treatment of those suffering from various maladies (and the contrast with the effective rehabilitative treatment of those committing criminal acts) shows the absurdity of our criminal processes and the benefits that would result from treating criminal behavior in the way we now treat illness. In this instance, a judge is condemning a man who has been convicted of the very serious *crime*—in Erewhon—of suffering from tuberculosis (consumption):

> It is all very well for you to say that you came of unhealthy parents, and had a severe accident in your childhood which permanently undermined

your constitution; excuses such as these are the ordinary refuge of the criminal; but they cannot for one moment be listened to by the ear of justice. I am not here to enter upon curious metaphysical questions as to the origin of this or that—questions to which there would be no end were their introduction once tolerated, and which would result in throwing the only guilt on the tissues of the primordial cell, or on the elementary gases. There is no question of how you came to be wicked, but only this—namely, are you wicked or not? This has been decided in the affirmative, neither can I hesitate for a single moment to say that it has been decided justly. You are a bad and dangerous person, and stand branded in the eyes of your fellow-countrymen with one of the most heinous known offenses.

(Butler 1872)

In his reflections on this process of "justice," the supposed visitor (*Erewhon* is presented as the first person account of a visitor to this strange land of Erewhon) expresses consternation that the Erewhonians cannot see the difference between the physical and the mental natures; but of course the point is that the visitor and narrator is caught in his own system of belief, which shares the same absurdity that plagues the Erewhonians:

I had fallen upon a set of people who in spite of their high civilization and many excellences, had been so warped by the mistaken views presented to them during childhood from generation to generation, that it was impossible to see how they could ever clear themselves. Was there nothing I could say to make them feel that the constitution of a person's body was a thing over which he or she had had at any rate no initial control whatever, while the mind was a perfectly different thing, and capable of being created anew and directed according to the pleasure of its possessor? Could I never bring them to see that while habits of mind and character were entirely independent of initial mental force and early education, the body was so much a creature of parentage and circumstances, that no punishment for ill health should be ever tolerated save as a protection from contagion, and that even where punishment was inevitable it should be attended with compassion?

(Butler 1872)

Whether Butler intended his reflections on psychological *treatment* of criminals seriously or only as satire of British customs, there certainly have been enthusiastic advocates of the rehabilitation (rather than retribution) policy of dealing with those who commit crimes and cause harm. One of the best known is Karl Menninger, a psychiatrist who vigorously promoted replacing prisons with programs of therapy:

Having arrived at some diagnostic grasp of the offender's personality, those in charge can decide whether there is a chance that he can be redirected into a mutually satisfactory adaptation to the world. If so, the most suitable techniques in education, industrial training, group administration, and psychotherapy should be selectively applied. . . . And if the *prisoner*, like some of the psychiatric patients, cannot be changed by genuine efforts to rehabilitate him, we must look *our* failure in the face, and provide for his indefinitely continued confinement, regardless of the technical reasons for it. This we owe society for its protection.

(Menninger 1959; see also Menninger 1966/1968, 261)

An even stronger statement of the therapeutic model was offered by Benjamin Karpman:

If you make a careful, intensive psychogenic study of every prisoner, but very few, if any at all, would be found who would not reveal that their criminal behavior is an unconsciously conditioned psychic reaction over which they have no conscious control. . . . If it be true, then obviously imprisonment and punishment do not present themselves as the proper methods of dealing with criminals. We have to treat them as psychically sick people, which in every respect they are. . . . In the future, it is the hope of the more progressive elements in psychopathology and criminology that the guard and jailer will be replaced by the nurse, and the judge by the psychiatrist, whose sole attempt will be to treat and cure the individual instead of merely to punish him.

(Karpman 1949, 604–605)

## Perils of the Sickness Model

It is not unreasonable to suppose that if we regard those who commit criminal acts as "sick," that will eliminate or at least ameliorate the desire for harsh treatment. Perhaps it would, at least in some people; but I suspect that those are people who are already repulsed by the harsh treatment of wrongdoers. In some cases classifying criminals as sick may prompt even harsher condemnation. As Joel Feinberg noted, adding a "sickness" element to wrongdoing may exacerbate rather than ameliorate the harsh attitudes of those who demand severe retribution against criminals:

Instead of being a kind of softening excuse, mental illness has become in some quarters a kind of hardening aggravation. Instead of saying, "He is mentally disordered, poor fellow, go easy on him," now some say, "He is a damned sicko, so draw and quarter him."

(2003, 141)

Motivated by the deep belief in a just world, there is a powerful tendency to link sickness with badness (severe sickness is bad, and in a just world bad things happen to bad people). The most obvious example is the deep-seated *moral* revulsion against leprosy (we still speak of really vile people as "moral lepers"):

> Leprosy has always carried the stigma of divine curse. "Flee the leper as you would flee the lion," said Mohammed. All over the world, and most markedly in countries like Japan which never had exposure to the Bible, the disease was taken as a sign of supernatural judgment. Hindus in India, who traditionally viewed leprosy as punishment for some crime in a former life, implemented repressive measures similar to those in Christian Europe. The official Leper's Act in India, which remained law until 1984, sanctioned mandatory incarceration for anyone infected with the disease.
>
> (Yancey and Brand 1997, 320)

Belief in a just world promoted the equation of leprosy with godly punishment of evil. Sadly, the tendency to link illness with wickedness has not been eliminated by modern scientific thinking. According to surveys by the Pew Research Center, in 1987 43 percent of U.S. citizens believed that "AIDS might be God's punishment for immoral behavior."

Leprosy and AIDS scare us; so do criminals. When the AIDS epidemic was at its most severe, there was something close to mass hysteria, and the fear of infection intensified the opprobrium directed toward AIDS victims. The same fear of contagion can be found in attitudes toward criminals. Dan Kahan—who celebrates the fact that prison inflicts "countless indignities" on inmates and "unambiguously marks the lowness of those we consign to it," also values imprisonment because "imprisonment removes offenders from our midst, shielding us from their contaminating influence" (1998, 1642). Criminals are—almost by definition—people who are disliked and disapproved of by society; adding a "sickness" element to that stigmatization may promote increased harshness and hostility, rather than sympathetic understanding. (And if the just world belief remains intact, we are likely to suppose that those offenders who are "quarantined" are—like lepers—justly deserving of such treatment.)

## Serious Challenges to the Therapeutic Model

Though elements of the therapeutic model—particularly as it emphasizes a public health orientation (Caruso 2016; Pereboom and Caruso, forthcoming)—are of great value, some aspects of that model raise questions. One problem for the quarantine/therapy model is noted by Michael J. Zimmerman: the difference between the level of knowledge when we quarantine an individual with a highly contagious disease and the level of knowledge when "quarantining" someone who poses a danger of criminal violence:

> In the typical case of quarantine, two facts stand out. First, the prediction that the person will spread the disease unless his movements

are suitably restricted is one that is based on solid scientific evidence. Second, the confinement that is imposed on the person in question is relatively short-term. If either of these points should fail to apply in a particular instance in which quarantine is proposed, the measure will be that much more difficult to justify. Unfortunately, this is precisely the problem that besets preventive detention under most present and, I would have thought, foreseeable circumstances: the prediction of future criminal activity is not based on solid scientific evidence, and the confinement would not be short-term.

(2011, 169)

In fact our knowledge of contagious diseases and how they spread is often limited, and sometimes we quarantine more stringently than the potential for contagion would justify. Nonetheless, our knowledge of contagious disease remains greater than our capacity for predicting violent criminal behavior—though predictive powers for violence are rapidly improving (Raine 2013).

Attacks on the therapeutic use of rehabilitative measures are sometimes gross strawman distortions, such as Clockwork Orange horrors. Nonetheless, some of the concerns raise problems worth noting. There are hazards in the rehabilitative/therapeutic model of dealing with criminals: the most obvious (but not the most basic) being the problem of indefinite sentences left in the hands of over confident and under-competent psychologists and psychiatrists. If we consider the current dedication to the nostrums of "Big Pharma" for treatment of psychological "disorders" (ranging from depression to shyness), the hard sell and weak research—sometimes research of very questionable legitimacy indeed (Angell 2004 and 2009)—in support of such drugs, and the billions that drug companies could reap by selling long-term pharmacological "cures" or "chronic disease treatment" medications to prison/asylum settings, then it is clear that not all therapeutic perils are strawmen. Furthermore, too often the "rehabilitation goal"—whether for "difficult" children or rebellious prisoners—is passive or even stupefied obedience. Drugs are often quite good at achieving that type of "cure."

If we favor therapeutic "rehabilitation," we must be acutely aware that there are programs that disguise themselves as rehabilitation when in actuality the "rehabilitation" involves very severe punitive measures. Sadly, these brutal "treatment" processes are not all stories from distant decades past. "Wet packs"—under the guise of therapy to "cool down" patients who were difficult to control—were in regular use well into the 1980s to punish adolescent girls in places such as the "Institute of Living" in Hartford: girls were stripped and tightly bound into sheets that had been packed in ice, and left in that condition for as much as 24 hours. The popular "boot camps" for juveniles—which peaked in popularity in the 1990s, but remain in existence to this day—often masked brutality under the guise of rehabilitation (Muscar 2008): they were built on notions of "tough love" more toughly punitive than loving, while the "rehabilitation" was primarily conditioning for abject submission.

We should be particularly concerned about claims that a rehabilitation program for offenders aims at "reintroducing them successfully into society" if that means making them acquiescent in menial tasks and lowly status. In neo-liberal society, there is good reason to fear such programs. That was a clear motive in some of the "boot camp" programs: "educate" these hoodlums to "accept their place." "Campers" were taught "skills" of how to follow orders and show up on time and dress "appropriately"; not skills of thinking for themselves, stronger self-reliance, and resilience. Obviously, those who favor the therapeutic model fiercely oppose harshly punitive measures that are imposed under the cover of therapy, but the danger of abuse does exist. That danger should not be exaggerated: the danger is certainly less than the actual abuses carried out under the retributive system. But the danger remains real.

## The Basic Objection to the Therapeutic Model

The therapeutic model seems quite different from any system based on belief in moral responsibility, and in many respects it is. But the therapeutic model and the just deserts model share a common framework, or at least a common deep assumption: the assumption that moral responsibility is the default setting, and denial of moral responsibility is a special *exception*. The most common and tempting proposed substitute for the moral responsibility system is the system that starts from the legitimacy of *excuses*, and then *expands* the range of excuses until it encompasses all behavior: as discussed in Chapter 6, this is an "excuse-extensionist" (Waller 1998, 57 and 2011, 206) model of the denial of moral responsibility. The therapeutic model is essentially a *sickness* model; and while advocates of the therapeutic model acknowledge that not all who must be "quarantined" are actually "sick," the model works from that basis.

When starting from *within* the moral responsibility framework, the operating assumption is that everyone is morally responsible *unless* he or she qualifies for a special excuse (she was drugged, or coerced, or ignorant, or temporarily insane) or exemption (he is a child, or senile, or permanently deranged, or otherwise long-term incompetent). Working within the moral responsibility system, the *universal* denial of moral responsibility must be based on the claim of universal derangement or incompetence. The key *real* problem for the therapeutic-quarantine model is that it is built on a basic assumption of the moral responsibility model: therapy and quarantine replace punishment because offenders are deeply flawed and thus excused or exempted from punitive just deserts. From P. F. Strawson on, it has been assumed that the denial of moral responsibility must be based on universal infirmity: an excuse-extensionist model that treats *everyone* as insane and incompetent and profoundly flawed (thus excused). But the universal denial of moral responsibility is *not* best understood as a sickness model. No doubt some offenders are insane, but most are not. They are flawed, certainly, as we all are in a variety of ways; but neither incompetent nor insane, and not that different from you and me.

The therapeutic approach has the advantage of incorporating a basic element of the moral responsibility system; but it likewise has the *dis*advantage of incorporating a basic element of the moral responsibility system. The advantage is that excuse-extensionism starts from the widely accepted "common sense" view of moral responsibility: we are morally responsible for our behavior *except* when we have a special excuse. Indeed, this is the basic view of criminal liability that is built into our criminal justice system. If you engage in criminal behavior, you are liable to punitive sanction *unless* you have some special excuse, which typically takes the form of an *affirmative* defense in which the burden of proof shifts to the defendant: you were temporarily or permanently insane, you acted under coercion, you were dealing with a special emergency, you were drugged.

Pereboom's well-known four-case argument is an excuse-extensionist argument. Pereboom starts from a case in which the moral responsibility system would *excuse* a wrongdoer from moral responsibility (because of manipulation which undermines the wrongdoer's power of control); and he then extends this case through three additional cases until he arrives at a standard nonintervention case in which the moral responsibility system would ordinarily count the wrongdoer as morally responsible. Pereboom argues that the last case is analogous to the earlier cases in all morally relevant respects, so we should draw the same conclusion: moral responsibility no more applies to the last case than the first, and so all of us ultimately meet the basic *excusing* conditions of the moral responsibility system. Therefore, no one legitimately can be held morally responsible in the basic desert sense: no one justly deserves blame or punishment. As Pereboom describes this process in a slightly different context:

> The best sort of argument against the claim that our practice of holding morally responsible is insulated from the skeptic's challenge involves what Wallace calls a generalization strategy—arguing from generally accepted excuses or exemptions to the conclusion that causal determinism rules out moral responsibility. . . . The excuses and exemptions that form the basis of this sort of argument would need to be generally accepted (but perhaps not uncontested), so that they are plausibly features internal to the practice of holding morally responsible. The manipulation argument is such a generalization strategy. The kinds of exemptions that I exploit in the four-case argument are due to deterministic manipulation, and it is a feature of our practice that we exempt agents from moral responsibility in the basic desert sense when they are manipulated in this way. It is also a feature of our practice that if no morally relevant difference can be found between agents in two situations,

then if one agent is legitimately exempted from moral responsibility in this sense, so is the other.

(Pereboom 2014, 155)

This is a powerful argument against moral responsibility. It starts from the basic assumptions of the moral responsibility system itself—the excusing and exempting conditions built into that system—and demonstrates that given the basic principles acknowledged internally to the system, holding people morally responsible cannot be justified. But what makes for a strong argument against the moral responsibility system—starting from its basic assumptions—does not produce the best *alternative* to the moral responsibility system. When seeking an alternative to the moral responsibility system, it is better not to build on a basic assumption of that flawed system: specifically, the assumption that denial of moral responsibility must be based on an exemption or excuse.

When tempted to think in terms of sickness, note that in many recent honor cultures (and perhaps some remaining honor cultures) a violent reaction to a mild affront or insult to one's honor or the honor of one's family was considered the virtuous act of a well-adjusted and morally sound individual. The same violent response in our contemporary dominant culture is classified as the criminal result of a profound lack of self-control coupled with a fragile self-image. And if we are tempted to think of "honor cultures" as a historical curiosity, we should note the rising popularity of "stand your ground" laws in various states across the United States: laws that are explicitly based on the "right" to use lethal force rather than "dishonorably backing down" from a threat.

Perhaps there is little likelihood that proponents of "stand your ground" laws will be classified as insane, but there are genuine dangers of wrongly classifying those who struggle against harsh circumstances as suffering from psychological disorders, a point that Focquaert, Glenn, and Raine emphasize:

We should be mindful that certain behaviors are easily misclassified as behavioral indications of an underlying disorder while in reality being expressions of normal variation in personality traits and behaviors. The risk of false positives is especially worrisome when faced with children and adolescents living in low socioeconomic, deprived neighborhoods and attending schools with high-delinquency rates. Behavior that reflects normal survival and coping strategies in such an environment may be misunderstood as exemplifying underlying disorders.

(2016)

Certainly, Pereboom does not regard all persons who are candidates for "quarantine" as suffering from psychiatric illness; to the contrary, he explicitly rejects that generalization:

Policies for making a detained criminal safe for release would address a condition in the offender that results in the criminal behavior. These conditions include psychological illness, but also problems that are not plausibly classified as illness, such as insufficient sympathy for other people, or a strong tendency to assign blame to others for whatever goes wrong.

(Pereboom 2001, 178)

But he does regard all those who are fit candidates for quarantine as significantly *flawed*. However, in many cases the people who do wrong are not so substantially flawed, but were in a *situation* (in some cases a deprived neighborhood, in others an avaricious corporate culture) that resulted in their participation in wrongdoing.

## Does the Therapeutic Model Eliminate Punishment?

Building on the excuse-extensionist basis for the therapy model, one supposed advantage of the therapeutic-quarantine model may instead be a liability. Advocates of the therapeutic model may claim that it offers the ideal solution to the problem of punishment, because it eliminates punishment altogether. The therapeutic model does eliminate punishment, but that stunning success is not entirely the result of its improved methodology. It owes much of that success to a narrow definition of punishment. If therapy for criminals is not *aimed* at producing some degree of pain or discomfort, then it does not count as "punishment"; and since the *purpose* of the therapeutic procedures is rehabilitation rather than the infliction of suffering, any discomforts suffered by the subject are not inflicted as punishment. When the dentist extracts a badly decayed tooth, the patient may experience some pain, or at least considerable discomfort; but rather than punitive, this is a therapeutic process in which some suffering cannot be avoided, though the dentist does not intend to cause suffering.

Although there is an important distinction, the therapeutic model cannot avoid something that closely resembles punishment, even if the goal is not punitive. Rather than imprisoning wrongdoers as a means of punishment, under the therapeutic model wrongdoers are held against their will in quarantine. While there may be rehabilitative goals as well, the quarantine is explicitly designed to coercively isolate the wrongdoer and prevent harm to others. Pereboom acknowledges such motivation for the quarantine process:

Ferdinand Schoeman has argued that if in order to protect society, we have the right to quarantine people who are carriers of severe communicable diseases, then we also have the right to isolate the criminally dangerous to protect society. . . . Suppose a person poses a danger to society by a sufficiently strong tendency to commit murder. Even if he is not in general a morally responsible agent, society would seem to have as much right to detain him as it does to quarantine a carrier of a deadly communicable disease who is not responsible for being a carrier.

(2001, 174)

Saying that this does not involve punishment is a bit like the infamous claim of the U.S. Air Force press agent: "You keep saying it's bombing. It's not bombing, it's air support." There is an important difference between quarantine of criminals while minimizing suffering, in contrast to the retributive intentional infliction of suffering. But even if we call it quarantine, we are still isolating criminals for the protection of society and coercively restraining those quarantined. While the "quarantine" conditions may be better than those in most prisons, this still involves the coercive and involuntary confinement of the criminal. When we "quarantine" the convicted child molester after that person has served a criminal sentence (but still poses a threat)—currently the closest thing in the United States to the therapeutic model—the "quarantine" looks and feels very much like imprisonment; indeed, it may occur in precisely the same facility, in the same cell. So whether we call it punishment or quarantine, we still have the question of whether such coercive confinement can be *just* in the absence of moral responsibility.

Whether we call it punishment, quarantine, or preventive confinement, when we lock someone up by coercive force, without the person's permission, and for the benefit of others rather than the benefit of the confined individual, we are imposing harsh treatment on that individual. It may well be true that we do not *intentionally* cause suffering to the incarcerated individual, but we know that we *are* causing that person to suffer. Sadly, the very fact that we are not *aiming* at punitive measures may weaken safeguards against mistreatment. A case in point is *Smith v. Doe* (538 U.S. 84), a 2003 case in which the U.S. Supreme Court ruled that the state of Alaska could impose onerous post-release regulations on a convicted sex offender although the crime had occurred long *prior* to the law imposing those regulations. As Vincent Chiao describes the Court's reasoning:

> Despite the significant stigma and harassment that accompanies public registration as a sex offender, the Supreme Court took the view that because the statute was intended to be part of a merely 'regulatory' regime aimed at fostering public safety, the statute was not punitive, hence was civil rather than criminal, and hence not subject to the federal Constitution's ban on *ex post facto* legislation.
>
> (Chiao 2013, 730)

As Chiao argues, this distinction between policies that *aim* at suffering and those that unavoidably *cause* suffering is based on the principle of double effect; and that is a shaky foundation with vigorous defenders (Scanlon 2008) as well as powerful critics (McIntyre 2001). Leaving aside the questionable principle of double effect, it is important to bear in mind that whether we speak of quarantine as regulation or punishment it will in either case involve unpleasant and perhaps harsh coercive treatment of offenders. As Chiao sums up the key question:

> The motivation for sex offender registries, unlike that of imprisonment or fines, may not be retributive, and hence . . . may not properly be considered punishment. But the question is not whether they are punishment. The question is to what degree they can be expected to harm those subject to them.
>
> (2013, 758)

This is more than a verbal disagreement over whether we wish to call it quarantine or punishment. It is a fundamental disagreement about whether we are participating in a *just* or an *unjust* process; and that is a difference that makes a difference. It is not really "quarantine" that is objectionable (adopting something of that sort is probably unavoidable), but the idea of feeling *comfortable* with quarantine as a solution. We are dealing with this unfortunate person's "sickness," and certainly not intentionally imposing suffering on that person, and in the process we are protecting society: we too easily conclude that there is nothing disturbing in the process. But while the punitive elements are no doubt minimized they still remain, and should be acknowledged as necessary but unjust. When we cannot avoid imposing unjust punishment (or "quarantine" or "detention"), we must avoid becoming comfortable with that injustice.

Whatever one's verdict on whether the therapeutic model eliminates punishment, there is no doubt that adopting major elements of the model would greatly *reduce* punishment. First, the quarantine and therapy would not *aim* at causing suffering, but would instead reduce suffering as much as possible, consistent with the goals of rehabilitation and public safety. Second, it would seek the least intrusive measures, and minimize the use of quarantine/incarceration. Third, it would emphasize "public health" (Caruso 2016; Pereboom and Caruso, forthcoming) measures that would seek to improve society so that the root causes of crime are targeted and fewer people would require quarantine or therapy. Whatever faults the therapeutic system may have, any morally decent system must incorporate those positive elements of the therapeutic model.

## Rehabilitation in a Coercive Environment

In addition to the concerns noted in the previous section, there is a substantial challenge for rehabilitation programs that operate in coercive settings. Central to the therapeutic/quarantine model is the importance of *rehabilitation* programs: those offenders who are coercively "quarantined" are not warehoused in locked facilities; rather, they are given the best rehabilitative measures available. Quarantine involves coerced and unavoidable suffering, including deprivation of freedom; fairness requires positive rehabilitation that can at least partially balance the negatives of quarantine. As Pereboom states:

> When a criminal is "quarantined," supposing that hard incompatibilism is true [and no one justly deserves punishment], then he is also made to experience a deprivation he does not merit, and from which society benefits. . . . It is a matter of fairness for society to do what it can, within reasonable bounds, to make the criminal safe for release. For society to repudiate programs for criminal rehabilitation because it is unwilling to pay for them could well involve serious unfairness.
>
> (2001, 178)

However, there are problems in offering rehabilitation measures to those who are coercively quarantined (or incarcerated). When we regard criminals as *sick*, there is a grave danger: we are tempted to classify them as psychologically sick and therefore *incompetent* to give consent. Their psychological impairment undercuts their competence, and they don't know what's really good for them. It becomes too easy to suppose that we are doing this "for their own good" when we lock them away or subject them to brutal "tough love" boot camps. Exacerbating the problem of consent is that the quarantine setting is what the courts would classify as an "inherently coercive environment": when the prisoner is offered the "choice" of participation in a program of rehabilitation, it is actually a "choice" between participating in rehabilitation (and thus becoming "safe for release") or remaining in quarantine indefinitely. In regard to the "free choice" of drug rehabilitation programs for prisoners, the Center for Cognitive Liberty and Ethics claims that:

> Being forced to choose between imprisonment or "medical treatment" with a pharmacotherapy drug is inherently coercive. There are very few things that people will avoid more than going to jail or prison. Informed consent is incompatible with inherently coercive situations that force a person to barter his or her natural neuro- and biochemistry in exchange for freedom.
>
> (Center for Cognitive Liberty and Ethics 2004, 13; quoted in Ryberg 2015)

If the rehabilitation program is being offered as a means of making the criminal "safe for release," then when the prisoner "freely chooses" to enter into a rehabilitation program there are serious problems with that "free choice."

Whether we classify it as imprisonment or quarantine, we are inflicting unavoidable (and unjust) suffering on an individual. Certainly it seems—and might be—legitimate to offer an *alternative* (Focquaert and Raine 2012): correction involving *reduced* harsh treatment if the offender with a drug problem will participate in a drug-treatment program or the violent offender works through an anger-management program. Whether we call the necessary confinement "quarantine" or (as I would prefer) treat it as "unjust punishment," there remains the serious problem of a "choice" of therapeutic alternatives within a coercive environment. Obviously, we must not make the harsh treatment (the punishment) so harsh that the "choice" of instruction is coerced ("either ten years in Attica, or work through this instructional self-help program"); but the strong requirement of *minimized* correctional harsh treatment offers some protection against such abuse. Still, there will inevitably be pressure to choose such programs (when they offer a reduction of harsh treatment and/or release from quarantine/incarceration).

Perhaps this problem cannot be solved, but it can be ameliorated. Though prison (and coerced quarantine) settings are inimical to full free choice, some such settings are a greater threat to free choice and consent than are others. When we offer a prisoner in Attica or Angola participation in a rehabilitation program as a means to reduced prison time, that is significantly more coercive than the same offer to a prisoner in Norway's Bastoy Island Prison; and one can reasonably expect that the quarantine facilities offered by Pereboom's program would more closely resemble Bastoy than Attica. Though the problem of coerced choice cannot be solved, neither should it be exaggerated. If it is acknowledged that quarantine/incarceration is sometimes necessary unless we have a rehabilitative program that will reduce the dangerousness of the offender, then the "coercive offer" of rehabilitation may be the lesser of two evils. As Jesper Ryberg notes:

> Surely, locking people up involves a much more forceful use of coercion (in fact compulsion) than what would be involved in the making of a coercive offer of treatment.
>
> (2015, 626)

It is also essential that the rehabilitative programs offered be such that residents might reasonably conclude that the programs provide genuine benefits (*beyond* any benefits of early release). Opportunities for addiction therapy, real educational programs, enhancement of self-control and self-efficacy, and anger-management treatment might be chosen whether or not one is in coerced confinement; the "rehabilitation" of mindless acquiescence is likely to be "chosen" only under harsh coercive circumstances.

## Limiting Punishment

There is a common fear that if we give up belief in moral responsibility (and especially if we adopt a *therapeutic* model), we will open the door to excessive punishment (or excessively harsh "treatment" imposed on too many people) and we will lose the protection of basic individual rights. In fact, eliminating moral responsibility from society threatens individual rights the way that eliminating lead from gasoline threatens health. Strong belief in moral responsibility does not *protect* individual rights and protect against cruel and excessive punishment, but instead produces a social environment in which basic rights are threatened and abused—or so it was argued in Chapters 6, 7 and 8. Nonetheless, there is a serious challenge for any system that rejects moral responsibility while admitting that punitive measures cannot be eliminated in the foreseeable future: how do we place *limits* and *restrictions* on the necessary use of punishment, *without* using the principles of just deserts? Part of the answer is simple: always use the *least* punishment that will serve the essential function. But the basic question remains: how do we set the limits on such punishment?

Michael Corrado—who rejects moral responsibility—struggles honestly and vigorously with that question (2013). He insists that we must keep the distinction between competent and incompetent and a corresponding distinction between *correction* and *therapy*. *Correction* (involving harsh treatment) can be applied only to those judged *competent* who commit bad acts (while therapeutic measures are reserved for those judged incompetent or insane). This would have the deterrent/enforcement effect we may require in order to have effective rules/laws in the society, while preserving protections against the power of the state over individuals. Corrado recommends that we use the term "correction" rather than "punishment" because (among other reasons) genuine *punishment* must be *justly deserved*; and because he rejects moral responsibility and just deserts, he believes we should not speak of punishment. That is certainly an important distinction. However, I prefer to keep the term "punishment," because this process still has a great deal in common with our traditional concept of punishment: it is imposed only on those who are competent and have committed a serious offense; it involves some degree of "harsh treatment" (though we will work to keep the harshness to a minimum); and it is imposed coercively (it does not require the consent of the punished). If we use a different word—this is correction, not really punishment—that may prevent us from facing forthrightly the *unjust* nature of the unavoidable punitive process.

We might well decide that we *must* punish a fraudulent stock broker (though like all of us, he does not justly deserve punishment), for otherwise the rules of conduct will be flaunted. But deeper scrutiny of the culture and history that shaped his greed would reveal more flaws in the system than in the particular individual. It is important to recognize that, so we will have strong motivation to *fix* the flaws in our social system that are producing such flawed persons (whom we must *unjustly* punish) and flawed situations. So we impose *punishment*, not therapy, because subjecting him to *therapy* against his wishes involves treating this competent person as if he were incompetent to make his own choices. Once we start down the path of *imposing* therapy, we lose valuable protections against the power of the state (Corrado 2013 and 2015).

Power corrupts, and the persons who employ this power may not be as conscientious and nice as Derk Pereboom and Gregg Caruso. As Corrado makes clear, there are important protections that we do not want to lose, even if we reject the notion of moral responsibility and just deserts. We do not want to lose *habeas corpus*, proportionality, rights to a fair trial and a presumption of innocence, the right of no legal punishment unless we have broken a law. (The fact that in the United States these protections are not working very well is not a reason to give them up altogether; rather, it is a reason to give up the moral responsibility system that works against such protections.) We need protections that a pure therapy system endangers: under therapy, we are not *punishing*, but providing beneficial treatment, and so the protections against the powers of the therapeutic state are of less concern. But in fact those protections remain very important indeed. We have already observed how "treatment" of sex offenders can swiftly erode away basic legal protections (Corrado 2013, 90). Allowing the state to exercise special powers in imposing therapy on competent persons gives the state an enormous power; and power has a long and terrible history of corrupting.

It is hard to acknowledge that we must treat people unjustly. But it is better to face that fact, and try to minimize it. Pretending that punishment is *just* makes a bad situation worse. We cannot (for the foreseeable future) avoid administering corrective "harsh treatment" to competent persons who violate our laws, but it will remain important to emphasize that the harsh treatment is *not* justly deserved. That emphasis will motivate us to find better ways of preventing lawbreaking that do not involve us in injustice, and will encourage us to keep the unavoidable harsh treatment to a minimum.

## Conclusion

Quarantine assumes that the *individual* is flawed, and that is the focus. Sometimes that is true, but by no means always. Often the real problem is the situation or cultural setting that prompts bad behavior. Even when we are dealing with the problem of flawed individuals, the most important question—the question rightly emphasized by the public health model—is what *caused* the severe problems, and what steps can we take to change those larger causes (whether the causes are social or a toxic physical environment). "What do we do with those who commit crimes?" That's a classic complex question, which fixes the narrow and shallow focus on the individual (and the individual's current state, rather than the forces that shaped that individual). A better question: What do we do about a *system* that produces this level of crime?

The therapy model has important virtues, particularly when the public health aspect is emphasized. But ultimately we must find a radical alternative to the moral responsibility system and its Tychonic variations: a model that makes a total break with the moral responsibility system and its powerful assumptions and pervasive influence. That model is now being developed, though not by philosophers. That should not be a surprise. Philosophers have been deeply immersed in just world beliefs, defending the moral responsibility system, saving human uniqueness, and insisting that ought implies can; and those commitments block the path to a genuine alternative to the retributive system of just deserts. The final chapters of this book explore that emerging new alternative.

# 11 The No-Blame System Model

We will not give up the moral responsibility system and change the way we deal with punishment until there is a replacement system in view; however, the emerging replacement need not be a finished product. When the Copernican System successfully challenged the Ptolemaic System, the Copernican System still had a realm of fixed stars, and those stars were relatively close to the Sun; it required cycles and epicycles (until Kepler, no one imagined that the orbits of the Earth and the other planets could involve anything other than perfect spheres). But it posed a radically different world view that could be developed and improved. There is now a serious challenger to the moral responsibility system, though that challenger will require development and refinement. And just as the Copernican System had to resist efforts to remold it into a Tychonic variation of the Ptolemaic System, so also this challenger to the moral responsibility system must resist powerful forces that would co-opt it and reshape it as merely a modification of the moral responsibility system.

The serious new challenger to the moral responsibility system is the *no-blame system* model. It was born in the grubby mundane world of the factory assembly line, and matured in industrial settings, air traffic control programs, and hospitals. Like the Copernican System, there was first an effort to reject it, followed by a vigorous campaign to co-opt it. The new challenger has been called by various names (occasionally reflecting significant modifications in the model): the system model, the no-blame system model, and—more recently, and with major unfortunate modifications—the just culture model.

## The System Approach

There are several distinctive features of the system approach that distinguish it from the work management models that are common in the United States, especially in factories but also in other work environments. First—and the feature that has drawn the most attention—the system model takes a very different approach to errors and mistakes and problems in the workplace and the production line. Rather than *blaming* or shaming an individual worker as the source of the problem, the system model treats errors and mistakes—whether large or small—as learning opportunities that can improve the workplace and the production system. A worker who reports an error provides valuable systemic information that can prevent future errors and improve the overall production process, and is thanked rather than blamed. The emphasis is on designing a workplace or an assembly line that prevents worker mistakes, rather than seeking perfect workers who never make mistakes. How far this approach is pushed—does it apply to negligent workers or drug-impaired workers?—varies according to the system version employed, and that will be a major issue in later pages. But all versions share a commitment to rejecting blame and punishment for errors committed by well-intentioned workers.

The second distinctive characteristic is an emphasis on *systems* rather than individuals. When a problem occurs, the underlying assumption is that there is a flaw in the system, and deeper inquiries are needed to find and fix the problem (in contrast to the traditional management assumption that the basic problem is a flaw in the worker who had the most immediate involvement when the error occurred, and the problem is solved once that worker is disciplined or fired). A worker's error is the start of serious inquiry, not the final answer. Was there a problem in the workplace that made this "an error waiting to happen" because of bad system design, or bad labels, or confusing steps? Was the training of the worker flawed? Is the system causing too much stress for workers in that part of the system, or leaving them too exhausted to work effectively? Was this worker assigned a role that was inappropriate for his or her abilities? Was this an error that should have been prevented by checks and protections that were not in place or that failed? Obviously, individuals are important, and indeed the system model—the third characteristic discussed below—emphasizes respect for individuals in every part or "level" of the system; but the importance of the larger *system* in promoting effective behavior as well as in causing and preventing mistakes must be taken very seriously.

The third characteristic of the system approach is a rejection of rigid hierarchy in the workplace, and in particular a rejection of any "division of labor" in which management supplies the brains and makes the decisions while the workers provide the brawn and hard labor and "don't get paid to think." In the system model, all workers are expected to use their intelligence and perceptiveness to detect problems—including small problems that could lead to big problems—and find ways to solve them, and all workers are empowered to stop the work (including the assembly line) if there is a problem that needs to be fixed, and the expertise and experience and perspective of each worker is respected and valued. Norman Bodek describes a basic element of the system model as it was employed in improving the quality of Toyota automobiles:

> *Jidoka* is one of the core principles of the Toyota Production System. It means applying the "human touch" to immediately address

manufacturing problems at the moment they are detected. *Jidoka* is used at Toyota to empower every worker to stop the assembly line whenever a quality problem is detected. The worker pulls a red cord and the entire assembly line stops, idling every machine and every worker on that line until the problem is solved or a remedy is found to prevent a defect from moving forward. When the line stops, fellow workers run over to the person who pulled the red cord to help them resolve the problem.

(Bodek 2011)

Everyone is a full participant in improving quality and identifying problems, and everyone plays an important role. Instead of rigidly policing and coercing work, the system approach encourages and recognizes good work and respects the abilities and cognitive capacities of the workers. Finally—the focus of Chapter 13—the system approach builds and relies on *commitment* from all workers to a shared project.

When the system approach is installed, then workplace problems and errors are greatly reduced. The reduction is the result of two parallel forces that follow from rejecting the blame and shame approach to workplace management. First, instead of blaming individual workers, mistakes and errors are evidence of *systemic* problems that need to be changed. When individual workers are not blamed and shamed for mistakes, they not only report serious mistakes but also the "harmless errors" that would have been ignored or covered up (to avoid blame). Under the system approach, "errors are learning opportunities": rather than suffering blame and shame, the reporting individual is recognized as providing information that improves systemic safety and efficiency. Errors are examined carefully, patterns detected, and changes made to prevent small untreated errors from growing into large and recurring problems. Second, when errors are blamed on an individual, deeper inquiry is blocked: the blame and the buck stop *here*, with the blamed individual. If inquiry goes deeper into the systemic causes of the problem, then it becomes obvious that the individual does not really deserve to be blamed. Preservation of a blame and shame model blocks deeper inquiry, rather than facilitating it. In contrast, when there is no insistence on blaming a flawed individual worker, then it is possible to probe deeper into the systemic causes of the problem and fix them: whether that problem lies in bad design of the production process, inadequate worker training, the mind-numbing and helplessness-inducing repetitiveness of the assembly line, or some other cause.

The success of the system approach in manufacturing led to its implementation in another industry that had a long history of errors, and where even small errors could and did have catastrophic results: the air traffic control system. The pressure on individual controllers was enormous. They were working in a complex fast-paced system, with procedures that were often confusing (such as flight names and instructions that sounded similar), constant handoffs from one control group to another in a different region, very little in the way of internal controls to catch errors before they caused problems, and a high pressure working environment in which any error could result in hundreds of deaths and was regarded as evidence of individual negligence. It is hardly surprising that controllers faced anxiety-induced problems ranging from depression to sleep-disorders to drug and alcohol abuse; and it is not surprising that their work suffered, and that they made strenuous efforts to cover up their errors or shift the blame elsewhere. "Harmless errors" were hidden and repeated, and became terrifying near-misses; the near-misses were blamed on negligent controllers who were disciplined or fired and "the problem was solved"; and the whole process led inexorably to airline catastrophes.

When the no-blame system model was installed, controllers were no longer blamed for errors, but were encouraged and commended for reporting errors. Collecting information on errors and where they were occurring was the essential step in finding the system component that was causing the errors and fixing the system before small errors caused disasters. Everyone worked together to report errors, find their deeper causes, and fix them—and to devise a safety system in which the inevitable errors would be detected and corrected *before* they became harmful. Sometimes, of course, the problem was in the individual controller: perhaps a once competent controller had been worn down by the unavoidable stress of the position; perhaps the controller had been trained badly; possibly the controller was simply not suited for this sort of stressful environment, and the screening program for controllers needed improvement; perhaps the controller was suffering from excessive stress that could be significantly reduced—in which case, there were probably multiple controllers suffering from the same error-producing problem—and stress-reducing adjustments were needed in the system. But if the problem was in the individual controller, that was vitally important information—information controllers were commended for reporting—that served as the *start* of the inquiry into the deeper systemic problem, and not as the answer to a problem that was solved once the individual controller was blamed and punished or fired.

While airline disasters are spectacular and receive enormous media coverage, there is another industry that causes many more injuries and deaths than the airline industry at its worst: the medical care industry, and especially hospital operation. The worst aviation year on record was 1972, when 2,429 people died worldwide in aviation accidents. The most conservative estimate of annual deaths in the United States (not worldwide) from errors and accidents in U.S. hospitals is 40,000, and the more likely number is between 40,000 and 100,000. If there is an industry needing a new way of preventing harmful errors, the U.S. hospital industry is a top candidate.

## Resistance to the No-Blame System Model

Some hospitals and medical practices have adopted the system approach to at least some degree, and there have been encouraging results. But the adjustment has not been easy. Several factors in the U.S. health care system make it difficult to implement a system approach, and there has been vigorous active opposition to the system approach. The problems for adoption of the no-blame system approach in medicine are matched by similar problems for the broader adoption of the no-blame system model in U.S. society. The first problem comes from those who regard a no-blame approach as demeaning, and the second from those who fear that the system approach would involve a demotion from their special status at the top of the pecking order. The first concern is fundamentally false, and based on misunderstanding. The second—the demotion from the top of the hierarchy—does involve an element of truth; but it is primarily a *promotion* of those who have been disempowered and disrespected, and that promotion is beneficial and long overdue.

Consider first the view that the no-blame system is somehow demeaning. From the perspective of some physicians—those who insist on an exalted and almost infallible status for physicians—it is not only careless and negligent and malicious behavior that must be blamed, but even honest errors by conscientious dedicated medical professionals should be subjected to blame and shame. If such errors are treated as *system* problems rather than due to flaws in individual professionals, that shifts the focus away from the character of the individual caregiver; and the individual caregiver is where the focus *should* always be. Edmund Pellegrino, champion of the virtue ethics approach to medical ethics, is the most trenchant and thorough critic of employing the system approach in medicine, and his criticisms are important in understanding the fierce opposition.

Virtue theory has its virtues, especially in an area like bioethics where the goals of the enterprise are reasonably well-defined: celebrating ideals can be beneficial. But it is counter productive if employed as an account of the best way to achieve those ideals. First, it overemphasizes *character* (and ignores situations and circumstances). And when it treats character as a special semi-miraculous power—a power able to rise above all problems and situations, and it is your own fault if you have character flaws and lack virtues—then it is a source of harm, and an impediment to understanding and fixing the problems: problems both systemic and individual (that ultimately are also systemic).

Pellegrino insists that the starting point for improving medical care and reducing error must be the individual *character* of caregivers, and that the benefits of improved *systems* are modest and perhaps illusory:

> Systems cannot make the professionals within them virtuous, but they can make it possible for virtuous professionals to be virtuous. . . . The moral sensibilities of each health professional must be preserved lest the system for error prevention become part of the problem. . . . Medical error takes place in a nexus of intricate human relationships. Health "care" is channeled ultimately through persons in unique relationships

far less subject to formularization than air travel, nuclear power production, or the manufacture of automobiles or complex pharmaceuticals.
No system of error detection or prevention can confine these intricate
human relationships within a set of preordained algorithms. . . . Overreliance on a systems approach can be as illusory as past overreliance
on the moral integrity of individuals. Even while systemic responses
are being designed, it will be necessary to reaffirm the moral nature of
medical error, and to retain the notions of blame, accountability, and
responsibility.

(2004, 84–85)

The complexity Pellegrino notes makes effective systems imperative. Greater
complexity requires detailed procedures such as checklists and group monitoring and universal vigilance, and makes reliance on individual virtue even
riskier.

Supposing that the problems can be fixed by focus on individual character
is a manifestation of what psychologists call the "fundamental attribution
error"—a subject for further discussion—but it is also a manifestation of a
still deeper problem. The problem is evident in the "solution" to medical
error proposed by Pellegrino:

Preventable or negligent harm as the result of error is a moral failure, whatever its legal status may be. Moral blame and culpability are
therefore unavoidable. Removing individual blame could conceivably
encourage better reporting of errors or more readiness to accept rehabilitative measures. It might also simplify litigation and standardize the
tort system. It could mitigate the punitive atmosphere and enhance col-
legiality and interprofessional communication . . .

However, despite these beneficial possibilities, there are the associate dangers of complacency and dulling of the moral sensibilities of
the humans in the system when either a "blame-free" approach or a
"blame-the-system" approach is adopted. The power of individual guilt
can be constructive as often as it is destructive. Personal accountability
is owed to the person injured. The deterrent effect of fear of shame and
blame is not safely ignored.

(2004, 86)

It is true that the deterrent effect of blame are shame is not safely ignored;
but the major deterrent effect is in deterring the reporting and examining
and understanding of errors and their sources. And the "complacency and
dulling" that Pellegrino legitimately fears are more likely enhanced by the
cover ups that the blame system promotes. I can be complacent, because
there wasn't a mistake at all (since no one could find it) or because the problem was *really* caused by someone else (usually a nurse, but sometimes the

patient) to whom the blame was shifted successfully. Diligent effort to find and fix the real problems—problems that are often deep and difficult—is the opposite of complacency.

The most revealing part of the quoted passage is the first two sentences: "Preventable or negligent harm as the result of error is a moral failure, whatever its legal status may be. Moral blame and culpability are therefore unavoidable." Even *if* we agree that "preventable or negligent harm as the result of error is a moral failure," it does not follow that it deserves blame; certainly moral blame is not "therefore unavoidable." We might conclude that the person causing the "preventable or negligent harm" is badly flawed—even a moral failure—but that the individual's serious moral flaws were the product of causal conditions (perhaps a brutally abusive childhood) that shaped the person's character in such a way that the person is incapable of conscientious effort and thus causes negligent harm. But there is a bigger problem in Pellegrino's claim that "preventable or negligent harm as the result of error is a moral failure"; and that problem is the common but mistaken assumption that when there is "harm as the result of error," there must be a specific person who is the key ultimate cause (and thus the appropriate object of "moral blame and culpability"). That is an erroneous assumption, and such a common erroneous assumption that psychologists have given it an impressive title: the fundamental attribution error (Ross 1977). It is the fundamental and common error of supposing that when someone commits an error or makes a mistake or acts badly then some *character* defect in that person must be the cause of the problem. Someone's behavior was bad or erroneous, so some *attribute* of that person must be the basic source of the problem. It is more likely that the problem lies in the structure of the larger *system* or *situation* in which the person "who made the error" was working.

## The Narrow Focus on Individual Character

It is hardly plausible to suppose that some two-thirds of the U.S. population have a deep character flaw that could cause them to inflict painful and (so they thought) deadly shocks on innocent strangers. But two-thirds of Milgram's (Milgram 1963) subjects were willing to inflict lethal torture on an innocent stranger because they were in a situation in which an authority figure in an authoritative setting urged them to do so and assured them it was the right thing to do. When pleasant, friendly—and probably anti-authoritarian—Stanford students were placed in the *role* and *situation* of being prison guards, they became so cruel and brutal (to fellow students placed in the role of prisoners) that the experiment was soon ended (Zimbardo 1974). We look at the prison guards at Abu Ghraib and conclude that they did awful things—which indeed they did—and so they must have awful character traits (which is quite doubtful); but of course no one wanted to look at the horrific larger situation and system that higher ranking military authorities and political opportunists had created.

At the other end of the spectrum, stopping to help someone in need is admirable behavior, and we are pleased when people exhibit the virtuous character trait of unselfish helpfulness. It seems obvious that a trivial situational influence—such as finding a dime in a phone booth—could have little impact on behavior that seems based in a generous and virtuous character trait. But when this was tested empirically (Isen and Levin 1972), what seemed obvious proved false. In the study, one set of 16 subjects found a dime in a phone booth, while 25 subjects did not. After each of the subjects left the phone booth, another person (who was part of the experiment) walked by and dropped some papers and then started to pick up the papers. Of the 16 subjects who found a dime, 14 stopped to help; of the 25 dimeless subjects, only one helped. Those who stopped to help certainly were not conscious of the positive influence of the lucky dime, and would no doubt deny that it played any role; but situational factors need not be consciously recognized to have a profound effect on behavior. In a somewhat similar study (Darley and Batson 1973) with Princeton Theological students, one group of experimental subjects completed a written task, and then each experimental subject was told to cross the quad to another building, and to please hurry since the experiment was running a bit late. Another group faced the same situation, with only one small difference: they were not urged to hurry to the next building. On the way across campus, the subjects from each group encountered an unfortunate person who appeared to be physically suffering. Of those encouraged to hurry, only 10 percent stopped to help; but in the absence of instructions to hurry, 63 percent of the subjects stopped and offered help. Again, one might expect that the character trait of caring helpfulness (or the lack of that trait) would be the major factor in whether help was offered; but any such trait appeared to have considerably less influence than a trivial difference in the situations.

At Toyota, the same workers who had produced cars notorious for their flaws were shifted into a different system—a system in which errors were no longer blamed on individual workers, and workers were respected for their intelligent efforts to find and fix the sources of error—and those same workers in the new system produced cars noteworthy for their mistake-free reliability. That is not to deny, of course, that shaped character plays a role in our behavior: after all, one third of Milgram's experimental subjects had the self-confidence and courage to defy the authoritative person demanding continued infliction of shocks. But it is to deny Pellegrino's widely shared assumption that character is the deciding factor in almost all behavior. It is better to look at the larger system that is the source of most problems. Blame and shame blocks such inquiries (and the problem is hidden, left unsolved, and continues to produce additional damage) or narrows the focus to an individual who is falsely attributed some egregious character flaw. Of course, it's nice when we accomplish things, and we like to claim the credit; and that is why people in positions of power and privilege are eager to claim that their admirable behavior is the result of admirable attributes (and ideally, admirable attributes that were "self-made"). But if we want to *understand* behavior—including positive and negative behavior, and erroneous behavior as well as negligent behavior and even malicious behavior (such as that of the Stanford "prison guards" and the Abu Ghraib torturers and abusers)—then we must avoid the powerful temptation of quick but shallow "explanations" in terms of character traits and bad people. Searching deep into the systems that profoundly influence behavior and that shape such character traits as we actually have is a harder but more beneficial path.

Sometimes, of course, the fault truly lies "not in our stars, but in ourselves, that we are underlings," or flawed in some other manner. For Pellegrino, that is the end of the story. For those interested in producing better behavioral results, it is only the start of the deeper and more important inquiry into *why* that character trait developed: what combination of social, cultural, biological, and environmental systems produced it.

Pellegrino offers a "personal integrity" and "individual character" solution to the problem of medical error: try harder, concentrate harder, be virtuous, honor the ideals of your profession. His "solution" focuses attention on the specific individual who is at most the end actor in a complex causal series and ignores the systemic problems that are causing error, burnout, and negligence. But Pellegrino insists that the only legitimate path to better health care must be through focus on *individuals* who bear complete responsibility—and deserve full blame or credit—for both medical success and medical error:

> The blame-free approach advocated by many in the patient-safety movement cannot erase the individual moral onus of preventable error. The physician or other health professional cannot blame the system for his or her failings. Organizational conformity cannot take the place of moral responsibility even if the system follows a no-blame rule. The physician or the nurse, in their respective realms, are the pathways through which harm or good comes to the patient. They are responsible for what they order, or the way they follow an order or procedure. They are responsible for monitoring the steps immediately preceding and following their personal functions in that process.
>
> (2004, 88)

It is true that physicians and nurses often "are the pathways through which harm or good comes to the patient"; but they function in complex systems, and improving those systems requires studying systems carefully and profoundly and openly. Blaming not only prevents the openness that is the pathway such investigation must follow, but it also calls a sharp halt to the inquiry by its insistence that the buck stops here with this individual who justly deserves blame. It is also true that the health professional should not "blame the system"; but not because the health professional justly deserves all the blame (or credit), but because thinking in terms of blame—whether individual or systemic—is counterproductive. The problem may be in over-work, or too many decisions (causing ego depletion), or too much pressure, or "accidents waiting to happen" (such as medications that look almost identical or the names of which are easily confused). When something goes wrong it is better to "pull the cord" and look hard for the problem, rather than narrowly focusing attention and blame on the last person in the causal chain.

Most critiques of the system model admit its advantages for dealing with errors, but—as in the *just culture* movement, which will be considered in the following chapter—insist on keeping blame and shame for cases of neg-ligence and other harmful behaviors that are not simply honest errors by well-meaning caregivers. But like Pellegrino, some doctors reject the system approach *altogether* and champion the individual blame culture.

Thousands of people die each year in the United States from medical mistakes, and many more suffer serious injury. The mistakes are the result of a system that almost seems designed to prevent the real problems from being discovered and solved. It starts with the basic moral responsibility belief that is a central element of the medical culture. Lucian Leape is deeply concerned with the problem of medical errors, and he notes that this deep individual moral responsibility orientation is at the heart of the problem:

> Physicians are socialized in medical school and residency to strive for error-free practice. There is a powerful emphasis on perfection, both in diagnosis and treatment. In everyday hospital practice, the message is equally clear: mistakes are unacceptable. Physicians are expected to function without error, an expectation that physicians translated into the need to be infallible. One result is that physicians, not unlike test pilots, come to view an error as a failure of character—you weren't careful enough, you didn't try hard enough. This kind of thinking lies behind a common reaction by physicians: "How can there be an error without negligence?"
>
> This need to be infallible creates a strong pressure to intellectual dis-honesty, to cover up mistakes rather than to admit them. The organiza-tion of medical practice, particularly in the hospital, perpetuates these norms. Errors are rarely admitted or discussed among physicians in pri-vate practice. Physicians typically feel, not without reason, that admis-sion of error will lead to censure or increased surveillance or, worse, that their colleagues will regard them as incompetent or careless. Far better to conceal a mistake or, if that is impossible, to try to shift the blame to another, even the patient.
>
> (1994, 1851–1852)

Individual air traffic controllers struggled to hide their mistakes, but disasters and near-misses made them impossible to hide. In medicine, the entire medical profession unites to hide mistakes, and even medical errors that result in tragic deaths are often concealed. This is not to blame the physicians who do so; instead, we must look at the system to see why cover-ups happen. An anesthesiologist administers an adult-sized dose to an infant, resulting in severe brain damage and ultimately death. What went wrong? The infant was undergoing surgery, and so there were already significant problems: a weakened heart gave out, an organ shut down. There are many possible "explanations," and if the medical community bands together to protect the errant anesthesiologist—who after all is one of us, and a good friend, and we must close ranks to defend ourselves from those predatory malpractice lawyers—then the error may never be revealed, and its deeper cause never discovered or examined or fixed. It is carefully concealed, its deeper causes are not scrutinized, and the underlying problem remains in place to result in additional tragic mistakes. Under the system approach, when there is a mistake we all made the mistake: a mistake we profoundly regret. The focus is not on the individual doctor who made a mistake and deserves opprobrium, but on the failure of the entire system and how to fix it. Small errors and close calls are not hidden, but instead reveal places where changes are needed in the system.

Like Pellegrino, Dr. Bruce Davis believes in the "just try harder" approach to medical error. Davis belittles the system approach as a "new age concept," favoring instead the traditional "blame and shame" method for dealing with errors and mistakes: "I don't see how this is any sort of improvement over the department based Peer Review and Morbidity and Mortality discussions we have traditionally used." But he admits that the traditional approach has not been effective:

> A valid criticism of our traditional peer review is that it hasn't worked very well to reduce medical error. I will accept that criticism on a system level. We do a poor job at making systemic changes.
>
> (Davis 2015)

That is hardly surprising, of course: a system based on blame and shame encourages covering up mistakes, rather than discovering them and seeking their causes; and when someone is *blamed* for the mistake, any inquiry into deeper systemic causes for the problem is blocked (since deeper inquiry into systemic problems would call into question the individual blame).

Davis embraces the traditional punitive model of blame and shame, and rejects the system approach; and while he acknowledges that "our traditional peer review . . . hasn't worked very well to reduce medical error," he rejects as inconsistent another criticism of that punitive model:

> We have also been taken to task for being too lenient with peers. . . . I'm not sure how we can be 'punitive' and too lenient at the same time.
>
> (Davis 2015)

But in fact it is easy to understand, for the punitive model of peer review not only blocks deeper systemic inquiry but also promotes deflecting blame away from those in the peer group who make mistakes. As Davis acknowledges about the peer review process: "Those who assigned the 'blame' did so with a certain amount of humility and respect. After all, it might be their turn the next meeting." So there is a strong tendency to not assign blame to one's "peers," since they might return the favor at the next meeting. And that tendency is increased by the fact that these peers are typically one's closest colleagues and often long-time friends. That tendency is further strengthened by a desire to circle the wagons and protect one's friends from the ultimate enemy: the personal injury lawyers. With such motives—and a closed peer review committee that bars outsiders—it is notoriously easy to avoid blaming one's friends and colleagues when mistakes happen. There is always the possibility of a complication that could not have been foreseen, a medical problem that "no one could have expected or fixed": so there really was not an error at all, and no one to blame and nothing in the system needs changing. If that doesn't work, blame can be shifted to the patient who did not follow orders concerning what to do before surgery, or whose lifestyle and poor health behavior caused problems no physician could fix, or who failed to provide accurate information concerning his or her medical condition. And if all else fails, the blame can be shifted to someone with considerably less power: a nurse or technician is often a convenient target. In fact, peer review committees are notoriously lenient toward their peers, with much less motivation to find and study the errors of their colleagues than to cover them up. It is the *punitive* blaming and shaming nature of the process that encourages "leniency" and cover-ups in its actual operation.

Dr. David Emmott—like Dr. Davis—insists that the peer-review process *is* the most effective method of preventing errors:

> The peer-review process, by its mere presence, deters mistakes even when its investigative techniques do not disclose clear-cut errors. The vast majority of physicians, by virtue of their personal drive for flawlessness, take personal pride in their work and are extremely sensitive to external scrutiny.
>
> (Emmott 2001, 29)

But the deeply ingrained belief that good doctors must practice flawless medicine causes the problems. It is not the "personal drive for flawlessness" that is the problem—everyone in medicine should share that goal, as should everyone in aviation and education and construction—but rather the assumption that good doctors never make mistakes (when of course no one can avoid making mistakes). In the system approach, errors are revealed and used to fix the flaws in the system, thus preventing more errors; in the blame and shame approach, errors are more likely to be hidden because physicians are indeed "extremely sensitive" to any suggestion that they made an error:

a physician who makes an error is a bad physician. In such a system, it is hardly surprising that doctors struggle to cover up their errors, or blame them on others; and it is not surprising that the physician's friends and colleagues on the peer review committee typically fail to discover "clear-cut errors," particularly clear-cut errors committed by a physician friend.

Rejection of the no-blame system—in favor of reliance on individual virtue—appeals to a deep tradition not only in medicine but in society: a tradition of individualism, in which personal characteristics (rather than situations and systems) are the crucial factors in understanding behavior. The following critique of the system approach comes from that individualist tradition:

> First, in their preoccupation with instrumental value, they tend to diminish the intrinsic value of an explicit emphasis on the moral agency of individuals. The idea that there is an inherent good in asking people to be good goes back to antiquity, but it is one that has special valence for the health-care professions. The term 'profession' has been linked to virtues—such as benevolence, compassion, mercy, and competence—since the earliest usage of the term.
>
> (Aveling, Parker, and Dixon-Woods 2016, 217)

*Why* some persons have stronger qualities of self-control and compassion and competence and other virtues is not addressed; but from this perspective, all such qualities are self-made, and are part of the myth of uniquely human powers: the special "moral agency of individuals." It is true, of course, that "asking people to be good" goes back to antiquity; but from antiquity to the present, it has never been an effective means of preventing errors or improving behavior or building better social systems. In the absence of any empirical knowledge of psychology or of social interaction, such facile admonitions were worthless, but probably did no harm; but when they block the adoption of more effective measures based on rigorous studies, then clinging to such a failed tradition is a serious impediment. Just try harder to be error-free, just be more conscientious. Fortunately, we did not apply that method—just admonish individuals to be more careful and conscientious—to air traffic control.

## Inclusive Systems

The system approach not only rejects blame and shame, but also rejects rigid hierarchy. *Everyone* is part of the effort to discover small errors that might become catastrophes, everyone contributes intelligence and experience and alertness to catch potential errors before they happen, and everyone participates in the effort to improve the system so that errors are reduced; or in brief, *everyone* is empowered to "pull the red cord." Dr. Davis cherishes the opposite approach: physicians—and especially surgeons—are at the top of the hierarchy, and all others have little to offer because they cannot really understand at my exalted level:

> The key here is that it is PEER review—review by other surgeons engaged in the same type of practice. I don't recognize a committee made up of an Internist, a Pathologist, a Cardiologist, and an Orthopedic Surgeon as a committee of my peers. They don't do what I do. They don't face the same decisions and problems that I do and have no frame of reference from which to analyze my actions.
>
> (Davis 2015)

Even physicians in other medical specialties are excluded from this elite group; obviously no nurses need apply. This scornful attitude toward anyone not in my elite group is manifested in a remark concerning Lucian Leape, one of the leaders in the system approach to reducing medical error. Davis describes "Dr. Lucian Leape, a professor of PUBLIC HEALTH (emphasis mine)"; and he concludes that Dr. Leape has nothing to offer, because "He is also not a surgeon. He does not understand the culture of the M & M conference and its power to offer both correction and forgiveness." In his scornful dismissal of Leape as a professor of public health who is "not a surgeon," one can hear the echo of his attitude toward others on the surgical team: "She's a NURSE," and so has nothing to offer in preventing errors and improving processes; her only job is to be quiet, follow my orders without question, and be deferential. In this atmosphere, no one dares pull the cord to prevent mistakes; and the only person in the room allowed to pull the cord is too arrogant to admit there is a problem.

The no-blame system model reduces errors, increases cooperation, and treats all workers with respect. In the process, it has a leveling effect on hierarchy. It is not only physicians and managers who are important, but *everyone* plays an important role in detecting and avoiding errors and improving the system, and *everyone* brings dedication and intelligence and perceptiveness to making the system work better. When errors are reduced—together with the *relative* status of those at the top of the hierarchy—then some at the top may regard the systemic improvements as being won at too high a price. For those who believe in the importance of *everyone* exercising take-charge responsibility and intelligent control, and the importance of everyone having a commitment to improving the organization through their own efforts and intelligence and dedication, this changed perspective of—and by—the workers is a substantial benefit. *Reducing* errors and *increasing* opportunities for more workers to practice take-charge responsibility and strengthen their self-confidence and enhance their dedication to the positive goals of the organization: those are mutually supportive processes.

# 12 No Limits on No-Blame

Perhaps the greatest problem for adoption of the no-blame system in medicine—and the problem of greatest relevance for the larger adoption of the no-blame system in society—is the powerful tendency to draw a line that places strict limits on what wrongs and mistakes can be classified as "no-blame," while leaving a substantial area where blame is regarded as legitimate and even mandatory.

When the no-blame system approach started to prove its worth in reducing errors and improving processes in manufacturing, air safety, nuclear safety, and medicine, there were some who saw the whole program as a threat. David Emmott, for example, complained that "Viewing healthcare not as an honorable profession but as a 'system' downgrades the product to a store shelf commodity" (2001, 30), though it is hardly clear why recognizing the systemic elements and issues in the practice of medicine should require that we no longer view healthcare as an honorable profession. Bruce Davis (2015) warned that the system approach is one of the silly "new age concepts" characterized by "diffused babble." And Edmund Pellegrino compared embrace of the no-blame system approach to a "utopian social engineering" scheme, on the same order as "the malignant social engineering of totalitarian states" (2004, 85).

More subtle opponents of the system approach take a different tack. Instead of condemning the system approach, they attempt to co-opt it. The no-blame system approach has some good ideas when it comes to dealing with simple errors. Instead of blaming and shaming, seek out the basic causes of the errors and fix them. But the no-blame system approach goes too far. We should forgo blame when an error is made by a conscientious healthcare provider who is doing his or her level best to provide the best care possible, but who makes an error because of bad labels or a particularly complex procedure or overwhelming pressures in dealing with special emergency cases; however, we should draw a line marking the difference between such innocent errors by conscientious caregivers—errors which should not be subject to blame—and errors that are the result of negligence or failure of concentration or failure to follow established rules and procedures. The former should be excused; the latter should be blamed, and subject to justly deserved punitive measures.

## Just Culture Versus No-Blame

Rejecting the no-blame system approach, this new system version was christened the "just culture" approach. Robert Wachter, an advocate of just culture (and a critic of the no-blame system model) states the basic premise of the just culture view:

> In the first few years of the patient safety movement, the pendulum swung too far toward systems. It is now swinging back toward individual and collective accountability. The ultimate success of our efforts to prevent harm will depend on ensuring that the pendulum comes to an optimal resting point.
>
> (Wachter 2012, 4)

But this is a pendulum that is firmly attached to a moral responsibility and just deserts pivot. The effort to break away from the moral responsibility system failed to escape the system's powerful gravitational pull. Why do we think it better to move back toward the middle, toward the "golden mean" of dropping blame for honest errors but keeping blame for negligence? Because that leaves us squarely in the old system. From inside the system of moral responsibility, excusing honest errors but blaming for negligence seems intuitively right; but that "intuition" grows out of the system itself, and the system is rotten and obsolete.

It is hard to let go of a system—whether the Ptolemaic or the moral responsibility system—that has dominated thinking for centuries, and it is not surprising that Tychonism (which maintained the basic ideas of the Ptolemaic System) became more popular than Copernicanism. Likewise, it is not surprising that a "revised" version of the new system—the *just* system approach—has become more popular than the no-blame system approach. The just system model keeps moral responsibility locked in place, just as Tychonism kept the Earth stationary. But the full advantages of the Copernican System could not be developed until the Ptolemaic System (and its Tychonic corruption) had been rejected, and the no-blame system approach cannot achieve full success until the moral responsibility system (including the Tychonic "just system" version) has been abandoned. The threat and reality of punishment may be necessary in some cases; the belief in *just* punishment is not, and is an impediment to understanding and improving society, character and behavior. We must reject just deserts and moral responsibility if we want to look harder and deeper at the real causes of our problems.

So long as we "excuse" errors and *blame* intentional and negligent acts, we stay within the moral responsibility system. At that point, the "just culture" system is just a Tychonic modification, and not a real break with the moral responsibility system. It easily accommodates—and co-opts—any effort at real reform. After all, by moral responsibility standards we should never blame for "honest errors": errors are largely luck, and luck is not supposed to enter into moral responsibility. Of course we know that everything in our lives includes an enormous element of luck, as Thomas Nagel (1979) and Neil Levy (2011) make painfully clear; but we easily ignore that fact under the Lethean grip of moral responsibility. Just culture (in which we forgo blame for honest errors by conscientious workers) is better than a total blame culture, of course; but it has the advantage of myopia over blindness, and is far from the optimum model.

*Just culture* does a fine job of dealing with "errors by well-meaning people," and certainly that is the most common problem in medicine. But it stops well short of fixing some major problems in medicine, because it is hamstrung by its devotion to moral responsibility—and by fear that it will appear "soft" on those our just deserts society insists on blaming and shaming and punishing. There are two basic problems. First, it is not so easy to draw a line between harm caused by the unintended error of a person of good character and harm caused by the intentional or grossly negligent behavior of a person of bad character. As Sidney Dekker notes:

> The problem is guidance that suggests that a just culture only needs to "clearly draw" a line between culpable and blameless behavior. Its problem lies in the false assumption that acceptable or unacceptable behavior form stable categories with immutable features that are independent of context, language or interpretation.
>
> (Dekker 2008)

Second, even if we *could* draw that line, it is a line that impedes our understanding and blocks deeper inquiries.

Consider the difficulty in drawing the line: a line, incidentally, that even those who favor blame and shame and just deserts acknowledge is difficult to establish. One of the most touching and honest accounts of the problems faced by physicians—in particular by physicians who are supposed to be incapable of error—was given by a young physician who practiced family medicine in rural northern Minnesota, Dr. David Hilfiker. In an essay published in 1984 by the *New England Journal of Medicine* Dr. Hilfiker candidly described his own struggle with the harmful medical errors he had personally committed. Prior to publication the journal editor, Dr. Arnold Relman, called Dr. Hilfiker to warn him of the potential damage to his career from publishing such a confession:

> I thought he was exposing himself to serious criticism. I wanted him to think about it carefully before confessing to a couple of serious mistakes that a lot of doctors would say could and should have been avoided.
>
> (Quoted in Frankel 1986)

Even aware of the criticism his account would generate, Dr. Hilfiker believed that he should publish the honest record of his own medical mistakes—mistakes of the sort that he believed other doctors also made, kept hidden away, and then faced a solitary struggle with the deep guilt and grief. As Hilfiker described the situation:

> Doctors hide their mistakes from patients, from other doctors, even from themselves. . . . Unable to admit our mistakes, we physicians are cut off from healing. We cannot ask for forgiveness, and we get none. We are thwarted, stunted; we do not grow.
>
> (Hilfiker 1984)

Hilfiker reported a variety of his own mistakes. One that he noted—when he misdiagnosed a severe ankle and foot injury—was from inadequate knowledge: "For primary care practitioners, who see every kind of problem from cold sores to cancer, the mistakes are often simply a result of not knowing enough." Another type of mistake resulted from carelessness:

> Often, I am sure, mistakes are a result of simple carelessness. There was the young girl I treated for what I thought was a minor ankle injury. After looking at her x-rays, I sent her home with what I diagnosed as a sprain. A radiologist did a routine follow-up review of the x-rays and sent me a report. I failed to read it carefully and did not notice that her ankle had been broken. I first learned about my mistake five years later when I was summoned to a court hearing. The fracture I had missed had not healed properly, and the patient had required extensive treatment and difficult surgery.
>
> (Hilfiker 1984)

Could we say Dr. Hilfiker was negligent for not having sufficient knowledge of medical developments in all the areas he must treat? As he notes, that is an impossible task for a rural general practitioner. But what about the problem that resulted from his admitted carelessness: "A radiologist did a routine follow-up review of the x-rays and sent me a report. I failed to read it carefully and did not notice that her ankle had been broken." Under the just culture/moral responsibility model, that careless error is one for which he justly deserves blame: case closed, source blamed, problem solved. If we look deeper, we might discover that the real problem is the lack of medical resources in rural and relatively poor areas, and the deep inequities in our society that make careless mistakes an inevitable by-product of overwork and stress and ego depletion. Rather than blaming the speck in Dr. Hilfiker's eye, perhaps we ought to consider the beam in the eye of our larger social system.

In the last and most painful and "shameful" category of mistakes, Hilfiker places mistakes that result from "a failure of will," when "a doctor knows the right thing to do but doesn't do it because he is distracted, or pressured, or exhausted" (Hilfiker 1984). Dr. Hilfiker's "failure of will" occurred after a stressful weekend of many hours in the emergency room, when an older woman complained of having chest pains all night. Dr. Hilfiker knew that the patient suffered from angina, but he had examined her the previous week, and dismissed this as another attack of angina:

> Some part of me knew that anyone with all-night chest pains should be seen right away. But I was under pressure. The delivery would make me late to the office, and I was frayed from a weekend spent on call, spent mostly in the emergency room. This new demand would mean additional pressure. "No," I said, "take her over to the office, and I'll see her as soon as I'm done here." About twenty minutes later, as I was finishing the delivery, the clinic nurse rushed into the room. Her face was pale. "Come quick! Mrs. Helgeson just collapsed." I sprinted the hundred yards to the office, where I found Mrs. Helgeson in cardiac arrest. Like many doctors' offices at the time, ours did not have the advanced life-support equipment that helps keep patients alive long enough to get them to a hospital. Despite everything we did, Mrs. Helgeson died.
>
> Would she have survived if I had agreed to see her in the emergency room, where the requisite staff and equipment were available? No one will ever know for sure. But I have to live with the possibility that she might not have died if I had not had "a failure of will." There was no way to rationalize it: I had been irreponsible and a patient had died.
>
> (Hilfiker 1984)

Of course, there were many ways to "rationalize it," and most doctors would have quickly taken advantage of those ways; but Dr. Hilfiker was too honest with himself to make use of such rationalizations. He made a mistake. It might well be classified as negligence: he knew better, he just didn't do what he knew was right because it was inconvenient. This was not a simple error; this was behavior that qualifies for "blame and shame."

Blame and shame blocks deeper inquiry: the buck must *stop* with Dr. Hilfiker's irresponsible behavior, *he* is the sole source of the problem and he is fully to blame. But even a modest inquiry undermines the conclusion that Dr. Hilfiker justly deserves blame. He is an extremely hard-working physician who has been on call all weekend, making difficult decisions for days on end. After making a series of difficult decisions requiring careful deliberation, there is a powerful tendency to lapse into quick non-deliberative decisions using whatever convenient heuristics are readily available: the problem of ego depletion (Baumeister et al. 1998). If there was ever a case of ego depletion, Dr. Hilfiker's decision is a strong candidate. But if we narrow our focus to the individual physician and this specific choice, we will not solve the problem, and probably will not even understand the problem.

Blaming Dr. Hilfiker is easy; solving the larger systemic problem is much more difficult.

Was this gross negligence, resulting from arrogance? If so, the doctor should be blamed and punished—according to the just culture perspective. Errors are blameless, but negligence requires blame and shame. But negligence has causes, just as error does. A lapse in dedication can occur just like a lapse in concentration, and doctors can burn out and give up. We need to know what causes such problems, and blaming the doctor does not get to the source. The problem in this case is not the individual physician, but the system that wears her down and enervates her, sapping her energy as well as her motivation and her judgment. Or if you insist, the problem *is* the individual physician who made a bad decision; but we still need to know the deeper causes that led to that bad decision. That is, we need to know, unless we suppose that the physician is a first cause, and the buck absolutely stops with her. She simply did not have the right character at that time, Pellegrino would say, and that ends the inquiry: we blame her for her character flaw, and the issue is settled. But the basic problem remains, is not understood, and is not corrected.

Robert M. Wachter recognizes the benefits of the "no blame" system approach to error, but insists that the model should not be extended too far. While no blame may be appropriate for medical personnel who make errors while conscientiously striving to deliver the best care possible, it is *not* appropriate when the error is the result of negligence or incompetence or carelessness. As Wachter states:

> Specifically, a "no blame" approach seems apt for some errors but not for others: the latter category includes errors committed by incompetent, intoxicated, or habitually careless clinicians, or by those unwilling to follow reasonable safety rules and standards.
>
> (2012, 1)

As an illustration of the kind of behavior that justly deserves blame, Wachter offers a fictional case in which a patient received a severe blow on the head while playing basketball, suffered severe headaches and became lethargic and vertiginous, and was taken to an emergency room in a rural hospital. The emergency room physician was concerned and requested that the patient be transferred to the care of a neurologist at the regional hospital. The neurologist refused, saying that the case did not seem to justify being moved to his care. The next day the patient's condition continued to deteriorate, and the local emergency room physician hospitalized the patient who was still refused admission to the regional center. The following day the patient was still worse, and the emergency room physician convinced someone at the regional center to accept the transfer. That night at the regional hospital the patient deteriorated further, moaning, and had to be restrained. The emergency room physician called the neurologist at home, but the neurologist declined to come to the hospital, saying he was familiar with the case and would evaluate the patient the next morning. The patient died during the night. The death might have been avoided had the neurologist come to the hospital earlier and started treatment; and Wachter's conclusion is that this is a case in which the neurologist's "refusal to come to the hospital to see a rapidly deteriorating patient seems like a personal failing," and the physician justly deserves to be blamed:

> Cases like this one illustrate that challenging lines must be drawn, lines that distinguish expected human frailties from levels of performance that fall below professional standards. The latter circumstances require an accountability approach.
>
> (Wachter 2012, 2)

Wachter is correct: this is a case in which the neurologist's behavior did not meet an acceptable standard. But is this so different from the case of Dr. Hilfiker's "failure of will" in which he "had been irresponsible and a patient had died"? In the case of Dr. Hilfiker, when we know all the details of his harrowing work, we recognize that the causes and circumstances resulted in a bad decision, but it does not follow that he justly deserves blame for that bad decision: exhaustion and ego depletion are the deeper problems, and blaming Dr. Hilfiker will not change the underlying causes that resulted in this bad decision. Blaming Dr. Hilfiker leaves the problems in place for the grossly overworked and overstressed physicians in such practices, and will result in more bad decisions. We know less about the neurologist who (like Dr. Hilfiker) plans to examine the patient later. But if we are willing to look harder and deeper—and not be blinded by the desire to assign moral responsibility and just deserts and blame and shame to the negligent neurologist—then deeper causes will not be difficult to discover. First, it is not unlikely that the neurologist also is dealing with ego depletion, after a long day of difficult and demanding treatment decisions. Another possibility is that the neurologist, like all of us, tended to place this case within a convenient "heuristic" that operated nonconsciously and prevented the neurologist from recognizing the need to switch into harder System 2 deliberation (Kahneman 2011) and consider the specific details of this particular case. Or maybe this is a neurologist who has been deferred to so often and obsequiously that he has become arrogant and overconfident, and regards his quick intuitive judgments as more reliable and authoritative than they in fact are. In any case, these are problems to be solved: problems that blaming the neurologist fails to address, much less fix.

Wachter quotes with approval a passage from James Reason, a champion of adding just deserts and blame to the "no-blame system" of finding and fixing errors and their systemic sources. Reason writes that in contrast to the "just culture" blame system:

> A "no-blame" culture is neither feasible nor desirable. A small propor-
> tion of human unsafe acts are egregious . . . and warrant sanctions,
> severe ones in some cases. A blanket amnesty on all unsafe acts would
> lack credibility in the eyes of the workforce. More importantly, it would
> be seen to oppose natural justice. What is needed is a just culture, an
> atmosphere of trust in which people are encouraged, even rewarded, for
> providing essential safety-related information—but in which they are
> also clear about where the line must be drawn between acceptable and
> unacceptable behavior.
>
> (Reason 1997, 195)

The complete rejection of just deserts does not offer offenders a "blanket
amnesty." A "blanket amnesty" remains within the moral responsibility
model: these are people who justly deserve blame and punishment, but they
are given amnesty. Rather than offering blanket amnesty, the essential step
is to recognize that no one—no matter how negligent or egregious his or her
behavior—justly deserves blame and punishment. Furthermore, it preserves
the distinction "between acceptable and unacceptable behavior."

When a person makes a mistake that places a patient—or an airliner—at
risk, that is *unacceptable* behavior; but blaming and shaming is not the best
way of preventing such behavior. Not blaming and justly punishing negligent
or drug-impaired or severely incompetent behavior would indeed "seem to
oppose natural justice," but "natural justice" is the product of a pervasive
and powerful system of belief in which moral responsibility and just deserts seem like "natural justice." That "natural" system is no more plausible
and fair than a "natural" system of ethnic prejudice, which probably has a
better claim to being "natural" than does the system of moral responsibility. Whether the problems are the result of "an error anyone could make,"
or substance abuse, or incompetence, or a "level of performance that falls
below professional standards," we still need to look at the causes and try to
fix the system so that they do not recur. Blaming and shaming blocks deeper
inquiry into those causes: when we find the individual who justly deserves
punishment "the buck stops there." As discussed later in this chapter, there
may be unfortunate situations in which we must punish; but in those sad
cases, it remains important to recognize that the punishment is not justly
deserved.

Fogarty and Mckeon (2006) note that badly structured health care organizations cause stress and discomfort in employees, and that in turn can
cause employees to perform substandard work: work that puts patients
at risk. When the whole system is working badly—placing demands on
employees that are seen as unreasonable and arbitrary, and functioning in
a manner that employees feel makes good quality work impossible—that
engenders a sense of helplessness: whether I work well or ill doesn't much
matter, because nothing good can come out of this system in any case, and
careful efforts are futile. In such circumstances we can blame and shame and

fire the negligent worker, but we will not fix the basic problem which results in a pattern of slipshod care. There are many other factors that can result in work that falls well below professional standards, and focusing blame on a "flawed individual" is easy and appealing; but it stops inquiries that could reveal systemic problems and/or situational stresses that are causing repeat instances of such substandard work (and that remain in place when we focus the blame on a single individual). Even in cases when the problem *is* due to the moral or professional flaws of a specific individual, when we *blame* that individual we call a halt to deeper inquiry (this individual justly deserves blame and shame and punishment, so the causes must *stop* with the blameworthy individual), and fail to discover the deeper causes that resulted in such character or competency flaws.

The spread of infection in hospitals is a very serious problem indeed. Eliminating it entirely is probably impossible, but there are simple effective measures that can substantially reduce the spread of infection. One of the most obvious is to have all medical staff who deal directly with patients wash their hands thoroughly before moving from one patient to another. Unfortunately, this simple preventive measure is too easily and too often ignored. The Cleveland Clinic Oncology Unit increased compliance (Weber 2008) from 24 percent to 94 percent through teamwork and pride in accomplishment, and without blame and shame.

Donald Goldmann is rightly concerned with the problem of hand hygiene, and in his frustration at repeated failures to improve hand hygiene among hospital staff, he recommended holding accountable and blaming and punishing for individual failure:

> True, the hospital and its leaders are accountable for establishing a system in which caregivers have the knowledge, competence, time, and tools to practice perfect hygiene. But each caregiver has the duty to perform hand hygiene—perfectly and every time. When this widely accepted, straightforward standard of care is violated, we cannot continue to blame the system.
>
> (Goldmann 2006, 122)

But many hospital units had the "knowledge, competence, time, and tools" to practice hand hygiene, and still had a very low rate of compliance. It was clear from a variety of studies that just having the *knowledge* was not sufficient to motivate the behavior; so how could the system be modified to encourage compliance, and what are the systemic factors that are making compliance difficult to achieve? We might blame and shame and punish, and perhaps by that heavy-handed method we could coerce some degree of compliance; but the deeper problem would remain, and manifest itself in other areas. It is not just that physicians fail to wash their hands; the same attitude may lead to careless work, refusal to consider warnings from other members of the team, a tendency to treat other members of the team in a demeaning manner (that undercuts the quality of their work). Strong punitive measures that are rigorously enforced might increase the amount of hand washing by physicians, but would leave the deeper problems in place.

Failure to follow established safety procedures—especially if done habitually—is an offense that the "just culture" perspective categorizes as justly deserving blame and shame and punishment: it is a moral failure of the individual, not the system, since the rules are clearly in place and the individuals at fault knowingly violate them. But closer scrutiny—the sort of scrutiny blocked by demands for blame and just punishment—yields better understanding. Sometimes the work demands are so heavy that only by implementing "work arounds"—procedures that work *around* the safety rules and policies—can the required work be accomplished. Rule violations often are not cases of negligence, or willful disregard for valuable procedures by workers who just don't care. Rather, many rule violators are conscientious workers who "work around" the rules in order to complete their work successfully. A study of railroad "shunters" (who perform the dangerous work of "shunting" freight cars onto different tracks and putting cars in order as trains are made up) found that violating safety procedures was fairly common, but was almost always the result of time pressure and an excessive workload, causing shunters to violate procedures in order to work more rapidly (Lawton 1998). Management can add another rule to the list and blame the violators, but that will not solve the basic systemic problems that are causing the safety shortcuts.

Often the rule violators are finding ways to cope with systemic problems in order to do their jobs effectively, or to provide better care for those in their charge. A famous—or infamous—case of a "work around" was the Montana case of the "Hospice Six": Six dedicated nurses at a hospice in the town of Helena, Montana, who found a way to provide morphine for dying cancer patients in intense pain. By Montana law, morphine must be dispensed by a pharmacist and requires a prescription from a physician. That rule may be quite legitimate: morphine, after all, is a dangerous and addictive drug. But the nurses in the case were facing a severe systemic problem: in the small town of Helena there were no 24-hour pharmacies, and for long hours every night there was no way to get a prescription for morphine filled. To exacerbate the problem, some physicians failed to phone in needed prescriptions during the hours when the pharmacies were open. Patients were spending hours in extreme agony—patients with bone cancer or stomach cancer who were in severe pain and for whom no relief was available during the long hours of a tortured night. For hospice nurses striving to make the last hours of dying patients as comfortable and pain-free as possible, that violated everything they were working to achieve. No one doubted the deep dedication of the nurses to their patients, and there was never any question of the nurses misusing the morphine in any way. To "work around" the severe problem, the six nurses began to collect leftover morphine donated by the families of patients who had died; this morphine was stored in a supervisor's desk, and was given to suffering patients who had a *prescription* for the morphine but who—because all pharmacies were closed, or because a physician had failed to phone in the prescription—could not obtain the desperately needed morphine from a pharmacist. Ruth Sasser, one of the nurses, described her reason for the "work around" thus:

> A few hours of severe pain can be an eternity. If it came down to the wire, I would do anything I could to help prevent someone from undue suffering. Nurses do what they need to do for the care of their patients.
>
> (Quoted in Shirley 1991)

Did the nurses violate important rules? Yes. And they were blamed and punished: all were placed on probation for three to five years. But that did nothing to fix the deep systemic problem that forced the nurses to work around the rules; to the contrary, once the nurses were blamed and punished, the assumption was that the problem was solved. But as typically happens with blame and "justly deserved" punishment, the real problem was not solved but ignored. A blame system deals swiftly with such a case: they willfully broke important rules—rules designed to prevent the misuse of potentially dangerous and addictive drugs—and so they justly deserve punishment. A no-blame system looks deeper into the causes, and finds deeper problems that the blame system leaves in place.

## Individuals Within Systems

What often looks like a problem caused by a bad *individual person* is more often a problem caused by a bad system, or a system that places good people in bad situations. There is strong temptation to look for a bad *individual* with *character* flaws: that is the deeply ingrained tendency that psychological researchers call the *fundamental attribution error* (Ross 1977; Doris 2002, 93). Not only is there a strong psychological inclination to attribute problems to some attribute or character flaw in a specific individual; also, the search for such an individual is almost always successful. Hollnagel and Woods provide important insight into *why* such searches succeed, and why those "successful searches" typically fail to find the real problem:

> Since no system has ever built itself, since few systems operate by themselves, and since no systems maintain themselves, the search for a human in the path of failure is bound to succeed. If not found directly at the sharp end—as a 'human error' or unsafe act—it can usually be found a few steps back. The assumption that humans have failed therefore always vindicates itself. The search for a human-related cause is reinforced by past successes and by the fact that most accident analysis methods put human failure at the top of the hierarchy, i.e., as among the first causes to be investigated.
>
> (Hollnagel and Woods 2005, 9; cited in Holden 2009)

The fundamental attribution error is deep and pervasive. The problem of theology students passing by a suffering individual, or the problem of American soldiers abusing prisoners at Abu Ghraib, is not basically a problem of character faults, but a problem of situation. Of course, some problems *are* caused by people with very bad character traits: problems caused by racists, for example, or by arrogant selfish people. Such problems happen, and such people exist. But even in those cases, blaming the bad individual blocks deeper inquiry into the basic and continuing problems that shaped the individual to be racist: problems that blaming the individual racist ignores. Of course, *fixing* such deep societal problems is a huge challenge; but blaming an individual hides the real problem from view, and does not even start the repair process. The deep problem remains in place for racist demagogues to exploit.

Suppose we find that one major source of problems in minimizing errors and improving health care is the arrogant and uncooperative behavior of some physicians. Now we have discovered the source—or at least *a* source—of our problems, and blaming those individuals is the answer and the solution. And indeed, it may well be the case that some physicians and their behavior are causing problems and blocking improvements. Those physicians display arrogant contempt toward other caregivers with whom they work, and make it clear that they do *not* want to be questioned—much less corrected—by any of the "lower status" workers. In those circumstances, the accumulated wisdom and observational powers of the other workers are underutilized. There are fewer professionals to perform the vital role of looking for possible errors and stopping bad or erroneous procedures before they cause serious harm or even death: no one is allowed, much less encouraged, to pull the cord and stop the dangerous process. If you are infallible, you do not need nurses telling you about possible mistakes; indeed, such warnings would seem to question your very worth as an infallible physician. Perhaps those physicians ignore important safety rules; or they keep other professionals waiting, thus wasting their valuable time and forcing them to work faster with greater likelihood of errors. These are flawed and even destructive behavioral patterns. But if we conclude that these are the persons to blame and justly punish, and so the problem is solved, then we fail to look deeper into the systemic causes of those personality problems. Such attitudes may be inculcated and encouraged by the culture, as seen (in the previous chapter) in Dr. Davis: "I was trained in a culture that emphasized the surgeon's personal responsibility for everything that happened to his or her patient." And of course that included taking all the credit when things went right, and being the infallible authority in the operating room.

The deeper problem is a system that—for traditional, cultural, and economic reasons (hospitals are dependent on the business brought to them by physicians, who could take their business elsewhere)—treats physicians with special deference that they are trained and acculturated to consider their right. Have they been taught to believe that a "real doctor" must act this way, and be totally in charge, and share responsibility with no one? Does this profession attract arrogant people, or create them? Part of the problem, of course, is sexism in the society: a sexism that was acquiesced in for many years by nursing schools, when female nurses were trained to be "properly deferential" to male physicians. If we look harder and deeper—and move beyond blaming—then it is not difficult to discover the causes of the "problem physicians" who arrogantly reject the valuable help of other professionals and shift the blame rather than dealing honestly with mistakes.

In a recent article in *CHEST*, physicians Bell, Delbanco, Anderson-Shaw, McDonald, and Gallagher gave an excellent overview:

> Medical culture, the set of values, hierarchies, and expectations embedded in the profession, is itself a barrier to collective accountability, especially when it is related to open discussion about mistakes. Historically, individual error has been seen as a moral failure, and doctors have been trained with the unspoken assumption of physician infallibility, the strong internalized message that doctors cannot, and do not, make mistakes. Although attitudes about discussing error are improving, we still need to change the messages (explicit and hidden) with which we train doctors if we expect them to share their mistakes or point out those of others [or welcome warnings about potential errors from other professionals]. Pervasive hierarchic frameworks, a strong culture of individualism, and lack of adequate psychological safety for reporting represent strong disincentives to speaking up . . .
>
> In addition, solving problems on the systems level remains far from the forefront of many providers' minds. The legacy of solo practice and its logical cousin, the "insular" mind, may inhibit doctors from taking an active role in a larger system. Extreme time constraints in the modern clinical environment limit system learning from problems as they arise, because pressed clinicians are more likely to seek quick fixes to the immediate problems of their individual patients. They are also less likely to ask for help, having been trained in a system where doing so is a sign of weakness.
>
> (2011, 522–523)

Certainly, there are problems caused by physicians with "bad attitudes" toward other professional caregivers, and arrogant attitudes that make them think they are above the rules (or that make them wish to *show* they are above the rules). But if we move beyond individual blame and seek to understand the systemic causes, those causes can be discovered; and having discovered the problem, we can work on solving it. The problem will not be easy to solve, but directing our efforts at the systemic sources will be a positive start.

We must screen out—or at the very least provide counseling for—those who view medical school as the path to unquestioned power and authority. Some physicians, of course, should not be in practice; just as some people cannot play center field for the Pirates, and some people cannot be good tugboat captains. But supposing that they justly deserve punishment is to blind ourselves to deeper causes and how they can be fixed.

A worker who engages in sabotage is the poster child for a worker richly deserving of blame and punishment; but even here, that response is myopic. When the General Motors plant at Lordstown, Ohio, geared up to produce cars at "maximum efficiency," it set in motion a production line that produced cars at a rate unmatched anywhere in the world. But the pace of the production line left workers severely stressed, and feeling like helpless cogs in an enormous and cruel system (Weller 1974; Waller 2015a, 161–162). They responded with a high rate of absenteeism and a steady stream of sabotage (such as gear shifts broken off). Blaming and firing the distressed workers might make management feel empowered, but it did nothing to fix the real causes. Blaming the workers who committed sabotage was an easy target and an "easy fix," but it was not actually a fix at all.

Systemic problems that cause errors can be examined and the causes understood and fixed; but systemic problems that cause flawed persons are out of bounds, because flawed persons cause themselves. But unless we are self-creating gods, then what is the source of the problems in ourselves? Sometimes it is the system in which we work; sometimes it is the system in which we grew up (which may have included abuse and lead-poisoning, not to mention racism); and sometimes it may be genetic. But we don't solve the problem if we blame and shame, any more than we solve problems in medicine when we employ that method for dealing with error. The answer to errors in medicine is to safely report small errors *before* they become large problems. The answer to character problems is giving people opportunities to gain early help without being shamed or blamed or penalized. Punitive sanctions seemed the only option for dealing with error, until we realized there was another and better approach. Now punitive sanctions seem the only way of dealing with neglect and refusal to follow the rules and malevolence—but when we look more carefully at the causes, we realize there are better alternatives.

That does not mean punishment is *never* to be employed; rather, looking deeper reveals that punishment is never *justly deserved*. Why does the culture make physicians—or a particular physician—arrogant, to the point of gross carelessness? The causes should be dealt with systemically, with punitive measures only as a very unfortunate mark of failure to fix the deeper problem. When you set up a system in which some people are treated with special favor, and any mistakes are blamed on others, and the favored people are treated (and regard themselves, or at least their ideal of themselves) as incapable of error or bad judgment, the result is bad behavior. Reckless arrogance may seem a mark of status. When something goes wrong, the patient didn't follow orders, or the nurses made mistakes. Indeed, there is a long history of blocking deep examination of mistakes when the mistakes were made by physicians. When mistakes are hidden, one can hardly expect to eliminate mistakes or their deeper sources. When punitive sanctions are meted out we may get reluctant compliance, but we will not solve the problems that are causing the basic difficulties: ongoing problems that result in other forms of destructive behavior. Punishment is sometimes unavoidable. But when we reach that unfortunate point and we suppose that it is a justified *solution*, then we stop looking for the deeper causes of the problem, we stop learning, and we stop improving.

The basic problem is not punishment; sometimes that cannot be avoided. Rather, the problem is in supposing that punishment is a just solution, that it is justly deserved, and that punishment solves the problem. When we stop blaming for errors, the errors are greatly reduced. When we stop blaming for other problems, we can take effective steps to discover and fix the real problems. Sometimes, because of deeper systemic failures, we may be required to punish; we are not required to add blame, for it is the blame that blinds us.

The *New York Times* (Wolfe 2003) published a piece on bad doctors getting away with lousy and negligent treatment; and that is indeed a serious problem. Of course we don't want bad doctors constantly "getting away with it"; but that is not part of the no-blame system approach. The unfortunate fact is that there are already bad doctors in the system who consistently "get away with it," and nothing is done. So we should not pretend that the blame system avoids a problem to which the no-blame system approach *might* be vulnerable. In such cases, punishment may be better than nothing; but it is not optimum, and insistence on just deserts blocks the search for something better and for the deeper knowledge that would make something better possible. In the moral responsibility system, punishment is the primary option we consider—so anyone who questions the desirability of such punishment appears to be favoring the continued tolerance of medical negligence. With limited understanding, and limited methods of gaining deeper insight, punishment may be the best we can do; but it is an admission of failure, not a reason to celebrate righteous retribution. We should still be seeking the better methods and deeper understanding that commitment to moral responsibility blocks.

## Very Bad Persons

Those who totally reject moral responsibility and just deserts are often challenged with a dramatic and difficult question that takes many forms, but fits this basic mold: What would you do with Robert Chambliss, the vicious unrepentant racist who murdered four young girls in the 1963 Birmingham bombing of 16th Street Baptist Church? My answer is simple: I would punish him, and severely. In our moral responsibility society, that is the only option open if we are to recognize and acknowledge that he did something horribly wrong. When punishment is the only option allowed for dealing with egregious behavior, then punishment is better than nothing.

Having grown up amidst the brutal racism and courageous civil rights activism of the deep South, the case of Robert Chambliss is one I vividly recall, and have cited before (Waller 2015a). In 1977, Chambliss was finally convicted—14 years later—of the bombing of the 16th Street Baptist Church (a predominantly African-American church that had been the site of civil rights gatherings), in which four young girls were killed and many people were injured. When Chambliss was convicted and sentenced to prison, I rejoiced: rejoiced within the context of the moral responsibility system of criminal justice that had for so long denied rights to African-Americans, and had refused to convict vicious white murderers when their victims were black. The conviction of Chambliss was a milestone, showing that crimes by whites against blacks would be prosecuted, even in Alabama; that African-Americans had rights, that African-Americans counted as real persons; that the long nightmare in which the rights of African-Americans were denied was ending—or at the very least, a vital first step toward recognizing those rights had been taken. Within the moral responsibility system, the conviction and punishment of Robert Chambliss was an important step and a wonderful victory. But it was the best solution available within a bad system, and far short of the optimum solution.

The conviction focused attention on the vicious crimes of Chambliss, and the vile nature of his brutal racist character; but there it stopped. The buck stopped with Chambliss, the inquiry stopped with Chambliss, as it had to stop if Chambliss was to be considered morally responsible for his terrible crimes. But the racist system remained in place: the system that shaped Chambliss and his visceral racism, the system of pervasive racism that permeated that culture and continued to support not only widespread discrimination but also more generations of racism, the system that remained available for exploitation by politicians in Alabama and across the country in national elections. That system remained in place, and the deeper causes of Chambliss's racist character and the systemic racism that shaped and sustained it were not subjected to scrutiny. Few people wanted to go deeper and examine the systemic racism, held in place by churches and political leaders and businesses and other forces: the deeper problems of which Chambliss was only a glaring symptom. Almost four decades after the conviction of Chambliss—and the narrow buck-stopping attribution of moral responsibility to Chambliss—racism remains a major problem in Alabama and across the country. Within the limits of the moral responsibility system, sometimes punishment is the best we can do; but we can do much better than the moral responsibility system and its principled blindness.

Obviously, we need to recognize severe character problems based in genuine character flaws. We can recognize and correct those faults more effectively—faults in ourselves as well as in others—when we don't blame.

In the absence of blame and shame we can acknowledge and deeply regret character problems in ourselves, seek effective ways to fix them, and sincerely apologize for them (Waller 2011, 190–199): it was our mistake, we are profoundly and genuinely sorry, and we are working to fix the basic problem. Sincere apology is often the greatest need of those who have been harmed. And when we recognize our own faults, and their causes, we will be less eager to condemn the faults of others.

The great virtue of the no-blame system approach is that we *learn* from our mistakes (and our near mistakes), and make the system better; so why should this *stop* at addiction, crime, sabotage? If you have negligent or addicted doctors, you have a systemic problem; if you are hiring negligent people, or creating negligent people, you have a systemic problem; if your workers are committing acts of sabotage—as at Lordstown automotive plant—you have a systemic problem. In all cases, blaming an individual doesn't solve it, but leaves the causes in place to produce more problems. Rather than a "just culture" that preserves moral responsibility, we need a "universal no-blame system." What works for errors also works for other faults and other problems. Just as finding the individual who committed the error does not solve the problem, so also finding the individual who commits a crime does not solve the problem. We do have to find who actually committed the crime; but that should be the crucial first step in the investigation, not the close of inquiry.

We will continue to have—and probably could not eliminate—the mild, useful, and all but inevitable social sanctions against those who offend. And for the foreseeable future, we will also require more severe punitive measures, perhaps including some form of imprisonment (a subject for the following chapter). But if we leave in place the belief that people *justly deserve* punishment, we are leaving in place a dangerous and destructive force that is always available for the unscrupulous (and their benighted followers) to wield in their "populist punitiveness" programs; and we are leaving in place a force that results—if not in blindness—then certainly in myopia.

This chapter has dealt with some of the problems of the blame and shame system, and why we should extend the no-blame system *without limits*—and the harm done when we revert to blame. By not blaming, we open up unlimited opportunities for deeper inquiry and understanding, and for discovering ways to improve both systems and individual behavior. But what are some of the positive features of a no-blame system? That is, what processes would a no-blame system encourage—other than deeper inquiry and better understanding, which is certainly a positive start—to produce better systems and better behavior? That will be the main topic of the next chapter, which will attempt to apply these lessons to the larger society and to questions of criminal justice.

# 13  A Universal No-Blame System

In his generous but critical review of *Against Moral Responsibility*, Daniel Dennett posed many tough challenges, but this was perhaps the toughest: "It is open to Waller . . . to propose a better game—and that actually is what he is trying to do—but here the most glaring deficiency in his project reveals itself: he doesn't give the specifics" (Dennett 2012, 8). Ouch. Dennett put his finger on the sorest spot, and pressed down hard. I didn't have such a plan, and I haven't managed to contrive one. Fortunately, others have. The really bad games—where the penalties are capital punishment and solitary confinement and poverty—are being played in stadiums that place great emphasis on just deserts. There are already better games being played, and they are games in which belief in just deserts is minimized. A still better game is being developed and practiced, and it shows what is possible if we move beyond blame and shame.

I did not invent the no-blame system model: that was the work of many people who developed and improved that model in manufacturing, air traffic control, and medicine; and who (at all levels of work) proved its benefits in the grubby workaday world. Nor did I come up with the idea of adopting the no-blame perspective in the larger social context: the social democratic corporatist countries have been moving in that direction for many years, and demonstrating the broad benefits of that social system. There is nothing original here. This is a brilliant proposal, but it is not my brilliant proposal. It is a promising way of looking at our problems, but it is not promising because it is philosophically promising; rather, it is promising because it has demonstrated its worth in many important contexts: through the efforts of line workers, nurses, managers, physicians, prison wardens, and systems engineers.

While improving the quality of cars and preventing airline disasters and reducing the number of mistakes among medical professionals are all worthwhile goals and heroic undertakings, the basic question of this book is broader, deeper, and even tougher: what do we do about the problem of *punishment* in our society? How do we handle the problem of crime? If we totally reject moral responsibility and blame and just deserts, how can we deal with criminal behavior? The moral responsibility system has an easy answer: give those who commit crimes their justly deserved punishment. Find the perpetrator, impose the punishment, and the problem is fixed. But in countries like Norway and Sweden, they have been doing the hard work of developing real solutions.

Blame, shame, and inflict justly deserved punishment: that is the easy answer, and in some ways a satisfying one. We have a visceral desire to see wrongdoers get their just deserts, and to see those who cause harm "get what's coming to them." The universal no-blame system model is not a feel-good system, and it offers no panacea. To the contrary, it threatens some cherished and satisfying beliefs: belief in a just world, as well as belief in just deserts. It demands difficult research, while moral responsibility encourages and justifies a comfortable halt of deeper inquiry. A. E. Housman wrote that "Ale, man, ale's the stuff to drink, for fellows whom it hurts to think"; a deep draft of moral responsibility serves the same purpose.

The goal is the total elimination of blame and shame and moral responsibility and just deserts and righteous retribution, with no Tychonic compromises. Moral responsibility should be eliminated entirely from our justice system, our medical system, our culture, and our lives. No one—whether a virtuous nurse or a negligent doctor, whether a racist terrorist like Robert Chambliss or a courageous reformer like Martin Luther King, whether a brutal murderer or a minimally decent person or a paragon of virtue—should ever be counted as morally responsible. We should abandon all efforts to make moral responsibility more positive or attractive, or reshape it into a form more compatible with our advancing knowledge of psychology and sociology and neuroscience. We should reject moral responsibility as thoroughly as modern chemistry abandoned phlogiston theory and modern medicine repudiated demon possession.

## Take-Charge Responsibility

There are many interesting and important arguments concerning what would be *lost* if we reject moral responsibility; some of those concerns (for example, those of Pellegrino and Roskies) have been addressed in earlier chapters; others—by a variety of insightful philosophers such as Robert Kane, John Lemos, Saul Smilansky, Daniel Dennett, Al Mele, Michael Moore, and John Martin Fischer—I have endeavored to answer elsewhere (Waller 2011 and 2015a). The focus in this book has been on the benefits of eliminating moral responsibility and replacing it with a universal no-blame system model, and dire warnings concerning the dangers and disadvantages of abandoning moral responsibility have received less attention. But there is one concern that is both important and particularly relevant: the concern that without moral responsibility, people would not and could not *take responsibility* for living well and contributing to their society and improving the systems in which they live and work.

Certainly, it would be terrible if all those dedicated people who have a strong sense of responsibility for providing the best health care possible for their patients should *lose* that sense. Nurses often feel profound responsibility for the care of their patients. Mary Mouat was one of the "Hospice Six" (discussed in the previous chapter). She was placed on probation and required to get special education and "rehabilitation" before being reinstated as a nurse. John Guy, the hospital administrator for St. Peter's Community Hospital (where the hospice was located) was outraged by the ruling: "I hope Mary Mouat isn't ever rehabilitated. What is she supposed to do, have a lobotomy and get rid of her caring and compassion?" (Quoted in Siegel 1991). Mary Mouat felt a deep sense of responsibility to care for her dying patients and find ways to relieve their severe suffering: loss of that sense of responsibility would be a profound loss indeed.

But the responsibility in question is not moral responsibility; instead (as discussed briefly in Chapter 5) it is what H.L.A. Hart (1968) called *role* responsibility, and I have expanded and called *take-charge* responsibility (Waller 1990, 64–71, 1998, 42–49, 2011,103–114 and 2015a, 182–186). Virginia Sharpe (2004) and Sidney Dekker (2009) also recognize the importance of distinguishing role responsibility from moral responsibility, though they employ a different terminology. Hart describes clearly the *role* responsibility that we can *take* for various roles and tasks:

> A sea captain is responsible for the safety of his ship, and this is his responsibility. . . . A sentry [is responsible] for alerting the guard at the enemy's approach; a clerk for keeping the accounts of his firm. These examples of a person's responsibilities suggest the generalization that, whenever a person occupies a distinctive place or office in a social organization, to which specific duties are attached to provide for the welfare of others or to advance in some specific way the aims or purposes of the organization, he is properly said to be responsible for the performance of these duties. . . . If two friends, out on a mountaineering expedition, agree that the one shall look after the food and the other the maps, then the one is correctly said to be responsible for the food, and the other for the maps, and I would classify this as a case of role-responsibility.
>
> (1968, 212)

The contrast between role (take-charge) responsibility and moral (just deserts) responsibility is easily marked. Consider Hart's sentry, who is responsible for sounding the alert at the approach of the enemy. The soldier could have that role responsibility—he was assigned the duty, or perhaps he volunteered to be sentry—while his *moral* responsibility for carrying out the role is quite doubtful. Suppose he fails miserably at his role responsibility: recent fighting has damaged his eyesight, and he fails to see the approaching enemy; or after two days and nights on the march he is physically exhausted and falls asleep (his efforts to stay awake are in vain). The sentry clearly had role responsibility, but even fervent moral responsibility advocates might well reject his moral responsibility while acknowledging that he did have role responsibility. Or on the other hand, suppose he does a superior job as sentry, and spots the enemy approaching at a great distance, and claims to deserve special credit for his superior sentry work. Someone might say: "No, you are just very lucky to be blessed with remarkable eyesight and a strong constitution, so you don't justly deserve special reward for your excellent vigilance." In that case, the sentry's *role* responsibility is certain, but his *moral* (just deserts) responsibility is challenged; and whether or not one regards that challenge as legitimate, the fact that such a challenge is clearly intelligible marks the difference between role and moral responsibility. Or perhaps the sentry was dozing, but the regiment's dog alertly barked at the approach of the enemy and awakened the sentry who then warned the camp. If the sentry insists that he nonetheless justly deserves credit for the warning—"after all, it was *my* responsibility to alert the camp if there was danger"—that will carry no weight: his role responsibility does not equate to just deserts responsibility.

We can indeed *take* responsibility if the responsibility in question is role (take-charge) responsibility; but moral responsibility does not work like that. I can voluntarily *take* the role responsibility of sentry; but I cannot *take* the moral responsibility of just deserts. If my friend does a lousy job as sentry, and the commander concludes that he justly deserves punishment for failing at his post, I might attempt to *claim* or *take* moral responsibility for my friend's misdeeds, but no one will treat such a claim seriously. The moral responsibility of just deserts is not something you can acquire merely by taking it. In contrast, role responsibility is precisely the sort of thing one can take, and taking such responsibility is a substantial part of a satisfying life. Being denied role or take-charge responsibility is not only demeaning but often debilitating. Suppose the department needs a course in modal logic, and you agree to fill that role: you agree to take responsibility for teaching modal logic. If someone then attempts to take the course away, or prescribe in detail precisely how you should teach the course, you will deeply resent it: "*I* have the responsibility for modal logic; and if I want your advice on the course, I'll ask for it." If someone tries to take control of your class, the implication is that you are incompetent to handle your role responsibility, that you cannot effectively exercise such control.

Daniel Dennett is deeply insightful concerning the psychological importance of taking responsibility:

> We want to be in control of ourselves, and not under the control of others. We want to be agents, capable of initiating, and taking responsibility for, projects and deeds.

(1984,169)

But while your role (take-charge) responsibility for the class is well-established, your *moral* or *just deserts* responsibility is another matter altogether. Role responsibility for teaching a class is certainly important; but as the quotation from Dennett suggests, there is a larger role: the role of being "in control of ourselves," the role of managing our own lives and making our own choices and decisions. Even more important than the take-charge responsibility I have for teaching my classes is the take-charge responsibility I claim for living my own life.

There are no doubt others who could run my life better than I can. But for those of us with a healthy sense of self-efficacy and self-confidence, it is vitally important that we have effective control of our own lives and decisions and choices. You may seek advice on some decisions from a trusted friend, but you still want take-charge responsibility for your own life: You decide what friend to ask for advice, whether to take that advice, and on what subjects. If you seek your friend's advice on a nice vacation spot, and she gives you unsolicited advice about your career or your love life or your religious views, or *demands* that you *follow* her advice, you legitimately will be angry: this is *your* life, not hers, and you will make your own decisions. This take-charge responsibility for your own life is psychologically valuable: being denied the right to make your own choices and decisions is a path to learned helplessness and profound depression. When people do not want to make such decisions, we fear that they have suffered severe mistreatment or have become profoundly depressed, or both. But my valuable take-charge responsibility for my own life and my own decisions does *not* imply that I also have *moral* (just deserts) responsibility for my own life and choices. Alice may handle her take-charge responsibility for teaching her courses better than Allen does, but having the take-charge responsibility is valuable for both (and there is no doubt that both *have* the take-charge responsibility for their courses). While someone might claim that both also have moral (just deserts) responsibility for teaching their courses well or ill, that will be an *additional* claim: a claim that can be disputed even if we agree that both have full take-charge responsibility.

We do want responsibility, and being deprived of responsibility is bad for our psychological health and our character development and our sense of worth. But the responsibility we want is the genuinely valuable *take-charge* responsibility, not the *moral* responsibility with which it is too often confused. Loss of take-charge responsibility would be a substantial loss indeed; but rejecting *moral* responsibility does not imply the loss of *take-charge* responsibility. To the contrary, take-charge responsibility thrives in the absence of moral responsibility: a world without moral responsibility is the optimum environment for take-charge responsibility. Fear of blame makes one reluctant to seize opportunities for take-charge responsibility. If you want to exercise take-charge responsibility for carefully monitoring the safety of a medical procedure, but you fear that if you speak up and warn of a possible danger you will be regarded as arrogant (who are you to question my expertise as a physician?) and if you are wrong you will be ridiculed and perhaps disciplined, then you are less likely to *take* responsibility for scrutinizing potential problems. Blame and shame are threats to the effective exercise of take-charge responsibility. Not only are moral responsibility and take-charge responsibility profoundly different, but moral responsibility is inimical to take-charge responsibility.

Virginia Sharpe (2004, 14) distinguishes (what she calls) a forward-looking *prospective* sense of responsibility from a backward-looking *retrospective* sense (with the retrospective sense concerned with "the assignment of blame"). Her prospective responsibility is clearly a variation on Hart's role-responsibility (she speaks of *roles* when describing it); but whatever terms are used, this is an important distinction, and Sharpe makes important points about the vital benefits of prospective/role/take-charge responsibility in the context of medical care:

> The forward-looking or prospective sense of responsibility is linked to theories and practices of goal-setting and moral deliberation. It is expressed in phrases such as "As parents, we are responsible for the welfare of our children," or "Democratic citizenship involves both rights and responsibilities." Responsibility in this sense is about the particular *roles* that a person may occupy, the obligations they entail, and how those obligations are best fulfilled . . .
>
> A systems approach to error emphasizes responsibility in the prospective sense. It is taken for granted that errors will occur in complex, high-risk environments, and participants in that system are responsible for active, committed attention to that fact. Responsibility takes the form of preventive steps to design for safety, to improve on poor system design, to provide information about potential problems, to investigate causes, and to create an environment where it is safe to discuss and analyze error.
>
> (2004, 13–14)

Sharpe sees great value in prospective responsibility, but negative value in the retrospective responsibility of blame: "the dominant strategy of blaming individuals will (continue to) be ineffectual and counterproductive in promoting safety" (2004, 7).

## Motivating Take-Charge Responsibility

The crucial question is how we empower people to carry out—to the best of their abilities—their important roles as parents, citizens, nurses, bakers, and teachers. Or more precisely, the crucial question is how do we accomplish that in the *absence* of blame and shame and just deserts and righteous retribution. That may seem a difficult or even impossible question to answer; actually, the answer is easy. Or rather, it is easy once we free ourselves from the punitive perspective of the myopic moral responsibility system—and that is not at all an easy task. From deep within the assumptions of the moral responsibility system, carrying out one's role responsibilities appears to be an odious obligation that must be enforced by means of blame and shame and punishment (with a leavening of praise and reward). But freed from the dark perspective of moral responsibility and just deserts, role responsibilities are not burdens but opportunities—not externally imposed obligations, but eagerly embraced ways of achieving personal goals and contributing to something worthwhile. Workers on an assembly line who are treated as merely interchangeable parts of the machine must be compelled to work by threat of punishment. Contrast that with workers whose intelligence and commitment and expertise are respected and valued, whose vital *role* in producing a worthwhile outcome is respected, and who have substantial autonomy and control in producing the work they value. Such workers eagerly engage in carrying out their role responsibilities to the best of their abilities, including preventing errors and improving quality.

From within the moral responsibility system, this seems like fantasy; without the blinders of moral responsibility, it is plain fact. The contrast between the two perspectives is described clearly in a paper by three professors of health management at the University of Missouri School of Medicine:

> The control-based model assumes that people are incapable of self-regulating their behaviors, and they need constant guidance, reward, and discipline from management. Consistent with this assumption, the natural emphasis of the control-based management is on monitoring employee behavior closely via a variety of control mechanisms. . . . In a control-based organization, hierarchy is tall and communication is quite anemic, mostly top-down. The focus of employee behaviors is on compliance, with procedures, instructions, and orders from the top.
>
> The commitment-based management, on the other hand, has two underlying assumptions: (a) People are capable of self-discipline, and given the opportunity and developmental experiences, they would like to seek responsibility and exercise initiative, and (b) people work best when they are fully committed to the organization, and they commit to the organization when they are trusted and allowed to work autonomously. The commitment-based approach relies on creating an environment that encourages the exercise of initiative, ingenuity, and self-direction on the part of employees in achieving organizational goals.
>
> (Khatri, Brown, and Hicks 2009, 316)

Of course some people are *not* capable of self-discipline, and not capable of carrying out their roles successfully; indeed, some may be so damaged or lacking in self-confidence (or fearful of blame and shame, from their history in that culture) that they reject opportunities for taking role responsibility. But these are exceptions that need help, not standard cases. Most foraging animals—humans included—strongly prefer lives of active control (Waller 2015b). The captured tiger pacing relentlessly in its narrow cage is no more representative of healthy behavior than is the miserable rigidly controlled factory worker who hates work and drinks heavily.

When we treat people disrespectfully as objects to be monitored and controlled, depriving them of opportunity to exercise autonomously their role responsibilities, the result is a punitive model that sinks into a destructive cycle. Khatri, Brown, and Hicks note that:

> The ubiquity of control-based management in health care organizations seems to be a major source of the culture of blame existing in them. . . . The control-based management does not allow much learning to take place in the health care delivery process and sets in motion a "vicious cycle" in which greater incidence of medical errors leads to greater control and regulation of employee behaviors, further strengthening the blame culture and finger pointing.
>
> (2009, 316)

Control-based management is top-down management, operating with the assumption that good work requires constant monitoring and strict rules and harsh discipline, with a minimum of worker flexibility. When things go wrong, look for the individual who made the mistake and discipline or fire that person. It is not part of the job of workers at or near the bottom of the hierarchy to make evaluations or seek improvements or prevent mistakes: that is the privilege of management, and management needs no help from underlings, whose only task is to carry out management directives with as little variation as possible. The function of those at the bottom of the hierarchy is to be controlled, not exercise control; to follow orders, not evaluate them; to acquiesce in management decisions, not participate in them. In contrast to control-based management, commitment-based management encourages worker autonomy. Every worker plays an important, intelligent, and satisfying role in the success of the enterprise.

## Contrasting Management Models

In Chapter 11 there was extensive discussion of another model for comparing management systems: the contrast between the "person-centered approach" and the "total system" approach. The person-centered approach is an individualistic approach to management, in which the focus is on the behavior of *individual persons*: when an error occurs, the solution is finding the person who committed the error and imposing discipline (blame and shame, termination, or even criminal negligence charges) on the flawed person who caused the problem (which of course encourages workers to hide problems and errors, or endeavor to shift the blame elsewhere). At that point the problem is solved, and any deeper systemic inquiries are precluded. In contrast, the total-system model treats errors as opportunities for discovering flaws and gaining knowledge and improving the system. The worker who reports a problem is a valuable contributor to the improvement of the system, not a weak link deserving opprobrium. James Reason describes the "person approach" that dominates traditional work settings:

> The longstanding and widespread tradition of the person approach focuses on the unsafe acts—errors and procedural violations—of people at the sharp end: nurses, physicians, surgeons, anaesthetists, pharmacists, and the like. It views these unsafe acts as arising primarily from aberrant mental processes such as forgetfulness, inattention, poor motivation, carelessness, negligence, and recklessness. Naturally enough, the associated countermeasures are directed mainly at reducing unwanted variability in human behaviour. These methods include poster campaigns that appeal to people's sense of fear, writing another procedure (or adding to existing ones), disciplinary measures, threat of litigation, retraining, naming, blaming, and shaming. Followers of this approach tend to treat errors as moral issues, assuming that bad things happen to bad people—what psychologists have called the just world hypothesis . . .
>
>   Blaming individuals is emotionally more satisfying than targeting institutions. People are viewed as free agents capable of choosing between safe and unsafe modes of behaviour. If something goes wrong, it seems obvious that an individual (or group of individuals) must have been responsible. Seeking as far as possible to uncouple a person's unsafe acts from any institutional responsibility is clearly in the interests of managers.
>
> (Reason 2000, 768)

Workplace models can be compared along two distinct dimensions: the system vs. person-centered models, and the control vs. commitment models. But a more adequate comparison combines those dimensions into two radically different approaches to workplace functioning. Person-centered and control models merge to form one approach, while the system and commitment models operate together to form a very different workplace orientation. The control/person-centered model is a hierarchical model in which the control is exerted from the top (in the service of goals mandated exclusively by those at the top), and those lower in the hierarchy are "well-functioning" when they carry out the orders of their superiors without question or error or deviation. When something goes wrong, it is because some flawed individual lower in the order failed to follow those orders correctly (through error or negligence or willful disobedience). In contrast, the total-system/commitment model has minimal hierarchy, treating all persons in the organization as vital elements of the system making thoughtful and perceptive contributions to the better functioning of the organization and the achievement of shared goals. When problems arise, everyone in the system seeks more information to solve the problem, and problems and errors reveal flaws in the overall *system*. In the system/commitment approach, everyone's *role* includes *taking* responsibility for making the system function as effectively as possible; but workers are not blamed and shamed for mistakes, which are a product of flaws in the larger system structure. In the individual/control approach, workers are not considered worthy or capable of *taking* important responsibility for the well-functioning of the organization, but must be vigorously controlled by those higher in rank; however, workers are blamed and shamed when something goes wrong. The ideal of the commitment/system approach is for all workers to share a common commitment to improving the system; the goal of the control/person-centered model is to effectively control each individual worker from the top down. In the person-centered/control workplace, close surveillance and the threat of blame and shame and justly deserved punishment motivate workers to follow orders from their superiors; in the total system/commitment setting, workers are motivated by the opportunity to achieve autonomous contributions to a shared commitment.

## Contrasting Social Systems

Some workplace systems follow the person/control approach, while others favor the system/commitment model of workplace management. On a larger scale, there are also contrasting social systems. Neo-liberal culture follows the person/control model while social democratic corporatist culture manifests the values of the no-blame system/commitment model. This comparison and contrast of social systems (Beckett and Western 2001; Cavadino and Dignan 2006a and 2006b; Esping-Andersen 1990 and 1999) has been an important topic of study for sociologists, and more recently has been the focus of criminologists.

While sociologists and criminologists describe several different systems of social structure—including the neo-liberal, conservative corporatist, social democratic corporatist, and Oriental corporatist—the clearest contrast has been between the neo-liberal and the social democratic corporatist cultures. The neo-liberal culture is characterized by extreme individualism: failure and success both are products of individual choice and initiative, and both blame and credit belong almost exclusively to the individual. "Rugged individualism" is regarded as an achievable ideal, rather than a false and shallow perspective on human behavior. As Cavadinio and Dignan note, in the neo-liberal society: "Economic failure is seen as being the fault of the atomized, free-willed individual, not any responsibility of society. . . . Crime is likewise seen as entirely the responsibility of the offending individual" (Cavadino and Dignan 2006a, 448). In contrast, the social democratic corporatist culture matches the system/commitment model, with greater emphasis on social inclusiveness, focus on systemic problems and solutions, and shared social commitments.

The same contrast applies to economic success and social well-being. The system/commitment approach to mistakes in the workplace emphasizes examination of the larger systemic and situational factors to find the source of problems, while the person/control model focuses narrowly on the individual who was the immediate source of the mistake. In like manner, social democratic corporatist cultures emphasize social connections and the importance of examining the social system and the deeper systemic causes of behavior, while neo-liberal society narrows inquiry to the specific individual who commits a crime or is an economic failure and the flawed attributes of that distinct individual. As Cavadino and Dignan draw the cultural contrast:

> Corporatist societies like Germany—and to an even greater extent, social democratic ones like Sweden . . . tend to pursue more inclusionary economic and social policies. . . . The communitarian ethos which gives rise to these policies—and which in turn is shaped by them—also finds expression in a less individualistic attitude toward the offender, who is regarded not as an isolated culpable individual who must be rejected and excluded from law-abiding society, but as a social being who should still be included in society but who needs rehabilitation and *resocialization*, which is the responsibility of the community as a whole. The corporate citizen, unlike the neo-liberal, is much more his brother's keeper—even if he has done wrong—with a strong sense that "there but for the grace of God go I"—in terms of both economic failure and criminal activity.
>
> (2006a, 448)

Just as the person/control model of workplace management fosters narrow focus on the individual and blocks deeper inquiry into *why* that individual erred, so the neo-liberal culture treats the offender as "an isolated culpable individual who must be rejected and excluded from law-abiding society" and scorns consideration of the systemic flaws that shaped the individual's flawed character and the systemic problems that placed the individual in situations and circumstances that resulted in criminal behavior.

The link between the individual person model and the neo-liberal culture is particularly clear in the neo-liberal culture of the United States, where neo-liberalism is exhibited in its purest form:

There is much about the USA in the last three decades which may have made it fertile soil for law and order ideology. To begin with, the ideology's conjunction of beliefs in free market capitalism and in the free will of the individual expresses a very American rugged individualism, which may help to explain the particularly strong burgeoning of punitive politics and its popular appeal in the USA. The neo-liberalism of American society is predicated upon individual responsibility in a way highly consonant with the law and order attitude. The American Dream is one in which every good individual has the opportunity to succeed whatever their initial disadvantages—a recurrent theme of feel-good Hollywood films with happy endings. . . . Consequently, economic failure is seen as normally being the fault of the individual and no responsibility of society (hence the minimal, safety-net welfare state)—and so is crime. . . . Social democratic societies have a different culture and a different, less individualistic and more sympathetic attitude towards both the economic failure and the criminal.

(Cavadino and Dignan 2006b, 51)

The person/control management style is also, like neo-liberal culture, a steeply hierarchical top-down model, in which those at the bottom of the hierarchy must be managed and controlled. When they break the rules that hold them in place, they justly deserve the punishment they brought on themselves by their own bad choices stemming from their own bad characters. This emphasis on *control* of those at the bottom of the hierarchy—whether at the bottom of the economic system or as targets of the criminal justice system (or both)—is powerful in the neo-liberal United States, with its widespread and still expanding surveillance and control system. This is a system in which people of lower status are *controlled*, rather than included and valued as committed members of the system; and with its myopic commitment to *individual* moral responsibility, it is not a system that encourages fixing the real problems, or even discovering what those problems are.

### The Surveillance System and its Effects

The powerful and interlocking elements of the U.S. neo-liberal system of surveillance and control are clearly described by Young and Petersilia (2016). The starting point for that system of control is the special *surveillance* aimed at blacks, who are heavily targeted for "investigatory" stops (as opposed to standard "enforcement" or "traffic safety" stops). These investigatory stops (Epp, Maynard-Moody, and Haider-Markel 2014) are aimed at gathering information about people who are often prejudicially treated as "automatic suspects" because of their race (and young black men are the most common targets). There must be a "justification" for the stop, but some trivial reason is always available (a broken tail light, driving slightly over the speed limit, failing to signal a lane change). Such stops make young black men more likely to be apprehended for an offense—such as an open container of alcohol, drug possession, a weapon without a permit—that others who are *not* targeted are just as likely to commit, but who are not the target of "investigatory stops" and so are not apprehended. Even if no arrest is made and no illegal activity discovered, information from the stop goes into the records and the people stopped become part of the surveillance system. Not only do such surveillance procedures result in disproportionate arrests for those targeted, but they also have a powerful effect on the attitudes and beliefs of those subjected to such intense surveillance:

> Disproportionate levels of investigatory stops of African Americans . . . encourage these drivers to bring to their encounters with police expectations of unequal and intrusive treatment, and to leave these stops deeply distrusting the fairness of the police and doubting their own equal status and liberty in society.
>
> (Epp, Maynard-Moody, and Haider-Markel 2014, 50)

The result of this intense surveillance is to make its targets feel like objects who are coercively controlled rather than full participants who are valued contributors to the society. As Young and Petersilia note, this focused surveillance "has created an environment of surveillance and control in which black citizens are made to feel culturally and legally subordinate" (2016, 1329). How do we *control* those individuals at the bottom of the social structure? That question comes from a person/control framework, and blocks consideration of a more positive question: how do we construct a *system* that fosters and values and rewards the *commitment* of all members of society?

Investigatory police stops—whether traffic stops or the notorious "stop and frisk" of young black men in urban settings—are a basic element of the pervasive surveillance society, but they are only one part of the system. Because surveillance information is widely collected and widely shared—not only by the police, but also by the courts, schools, social services, hospitals, housing authorities, employers, and banks—and because such information becomes a *permanent* part of one's record, anyone who might be a target of arrest (or fears that he or she is a target) tries to avoid places where such information might be gathered or employed. A young man is involved in a high school fight, or is caught with a small amount of marijuana, or shoplifts a pair of sunglasses—offenses that would probably be dismissed with a stern warning for a suburban high school senior with affluent parents and a well-connected attorney—and now has a criminal stain on his record. As Alice Goffman (2014) details the problem, this can and often does result in a downward spiral: the young man is locked into the system, and becomes a suspect when the surveillance net places him near the scene of a crime; a warrant is issued for his arrest, and now he is "on the run," fearfully avoiding anything that would reveal his whereabouts to the police (he is painfully aware that being innocent of the charges against him is no protection against criminal conviction). As Young and Petersilia sum up the problem:

> The constant surveillance presence of the criminal justice system has several corrosive consequences, including fostering mistrust of the police, amplifying existing inequalities, and . . . creating a kind of "liminal," "second-class," or "peripheral" citizenship from which it is difficult to escape. In important ways, the modern criminal justice apparatus destabilizes lives, particularly those lived in poor and minority communities. Instead of helping people gain stability, the system actually frustrates people's chances of getting jobs, keeping their housing, and staying out of trouble.
>
> (2016, 1322)

The "second-class" citizenship that is part of the harsh surveillance society is characteristic of neo-liberal culture as well as the person/control model of management, both of which feature rigidly hierarchical structures and a powerful control apparatus that focuses blame and punishment on specific individuals while rejecting examination of the deeper systemic causes. Those caught at the bottom of the economic heap have only themselves to blame for their failure, and structural forces that keep them in their lower economic status are not part of the investigation. The young man who is hemmed in by a surveillance society and blocked from housing, social services support, educational opportunities, and employment turns to criminal activity as the only path open; but he *chose* to commit the crime, he is the one guilty of the crime, and—from the myopic individualist perspective of the neo-liberal culture—he is totally responsible, and no deeper systemic inquiries have any relevance.

Most crimes are not errors; but like errors, they can provide us with valuable information. What they teach us, if we are open to learning, is that in almost every case the crime involves a problem in the society. We need not probe very far into the systemic problems to discover a multitude of deeper causes of criminal tendencies and criminal behavior: inferior educational opportunities, lead poisoning, racism, poor housing, inadequate health care (including poor or nonexistent prenatal care), dysfunctional families, a brutalizing juvenile justice system, absence of living-wage employment opportunities, a demeaning and stultifying surveillance system, daily assaults on pride and dignity by police stops and searches; in short, a dignity- and self-confidence-destroying system that shapes despair rather than fortitude, and alienation rather than commitment. So long as we insist on focusing the blame and moral responsibility and retribution on the individual who—at the end of all these systemic causes—commits a crime, then we comfortably avert our attention from the deeper systemic causes. The buck stops with the individual criminal, and no deeper inquiry is relevant or allowed.

The deep *systemic* nature of the crime problem is clearly recognized by Young and Petersilia:

> Popular conversation tends to center on overincarceration and police brutality—and with good reason, as both exemplify the system's worst tendencies: biased, expensive, disproportionately harsh, and violent. But suppose that through police training and selective decarceration, we successfully curtailed these problems. We would have fewer people in prison and fewer needless civilian deaths at the hands of police. Both outcomes would be positive, and thousands of lives would be improved or even saved. At the same time, we should not mistake elimination of negative outcomes for the repair of a broken system. It is akin to trying to fix healthcare by developing affordable medicines to cure the most severe diseases. While the medications *should* be developed because they would heal many people, we should not mistake their development for changing the way healthcare itself operates. Similarly, if we do not repair the most basic, day-to-day processes that comprise the criminal justice system, we can expect new problems to take root.
>
> (2016, 1343)

Young and Petersilia offer valuable insights into the importance of doing more than fixing symptoms of the deeper problems in our criminal justice system; but changing "the most basic, day-to-day processes that comprise the criminal justice system" will require more than making *repairs* to the system. One, it requires a different approach altogether, that rejects the individualistic neo-liberal control model in favor of a *system* approach that promotes deeper inquiry into the causes of problems. Two, it needs a *commitment* approach that embraces inclusiveness and emphasizes opportunities for exercising take-charge responsibility toward shared worthwhile goals. Three, there must be a move toward a genuinely inclusive society that more closely resembles the social democratic corporatist model rather than the neo-liberal. Those three requirements coalesce into *one* requirement, taken from three perspectives: the democratic corporatist society is characterized by a strong *systemic* (rather than "rugged individualist") orientation and by an *inclusiveness* built on shared value commitments (as opposed to a top down control-surveillance policy).

Replacing a control model with a commitment model—a system in which people have a genuine stake in the society and an important role in making a positive and recognized contribution to it—does not result in a higher level of crime, just as rejecting the control model in industry does not result in a higher level of errors and mistakes. When the no-blame system model replaced the individual/control model in air traffic control, the result was less intrusive control *and* dramatically fewer mistakes. Compared to neo-liberal cultures, social democratic corporatist cultures impose less control, foster greater commitment, and have less crime. Rather than a harsh control or "get tough" approach to policing, Meares advocates a "rightful policing" approach. As Meares describes this approach:

> Procedural justice matters a great deal in civil society. One important consequence of people's perceptions of procedural fairness . . . is that they lead to popular beliefs of legitimacy . . . Research shows that people are motivated more to comply with the law by the belief that they are being treated with dignity and fairness than by fear of punishment. In fact, being treated fairly is a more important determinant of compliance than formal deterrence. When police generate good feelings in their everyday contacts, people are motivated to help them fight crime. All of this encourages desistance from offending, law-abiding and assistance to the police, contributing to lower crime rates.
>
> (Meares 2015, 6)

Or another way of putting it: when people are motivated to work toward a common goal in which their abilities and their contributions and their persons are respected, there is less need for a control-deterrence approach that coerces compliance through punishment and the threat of punishment. What is true in the factory also applies to the larger culture.

## Would It Work Here?

"It wouldn't work here." That is a popular refrain among Americans who observe a well-functioning and far superior system in another country, but nonetheless reject applying that system in the United States. The single-payer health care system of Canada provides excellent medical care for all its citizens, is superior on almost every health measure from life expectancy to vaccination rate to infant mortality rate, and costs much less per capita: but "it wouldn't work here." Norway's prison system is much less costly than that of the United States, Norway's crime rate is a fraction of the U.S. crime rate, and the recidivism rate is much lower than in the United States; but "it wouldn't work here." Many European countries provide excellent higher education opportunities to their students at low tuition rates, thus avoiding the crippling student loan debts that burden so many people in the United States; but "it wouldn't work here." And that is likely to be the response to the implementation of a no-blame system/commitment approach in the United States: it wouldn't work here. In this case, that narrow perspective may be correct. The United States is probably one of the least promising countries for the adoption of anything approximating the no-blame system model. The United States has cultural commitments that make adoption of such a system unlikely or even impossible: a commitment to rugged individualism, a deeply embedded retributivism, a pervasive neo-liberal outlook. Some other countries and cultures—such as those of Scandinavia—are much more fertile ground for the seeds of no-blame system/commitment to take root and grow; in the United States, those seeds are likely to fall on rocky and barren soil.

Can a system/commitment/no-blame approach work in the United States? Probably not: No more than a polar bear could thrive in the Sahara. But cultural environments can change. Look at the United States of 1950, and try to imagine the election of an African-American President less than 60 years later; or consider the vile treatment of homosexuals in the United States of 1950, and try to imagine the possibility of joyful celebration of same-sex marriages in considerably less than four score years. This is not a prediction that the no-blame system approach will be widely celebrated in the United States within a few decades. Rather, the point is that there *is* an alternative approach to the retributive system: an approach that does not—and may never—do away with punishment entirely, but that views punishment in a very different light: not as righteous retribution that solves the problem, but as a deeply disturbing mark of societal *failure* to solve problems that require devoted efforts to find real systemic solutions.

No-blame system/commitment runs counter to hierarchy, counter to radical individualism, and counter to the moral responsibility system, all of which flourish in the neo-liberal United States. It is not surprising, then, that the remarkable success of the no-blame system model has generated strong opposition: not because no-blame fails, but because it works. Its success challenges some deep American values: values of top-down management, blame and moral responsibility, and rugged individualism. If knowledge is better than ignorance, then no-blame is a better system; but the resistance will be powerful and the temptation toward Tychonism strong.

To gain the advantages of the new system, we must adopt the new system. We moved beyond honor killings to retribution; some cultures are now pushing beyond retribution, but we must take the full step beyond retribution into a better understanding. It was not so long ago that we could not imagine moving beyond an honor system; now, for those who have made that move, the honor system seems barbaric. When we finally move beyond the retributive system, the myopic moral responsibility system will be seen as perversely cruel: why would a society refuse to look at deeper causes and try to fix them? If we abandon a blame and shame and just deserts system, we must look for something else. That something else is *not* a revised version of blame and shame; rather, it is a system in which people are respected as valued contributors to a worthwhile social system: a system in which people value the responsibility they *take* for the effective operation of a system in which they are respected full participants. It is a system in which people have genuine opportunities to succeed at taking appropriate levels of take-charge responsibility, a system in which they have the tools and resources and learned abilities for success at exercising take-charge responsibility and contributing to shared social commitments, and a system in which policies of blame and shame do not cause them to *fear* taking responsibility.

In Norway's Bastoy Island prison, inmates have take-charge responsibility for getting ready in the morning and preparing their lunches; but they also have meaningful take-charge responsibility for significant jobs in which they can take genuine satisfaction. We must sometimes imprison (though very rarely). But prison should not be a place where one is further deprived of all control—perhaps in the desperate helplessness and hopelessness of total isolation—but rather a place where residents can begin to effectively take responsibility and exercise control and make a contribution. At Bastoy Island, prisoners make choices and take responsibility for their jobs, and have considerable autonomy in their work. Instead of shaming and degrading and breaking down prisoners, the prisoners build a stronger sense of their own ability to exercise effective control and gain respect and make a contribution. When they leave prison, the emphasis is on continuing the process of integrating people into meaningful autonomous roles in the workplace and in society. In Norway and other European countries, no imprisoned citizen ever loses the right to vote: prisoners remain full citizens of their countries. In the neo-liberal United States, almost all inmates are deprived of the right to vote, and in many states that deprivation is permanent for all convicted felons. It is not difficult to determine which society promotes greater inclusiveness, shared commitments, and individual dignity.

The neo-liberal individualistic hierarchical blame and shame society of coercive control and increasing surveillance is not working. Perhaps transforming that society into a no-blame system/commitment structure is an impossible goal. But at least there is a genuine alternative available if we wish to try.

# 14 Conclusion

"What do you do about punishment?" That is a scary question for those who deny moral responsibility. Not because it is impossible to answer, or even difficult. The answer is obvious: minimize it. Use as little punishment as possible, of the mildest possible variety. Punishment is bad, it is always unjust, and we should punish with caution, concern, reluctance, and regret—and *never* more than necessary. That's the easy part.

"What do you do about punishment?" That is not a scary question because it is hard to answer, but because it is hard to face. It forces us to confront a painful reality that belief in moral responsibility shields from view. When we recognize the spurious nature of moral responsibility, *and* we realize that punishment cannot be eliminated—that for the foreseeable future any functioning society must sometimes punish people—then we are forced to recognize both that punishment is *unjust* and that we cannot avoid active participation in the injustice of punishment. We must live in a society that imposes unjust punishment for our benefit and on our behalf. While we can and should minimize that injustice—and there are major steps we can take toward that goal—we cannot eliminate punishment and the injustice it inevitably involves. What we can do, however, is view punishment from a clearer perspective, and recognize that the quest to make punishment justly deserved is not only futile but harmful.

It is hard to relinquish the comforting blinders of moral responsibility. Renouncing moral responsibility means not only facing up to the injustice of punishment, but also threatens another deep source of comfort: belief in a just world. We live in a world in which injustice—in the form of unjust punishment—cannot be eliminated, and unjust punitive behavior cannot be avoided. It is comforting to believe that whatever we *ought* to do we can do, and anything we *must* do will be just. We employ a variety of defense mechanisms to protect our deeply implausible nonconscious belief in a just world: the (apparently innocent) rape victim "led him on," karma will eventually (perhaps in a future life cycle) restore the balance of justice, terrible Earthly injustices are all part of a larger divine plan and "we'll understand it better by and by." Stripping away the protective belief in moral responsibility and just deserts requires us to confront our own painful role in inevitable injustice, and after such knowledge it is tough to restore the comfortable belief in a just world. It is hardly surprising, then, that both philosophers and the folk struggle to retain belief in moral responsibility, even when encroaching scientific naturalism has long since destroyed the miracle-working world that is its essential habitat.

## The System-Secure Obvious Truth of Just Deserts

In *The Dry Salvages*, T. S. Eliot wrote of "what was believed in as the most reliable" and "therefore the fittest for renunciation." Some beliefs that are "believed in as the most reliable" may be worth preserving; but there are also some that hold their positions of certainty because they are central to a system of beliefs that has long endured and from which we are reluctant to part, even if that system of beliefs has become obsolete and dysfunctional. Such beliefs are "the fittest for renunciation," but also the hardest to renounce. They seem to be fixed comfortable certainties—as indeed they are, from within the widely accepted traditional system.

The previous chapter championed the no-blame system/commitment model, as a replacement for the moral responsibility system that is currently entrenched. In that new system no one ever justly deserves punishment, but punishment must sometimes be imposed. It is not surprising that the proposal of such a system prompts incredulity as well as outrage. How can we punish and say it's not justly deserved? It is not just crazy but morally repulsive. "You don't deserve to be punished, but we are going to punish you anyway." Punishing someone who doesn't justly deserve to be punished, but who is erroneously believed to be guilty and justly deserving of punishment: that's very bad. Punishing someone we *know* does not justly deserve to be punished: that is morally abhorrent.

It does look crazy. When a proposal looks that crazy, one possibility is that it truly is crazy. Another possibility is that it looks crazy because it is radically different from a broadly accepted system. In his examination of clashes between competing systems of thought, Wittgenstein noted the harsh conflict that can result: "Where two principles really do meet which cannot be reconciled with one another, then each man declares the other a fool and a heretic" (Wittgenstein 1969, 81e). From within the moral responsibility system, it is ridiculous to claim that someone like Bernie Madoff—who knowingly and purposefully carried out a massive swindle—does not justly deserve punishment. It is even worse to claim that though he does not justly deserve punishment, he should nonetheless be punished. But what appears ridiculous from within the rules of one system may be a claim worth considering when we are judging the merits of competing systems. As Wittgenstein noted: "It would strike me as ridiculous to want to doubt the existence of Napoleon; but if someone doubted the existence of the earth 150 years ago, perhaps I should be more willing to listen, for now he is doubting our whole system of evidence" (1969, 26e). Saying that Bernie Madoff does not deserve punishment (from within the moral responsibility system) is ridiculous; but saying no one ever just deserves punishment, but punishment cannot now be eliminated from our unjust world: that proposes a competing system. The question is then which *system* is better. When systems are in dispute, you cannot—as Wittgenstein notes in his criticism of Moore's "refutation of idealism"—hold up a hand and refute idealism: you cannot appeal to a truth that is obvious and indubitable from deep within a system to refute a competing system.

The question is not whether punishment is sometimes justly deserved from within the principles forming the moral responsibility system: certainly it is. Nor is the question whether punishment is justly deserved from within the no-blame system/commitment model: certainly it is not. Rather, the question is which of those *systems* we should prefer. When we place the systems side by side, they have strikingly different features. First, the no-blame system model regards punishment as a terrible wrong, and is devoted to minimizing punishment and its harshness; the moral responsibility system treats punishment as righteous retribution that is just and good, and panders to rather than mitigates the powerful strike-back desire. Second, the no-blame system rejects blaming and shaming; and shaming—rather than improving behavior and character—imposes further harm on character that has already suffered damage while increasing the propensity toward violence (Gilligan 2001). Shaming often marks the shamed person as permanently bad and further alienates that person from the community, creating a deep divide between offenders who suffer shame and punishment and the community that blames and shames. Shaming promotes defensiveness or hopelessness, makes it harder for the person who did wrong to carefully examine the deeper flaws that caused the problem, and blocks efforts at reform and restoration to the community. Third, the no-blame system approach insists on looking more deeply and broadly to find the real sources of problems: the buck does *not* stop with the punished person. It seeks causes in larger situations and systems and looks deeper at the systemic causes of individual flaws. The moral responsibility system is constructed on a "buck stops here" individualistic foundation that blocks deeper inquiry. Finally, the moral responsibility system was designed to preserve the naturalistically implausible belief in a just world (by making unavoidable punishment justly deserved); in contrast, the no-blame system confronts the fact that the world is not just and punishment is not just, and uses that insight to ameliorate the natural desire for harsh punishment.

In the no-blame system/commitment program we all work toward a shared commitment to make the system better. The punished person is not an alien, but someone who—ideally—is not only restored to the community but restored to the commitments of the community. Instead of blamed and shamed and distanced, the offender helps us understand the problems in the system. Through such knowledge the offender can be helped, and can in turn help improve the system by identifying the deeper problems. Together we can look for and fix the fault in the system, a process in which the offender plays a valued role and is recruited to a shared commitment. One system is based on the belief in a just world (that is profoundly implausible from our naturalistic perspective), blocks deeper inquiry, and promotes harsh treatment. The other rejects belief in a just world, embraces a thorough naturalism, encourages deeper and broader inquiry, and strives to minimize harsh treatment and improve the social system. It should not be a difficult choice.

## Protecting Basic Individual Rights

Without the moral responsibility system we must confront the harsh reality of punitive injustice in an unjust world. But there are other supposed perils of the elimination of moral responsibility, and while they provoke genuine fears, those fears—like fear of ghosts, or fate, or hell—are not realistic. One of those fears—fear that without belief in moral responsibility we would be in danger of "vanishing away"—I have discussed elsewhere (2015a, Chapter 9). Another such false fear: moral responsibility offers protection for the innocent, and without moral responsibility that protection will be lost. As discussed in Chapter 7, strong belief in moral responsibility endangers rather than protects the innocent. Still, there is a legitimate concern: moral responsibility was *supposed* to promote protection of the innocent and other basic rights; without moral responsibility, what protections will we have?

Someone might suppose that in denying moral responsibility we destroy any distinction between the guilty and the innocent. Robert Harris was guilty of willfully murdering two young men; Bernie Madoff was guilty of planning and executing a massive fraud. The fact that neither Harris nor Madoff nor anyone else is morally responsible for their bad acts does not alter the fact that Harris and Madoff were guilty of serious crimes while most of us are innocent of those crimes. Neither the guilty nor the innocent are morally responsible, and neither the guilty nor the innocent justly deserve punishment; but the distinction between guilt and innocence remains.

"If we lose moral responsibility, then we lose vital protections of our individual rights and values, such as protection of the innocent." That is such a strong fear that some (Smilansky 2000) who are skeptical about the plausibility of traditional justifications of moral responsibility insist that we should maintain the *illusion* of moral responsibility. That is like maintaining the illusion that the Maginot Line will protect us from invasion: it provides a false sense of security, and that false sense comes at a high price.

Social systems and cultures with strong commitment to individual moral responsibility and just deserts—such as the United States—provide fewer actual protections against convicting the innocent, are more willing to violate the basic human rights of prisoners (for example, by exposing them to severe psychological damage in long-term isolation), are less committed to fair trials, offer less support of basic needs (such as food and housing and health care and educational opportunity), less protection of the basic right to vote, less protection (in the United States) of *habeas corpus*, less protection (in the UK) of the right to silence. Commitment to moral responsibility is more likely to jeopardize than protect basic human rights. So by denying moral responsibility, we are not losing an essential protection; rather, we are losing an illusory protection, and eliminating a serious threat. Rejection of moral responsibility and just deserts facilitates development of genuine protections for basic rights. Recognizing that moral responsibility affords only bogus protection is an incentive to take *effective* steps to protect those basic rights and liberties we legitimately cherish.

It is important to recognize and protect fundamental principles protecting individual liberty. There must be no punishment of the innocent, no incarceration without proper *habeas corpus* safeguards, basic rights of freedom of speech and the press and conscience must be protected, and the right to silence must be respected. Such principles serve as checks on the dangers of power; and it is the powerful that control the fearful mechanisms of punishment. We value those checks not because we cherish moral responsibility, but because we rightly fear concentrated power that can control and manipulate and render helpless.

A good *start* to protecting individual rights is preventing concentration of wealth and power in the hands of a few individuals. Belief in individual moral responsibility and "self-made men" exacerbates that peril: those who accumulate wealth did it on their own, owe nothing to anyone, and are entitled to use their wealth as they please (including manipulation of the political process); and those in poverty have only themselves to blame. When we add the belief in a just world—closely linked with belief in moral responsibility—then it becomes doubly obvious that the wealthy justly deserve their good fortune, while the poor are also receiving that which is due them, and grossly inequitable distribution of resources is a legitimate element of just deserts.

Other than concentration of wealth and power, fear is the greatest threat to individual rights and liberties. The best protections against fear are deeper understanding and broader knowledge, and belief in moral responsibility blocks that deeper understanding. Individual moral responsibility requires that "the buck stops here" with this individual's act, and where the buck stops inquiry also ceases: either because the individual made a miraculous first cause choice (through the special power of will or perhaps the exalted power of reason), or any further inquiry is ruled (by compatibilists) irrelevant and out of order. Prime Minister John Major favored a harsher punitive blame policy against juvenile crime in the UK, and he was right about the way such a policy functions: "Society needs to condemn a little more and understand a little less" (1993, 8). The policy also works in the opposite direction: when we insist on understanding more, and seeking out the deeper social, conditioning, developmental, and genetic causes for criminal behavior, then we are less inclined to blame (Alicke 2000; Indermaur et al. 2012). Along with less blame, the greater understanding reduces fear, and makes us less vulnerable to "populist punitivism" and manipulative efforts to frighten us into accepting restrictions and deletions of our basic rights and liberties in the name of a "war on crime."

The cycle can be either vicious or virtuous: we blame more, and block understanding, and the criminal perpetrator seems less understandable and therefore scarier so we blame and punish and isolate still more. When this is ratcheted up into intense blame and a frenzied strike-back desire for "righteous retribution," then concern about "punishing the innocent" is overwhelmed by the extreme strike-back desire, as with the Central Park Five. Or we blame less, and understand more, and that understanding reduces the desire to blame and shame and ostracize.

These cumulative effects are not difficult to trace. The more narrowly we focus on the wrongdoer, and the more we refuse to look harder at the wrongdoer (and particularly refuse to identify with the wrongdoer or try to understand what prompted the behavior and the deeper causes, and refuse to walk a mile in his shoes because he is so different from us) then the crime and the criminal look inexplicable and unpredictable and especially dangerous. We are fighting a "war on crime," a "war on drugs," and a "war on terrorism"; and during wartime we must adopt special policies: suspending *habeas corpus* (in the Patriot Act); expanding surveillance (with fewer restrictions and protections); in the UK, doing away with the "right to silence" (and thus the right to be presumed innocent until proven guilty) because "too many criminals were hiding behind it"; employing methods of torture to extract confessions and information from terror suspects (in the guise of "enhanced interrogation"); imposing Draconian penalties (such as "three strikes" legislation allowing life imprisonment for three felonies); imprisoning in conditions of psychological torture and permanent psychological damage (in the total isolation cells of Supermax Prisons). These are special "war provisions"; but the "war" never ends. As understanding and empathy wane, so fear and loathing and condemnation and harsh measures take their place. It also works in the opposite direction. Even if we do not reach the point of "to know all is to forgive all," we gain in understanding of deeper causes, and that in itself softens the harshest punitive attitudes. When we look deeper at the causes that shaped the criminal (and that could have likewise shaped us, had we been less fortunate in our environmental histories), we are less likely to see the criminal as radically different and scary. Furthermore, we see that the causes of criminal behavior include *us*: our society shaped the criminal, and even if we did not actively participate in fostering those conditions, we acquiesced.

Finally, if we are serious about protecting individual rights and liberties, we must push for broader and more systematic protection of those rights. Reading suspects a Miranda warning, providing indigent defendants with grossly overburdened defense counsel who have little time for anything more than a quick consultation on a plea bargain, guaranteeing the "right to vote" without any real impact on the selection of candidates and with little or no power to influence legislation: such "liberties" fall far short of genuine commitment to the exercise of individual choice and control. When the overall system operates through surveillance and control and manipulation of the population (rather than fostering commitment to shared goals) then it is not surprising that rights and liberties are under threat. A genuine commitment to individual rights and liberties is not confined to the limited and often meaningless choices made in a voting booth; rather, it must be part of daily life: in schools, workplaces, long-term care facilities, and the other venues where we live our daily lives. Protecting individual rights and liberties requires protecting and enhancing opportunities to make meaningful choices and exercise take-charge control in broad areas of our lives, including particularly our work lives. It is not impossible to manipulate those who have the opportunity to exercise and strengthen their capacities for effective take-charge responsibility in a workplace environment characterized by commitment rather than hierarchical control; but it is more *difficult* than manipulating those who live under the constant shadow of a surveillance/control/blame culture. Protecting individual rights begins at home, at school, in the workplace, and in daily life.

## Free Will and Open Alternatives

The moral responsibility system claimed free will as a condition for moral responsibility; and as the flaws in the moral responsibility system become clear, there is a danger of throwing out the free will baby with the moral responsibility bath water. Unlike moral responsibility, free will is valuable; and appreciating its *actual* value is a positive step in protecting the basic rights and liberties that support and enhance free will. Human animals do not and cannot have a free will that supports moral responsibility (so long as we are mortals and not self-made deities); but natural free will is naturally valuable, independent of any supposed support for moral responsibility. Separating free will from moral responsibility reveals the real value of natural free will for animals like ourselves.

The philosophical debate over free will is primarily between two camps: the libertarians, who base free will on open alternatives and special unconstrained choices; and the compatibilists, who regard the capacity for control as the key to free will. Both camps offer valuable insights: it is true that both *choice* among open options and *control* are vital for free will. But those genuine insights into choice and control are badly distorted by two major problems. First, both camps endeavor to craft an account of free will that can carry the unbearable burden of moral responsibility. To make matters worse, the long struggle between libertarians and compatibilists has resulted in each side rejecting any collaboration with the enemy. As a result, compatibilists (such as Frankfurt and Fischer) insist that given sufficiently strong control, free will can flourish in the complete absence of alternatives; and libertarians attempt to make open alternatives strong enough to support free will with no need for substantive control. Both sides are driven to extremes in order to make their *half* accounts of free will do the job that requires *both* open alternatives and effective control. When those inadequate half accounts of free will are also required to carry the weight of moral responsibility, then their genuine insights are twisted beyond recognition, and certainly beyond any value for human animals. The first step is to cleanse open alternatives of its libertarian exaggerations and effective control of its compatibilist distortions. *Natural* choice and control combine in a free will that is valuable for humans and other animals.

Foraging animals have both a psychological and a practical need for open options. The options we need are not miraculous first-cause options, which are of no value to animals that evolved without divine attributes; and not infinite options, which are of negative value to animals lacking infinite rational powers (Iyengar and Lepper 2000). They are the mundane alternatives that enable us to maintain open possibilities and alternative paths and handy escape routes, and empower us to make choices and try new plans. J. Lee Kavanau, in training feral white-footed mice to run a maze, was frustrated by the behavior of mice that had thoroughly mastered the optimum path but occasionally deviated onto "incorrect" routes. After many frustrating trials he recognized something important about the behavior of white-footed mice—an insight that applies equally to humans:

> Actually, these responses are incorrect only from the point of view of the investigator's rigidly prescribed program, not from that of the animal. The basis for these responses is that the animal has a certain degree of variability built into many of its behavior patterns. This variability is adaptive to conditions in the wild, where there are many relationships that are not strictly prescribed. . . . The habit of deviating fairly frequently from stereotyped "correct" responses, together with a high level of spontaneous activity, underlie the remarkable facility with which white-footed mice can be taught to cope with complex contingencies.
>
> (1967, 1628)

More recently, Björn Brembs neatly summarized the great importance of behavioral options:

> Beyond behaving unpredictably to evade predators or outcompete a competitor, all animals must explore, must try out different solutions to unforeseen problems. Without behaving variably, without acting rather than passively responding, there can be no success in evolution. Those individuals who have found the best balance between flexible actions and efficient responses are the ones who have succeeded in evolution. It is this potential to behave variably, to initiate actions independently of the stimulus situation, which provides animals with choices.
>
> (Brembs 2010)

Being locked into circumstances that limit or destroy our options—whether the limiting circumstances are a rigid assembly line, a prison cell, ignorance, lack of confidence, addiction, or poverty—deprives us of a basic element of free will; and it also deprives us of a basic liberty. The choices of religious belief, freedom of association, freedom of conscience, freedom of speech, and freedom of movement are of obvious importance. But we also need choices of how to carry out our work, and what sort of work we want to do; choices of what to eat, and when; when to go to bed, or take a bath, or socialize: the everyday choices that institutions—including prisons and long-term care facilities—often eliminate. Mundane choices are at least as important to our free will and our psychological well-being as the big choices celebrated as "inalienable rights."

Neither white-footed mice nor humans have any need for first-cause *ab initio* choices. Even if we could make sense of such choices—it is hard to imagine exactly who is *making* such choices, or on what possible basis—they are not the choices we require. Whether pigeons, white-footed mice, chimpanzees, or humans, we do *not* need contra-causal choices that transcend all interests and environmental influences; rather, for our choices to have value they must be generated by and adapted to our natural environments. We want choices that can *respond effectively* to changing needs and desires and situations. We need *practice* at choice-making, and the confidence that we can choose effectively. Workplaces that enforce rigid behavioral patterns not only deprive us of an important psychological benefit, but also weaken our capacity and confidence for effective choice-making outside the workplace. We want to make intelligent choices, based on our own values and interests and commitments.

The desire and need and capacity to make choices is not a miracle-working uniquely human power. It is a highly adaptive natural preference found in many species, including pigeons (Catania 1975; Catania and Sagvolden 1980; Cerutti and Catania 1997), rats (Voss and Homzie 1970), mice (Kavanau 1967), monkeys (Suzuki 1999), and humans (Suzuki 1997 and 2000). "Spontaneous" behavior that opens new options has been studied in fruit flies (*Drosophilia*) (Heisenberg 1994; Heisenberg; Wolf, and Brembs 2001; Brembs 2011), including studies of the brain structures involved in such spontaneity (Solanki, Wolf, and Heisenberg 2015). The value of choice is sufficiently great that we have evolved to desire it for its own sake (Morris and Royle 1988; Bown, Read, and Summers 2003; Kunar, Ariyabandu, and Jami 2016). As Catania and Sagvolden note, this is not a surprising result:

> Given that food supplies sometimes may be lost to competitors or may disappear in other ways, an organism that chooses patches of the environment in which two or more food supplies are available will probably have a survival advantage over one that chooses patches of the environment containing only a single food supply.

(1980, 85)

The strength of the deep desire for choice is demonstrated by not only behavioral but also neuropsychological studies. When Leotti and Delgado "tested whether the mere anticipation of personal involvement through choice would recruit reward related brain circuitry, particularly the striatum" (2011, 1311), they found striking results:

> In summary, we obtained behavioral evidence that choice is desirable, and, furthermore, we found that anticipating an opportunity for choice was associated with increased activity in a network of brain regions thought to be involved in reward processing.
>
> (Leotti and Delgado 2011, 1314; see also Bjork and Hommer 2007, and Leotti, Iyengar, and Ochsner 2010)

There is also evidence for the learning process that enhances the desirability of choice (Cockburn, Collins, and Frank 2014).

Maintaining open choice options is sufficiently desirable that animals (including humans) pass up greater immediate benefits in order to preserve the possibility of future choices. Viewed from the evolutionary perspective, this makes survival sense:

> We suggest that a preference for choice over no-choice is a heuristic that has emerged because, in evolutionary terms, it has usually led to the best outcome. Our ancestors would have quickly learned that it is better to hunt in an area where there is a choice of prey (both in number and species), than in an area where there is little if any choice. Indeed, it is likely that they would not have had to learn at all—the research showing that animals prefer choice over no-choice paths . . . suggests that the preference for choice may be a fundamental part of our natural endowment.
>
> (Bown, Read, and Summers 2003, 307)

Choice among open alternatives is a vital element of free will. Unfortunately, in the effort to justify claims of moral responsibility and just deserts, the mundane open alternatives actually valued by butchers, bakers, and white-footed mice were not sufficient. Instead of real and valuable choices among paths, food sources, and work procedures, the choices became mysterious and miraculous first-cause choices, transcending all personal characteristics and environmental contingencies. In that process the vital and valuable daily mundane choices were banished from the free will repertoire of uniquely special humans, and their fundamental importance for free will was unappreciated and unprotected. Such choices are made by humans as well as other animals, but free will and the moral responsibility it supports must be the *exclusive* property of humans. As a result, *basic* everyday acts of free choice were ignored. Those mundane choices are the essential foundation of our natural free will and take-charge responsibility.

## Free Will and Control

In addition to open choices, the effective exercise of *control* is the other essential element of animal free will. As with open alternatives, the obsession with making free will support moral responsibility resulted in distortion of this basic need. There are two problems with contemporary philosophical treatments of control. First, most contemporary naturalistic philosophers could not accept the miraculous first cause choices put forward by the traditional libertarians. Unfortunately, compatibilists then rejected *all* accounts of open alternatives as an essential part of free will. As a result, control had to carry the full weight of free will (Fischer 1994, 216) in addition to bearing the impossible burden of moral responsibility. Second, because control was *the* element of free will and—philosophers generally assumed—free will must be uniquely human, the *control* had to be uniquely human rather than the effective control of common behavior valued by humans *and* other animals. Harry Frankfurt, for example, was in search of a control that only humans could exert:

> It is my view that one essential difference between persons and other creatures is to be found in the structure of a person's will. Human beings are not alone in having desires and motives, or in making choices. They share these things with the members of certain other species, some of whom even appear to engage in deliberation and to make decisions based upon prior thought. It seems to be peculiarly characteristic of humans, however, that they are able to form what I shall call "second-order desires" or "desires of the second order."
>
> (Frankfurt 1971, 6)

Second-order reflection is the capacity to *reflect* on my desires, and make them my *own* by reflectively approving of them. This uniquely human higher-order reflection (*without* open alternatives) must then provide all the control needed for free will and moral responsibility. That is the point of Frankfurt's philosophically famous willing addict:

> The willing addict's will is not free, for his desire to take the drug will be effective regardless of whether or not he wants this desire to constitute his will. But when the takes the drug, he takes it freely and of his own free will. I am inclined to understand his situation as involving the overdetermination of his first-order desire to take the drug. This desire is his effective desire because he is physiologically addicted. But it is his effective desire also because he wants it to be. His will is outside his control, but, by his second-order desire that his desire for the drug should be effective, he has made this will his own. Given that it is therefore not only because of his addiction that his desire for the drug is effective, he may be morally responsible for taking the drug.
>
> (Frankfurt 1971, 19–20)

Frankfurt's higher-order reflectiveness is valuable, though hardly a common occurrence; and it is, so far as we know, a uniquely human capacity. But while this exclusive focus on reflective control and humanly unique reflective processes is a fascinating philosophical exercise, it yields a distorted view of animal free will. First, of course, it leaves out the important element of open alternatives, vital for both psychological health and adaptive foraging behavior. Second, it focuses too narrowly on one—quite limited and infrequently employed (Haidt 2012, Kahneman 2011)—special human *enhancement* of free will, while ignoring the importance (for humans as well as other species) of exercising control over a vast range of mundane behavior. Seligman's dogs (Seligman 1975) may not have reflectively considered their cruel plight, but they certainly had an enormous need for exercising control, and a very painful and psychologically debilitating experience when they were deprived of control to the point of developing learned helplessness. Finally—as discussed in the following section—Frankfurt's model ascribes free will in some of the cruelest cases of free will deprivation.

The psychological importance of exercising *control*—and not being the puppets of external controllers or the playthings of Fate or the prisoners or powerful controlling forces—is clear, and research has demonstrated the value of having control in many settings. Some of the most striking research results have demonstrated the importance of control—including especially the mundane areas of control such as the control of meal times, menus, privacy, and bed times—for the life satisfaction and physical health of those in long-term care facilities (Langer and Rodin 1976; Schulz 1976; Schulz and Hanusa 1978; Rodin, Rennert, and Solomon1980; Schorr and Rodin 1982; Rodin 1986; Rodin and Timko 1992; Schulz, Heckhausen, and O'Brien 1994). Control involves being able to make things happen, the capacity to put one's decisions into effect, the ability to actively influence the course of events. Control has obvious value for humans, but research has also shown its desirability to other species, including white-footed mice (Kavanau 1963 and 1967), rats (Singh 1970; Joffe, Rawson, and Mulick 1973), laying hens (Taylor, Coerse, and Haskell 2001), marmosets (Buchanan-Smith and Badihi 2012), and monkeys (Hanson, Larson, and Snowdon 1976; Mineka, Gunnar, and Chapoux 1986).

The range and variety of studies demonstrating the value of control for humans is remarkable. The profound value of having control—and the severe problems that result from loss of control (Seligman 1975)—have been well-documented (Thompson and Spacapan 1991; Wallhagen and Brod 1997; Lachman and Weaver 1998; Lang and Heckhausen 2001; Leotti, Iyegner, and Ochsner 2010; Inesi et al. 2011; Ross and Mirowsky 2013; Leotti and Delgado 2014; Lammers et al. 2016), and those problems apparently occur not only in humans and dogs but also in fruit flies (Yang et al. 2013). The effective exercise of control—or even the *belief* that one can exercise control—(Golin, Terrell, and Johnson 1977; Taylor 1983; Taylor et al. 2000)—prevents depression (Silver and Wortman 1980;

Devins et al. 1981; Devins et al.1982; Taylor 1983; Devins et al. 1984; Brewin 1985; Benassi, Sweeney, and Dufour 1988; Ross and Mirowsky 1989; Mirowsky and Ross 1990; Thompson et al. 1993; Barder, Slimmer, and LeSage 1994; Kunzmann, Little, and Smith 2002; Rabbitt et al. 2004; Joekes, Van Elderen, and Schreurs 2007; Mirowsky 2013) and strengthens the immune system (Langer and Rodin 1976; Schorr and Rodin 1982; Skevington 1983; Rodin 1986; Bandura, Cioffi, Taylor, and Brouillard 1988; McNaughton et al. 1990; Wiedenfeld et al. 1990; Kamen-Siegel et al. 1991; Rodin and Timko 1992). People who believe they have some control over a painful stimulus endure the suffering more easily and feel less stress (Bowers 1968; Corah and Boffa 1970; Staub, Tursky, and Schwartz 1971; Langer, Janis, and Wolfer 1975; Averill, O'Brien, and DeWitt 1977; Pennebaker et al. 1977; Reesor and Craig 1987; Turk and Fernandez 1990; Arnstein et al. 1999). This research on pain and control has a positive application for dealing with the pain suffered by hospital patients. When patients can *control* their own access to analgesics by pressing a button on a pump, they require significantly less medication than when pain medication is provided by staff (Hill et al. 1990; Hill et al. 1991; Mackie, Coda, and Hill 1991; Ballantyne et al. 1993; Ripamonti and Bruera 1997; Momeni, Crucitti, and DeKock 2006).

The opportunity to exercise control is essential to our freedom and well-being, but that exercise requires not only opportunity but also capacity. A vital part of that capacity is the self-confidence that one can effectively and competently exercise control, that one can perform well and achieve one's purpose. A central part of that is having what Albert Bandura called a strong sense of "self-efficacy" (1977, 1982 and 1997; Schunk 1981; Bandura and Cervone 1983; Haidt and Rodin 1999): the belief in one's own powers and competence in the relevant sphere of activity. Developing the essential sense of self-efficacy requires support, as well as safe opportunities to practice exercising effective control: a strong sense of self-efficacy is unlikely to flourish in an environment of top-down rigidly controlling management that disapproves of workers exercising autonomous judgment and that inflicts blame and shame for any mistake.

## Natural Free Will

Libertarians emphasize—and often apotheosize—choice-making while compatibilists focus on control and "authenticity" and reflective approval with no alternatives needed. But *both* control and choice among open alternatives are essential elements of animal free will. Choice without control is frightening, rather than free; control without choice is obsession, not freedom. The classic libertarian *first cause* "choice" hardly seems like a choice at all. Such "choices" cannot be based on our values and preferences, nor can they be influenced by environmental and situational factors; it is not even clear *who* is making this extraordinary godlike "choice". On the other side, consider the now classic philosophical example of control without open alternatives: Harry Frankfurt's willing addict, who has *no option* and will inevitably take drugs, but who reflectively approves of being a drug addict and reflectively wills to remain enslaved by his addiction. This is a fascinating example that has enthralled philosophers for decades; but whatever else it may be, it is not an example of free will. When we closely examine a "willing addict" or "happy slave," the examination does not reveal someone whom we regard as acting freely. The slave who struggles to escape his cruel bondage is not free, as Frankfurt would acknowledge. But suppose the slave's attempts to escape are brutally punished, and the only gains from attempts to assert free choice are increased suffering and heavier chains. Eventually—like Martin Seligman's dogs, that after receiving repeated inescapable shocks ultimately abandon all efforts at escape and cower in learned helplessness—the fiercely independent slave is broken, and he embraces his enslavement and reflectively approves of his total servitude. At this point, on Frankfurt's *control* (without open alternatives) model, the slave has gained free will: he cannot be other than a slave, but he reflectively approves his condition of enslavement. But this is a cruel parody of free will, and nothing like the genuine natural article (Waller 2011, 60–66). The slave who struggles to be free of enslavement is not free; but the totally defeated and hopeless slave is even further removed from free will.

The libertarian and the compatibilist each recognizes an essential part of natural free will (though they then distort them). When we combine the insights of libertarians (choices among open alternatives) and compatibilists (control) then we can see the real value of animal free will (Waller 2015b, 139–145), and how to enhance it. The *control* essential for free will includes the mundane control so often lost in institutional settings and workplaces and impoverished environments and repressive political systems. The requisite *choices* include choices that the relatively "well-off" often take for granted as we exercise take-charge responsibility: choices of what to eat and where and when, where to live, what career to pursue, how to arrange our work process, what college to attend, what leisure activities to enjoy; and we forget how many people have very limited opportunities to make such choices and exercise effective take-charge responsibility and control in their work, their daily activities, and their lives. If we value the exercise of free will and the *taking* of take-charge responsibility, then we must actively promote a system of educational and employment opportunities, workplace autonomy, and social support that protects and enhances the actual enjoyment of the basic liberties involving both effective choice and control.

Developing and protecting the basic freedoms that support the exercise of free will—including the mundane workaday freedom that is the foundation for effective exercise of free will—requires a *commitment* rather than a control-surveillance society and workplace. Work in a control-surveillance atmosphere limits and atrophies exercise of freedom; commitment models enhance it. We cannot pretend an allegiance to free will and basic liberties if we are indifferent to their exercise in work and living environments. While residents of long-term care facilities should certainly have the right of free speech, they should also have the basic right to choose meal times and bed times and bath times, as well as the right to privacy.

We do not need miracles for free will, and we must not rely on miraculous powers of free will to protect basic rights and freedoms any more than we would rely on miracles to protect health. Free will is not a uniquely human esoteric power, but a natural process that can be enhanced or weakened. Protections of basic liberties are built into the no-blame system/commitment work management model: the protections *inherent* in seeking the *voluntary* commitment of workers who take an intelligent self-directed interest in doing the task well, as opposed to coercively controlling workers into rigidly performing a set task. By recognizing what free will really is (and freeing it from the burden of moral responsibility) we can more effectively protect it from threats and develop an environment—social, workplace, and political—in which it thrives.

## Beyond the Moral Responsibility System

The contest between the moral responsibility system and a workable replacement system is fundamentally a struggle between limiting and blocking deeper inquiry and pursuing inquiry without limits. John Major was correct: if we want to blame more, we must understand less. Commitment to moral responsibility blocks deeper inquiry, justifies harsh treatment, comforts us when we should not be comforted, and prevents the development of better alternatives. We now know more about deeper psychological and situational causes, and how to shape better character and better behavior. We have better methods of working with those who commit acts that cause harm and threaten society: methods such as those proposed by James Gilligan (2001), who recognized the destructive force of shaming and promoted placing prisoners in residential settings in which they could develop knowledge and skills and exercise take-charge responsibility; and the methods now employed in the Norwegian prison system.

The alternative to the moral responsibility system is an enhanced social democratic corporatist system that promotes commitment—for all aspects of society, including the workplace and the criminal justice system—rather than surveillance-control. It is not a system that eliminates punishment, but it minimizes punishment and treats it as symptomatic of a systemic flaw rather than as righteous retribution. It encourages rather than suppresses deeper inquiry into the causes of behavior—including errors, social alienation, and criminal behavior. It seeks to *fix* systemic problems rather than halting inquiry by focusing blame on an individual.

From *within* the deep assumptions of the moral responsibility system, this alternative—which is already partially implemented and positively productive in many quarters—may appear an unrealistic fantasy. To the contrary, it honestly confronts a very harsh reality indeed: a reality of unjust punishment in our unjust world that we make enormous efforts—both folk and philosophical—to avoid acknowledging, and that the moral responsibility system rigorously conceals from view. What *is* unrealistic is a policy based on belief in a just world, the fundamental attribution error, libertarian miracles, an aggrandized conception of human rational powers, and compatibilist insistence on rejecting deeper inquiry because "the buck stops here" with "self-made men." What is *real* is a social democratic corporatist culture that minimizes punishment and maximizes social support and cherishes basic individual rights (such as the right to vote and the right of genuine opportunity). What is real is a no-blame system/commitment work management program that respects worker autonomy and intelligence, minimizes oppressive punitive control, reduces errors, promotes better understanding and effective improvement of work procedures, and produces better results with greater efficiency. What is real is the strong naturally supportive connection between the no-blame system/commitment workplace and the social democratic corporatist culture.

There exists a freedom-enhancing no-blame system/commitment *alternative* to our radically individualist society of oppressive surveillance, hierarchical top-down control, harsh punishment, limited inquiry, and righteous retribution. That alternative will neither eliminate punishment nor make punishment just. But it will honestly expose the inescapable *problem* of punishment to a new perspective, deeper inquiry, and better understanding.

# References

Alicke, Mark D. 1992. "Culpable Causation." *Journal of Personality and Social Psychology* 63 (3): 368–378.

Alicke, Mark D. 1994. "Evidential and Extra-Evidential Evaluations of Social Conduct." *Journal of Social Behavior and Personality* 9 (3): 591–615.

Alicke, Mark D. 2000. "Culpable Control and the Psychology of Blame." *Psychological Bulletin* 126 (4): 556–574.

Alicke, Mark D., and Teresa L. Davis. 1989. "The Role of *A Posteriori* Victim Information in Judgments of Blame and Sanction." *Journal of Experimental Social Psychology* 25 (4): 362–377.

Alicke, Mark D., Teresa L. Davis, and Mark V. Pezzo. 1994. "*A Posteriori* Adjustment of *A Priori* Decision Criteria." *Social Cognition* 12 (4): 281–308.

Alicke, Mark D., David Rose, and Dori Bloom. 2011. "Causation, Norm Violation, and Culpable Control." *Journal of Philosophy* 108 (12): 670–696.

Alicke, Mark D., Michael F. Weigold, and Scott L. Rogers. 1990. "Inferring Intentions from Motive and Outcome: Effects on Responsibility Judgment." *Social Cognition* 8 (3): 286–305.

Alicke, Mark D., and Tricia J. Yurak. 1995. "Perpetrator Personality and Judgments of Acquaintance Rape." *Journal of Applied Social Psychology* 25 (21): 1900–1921.

Amnesty International. 2012. "Cruel Isolation: Amnesty International's Concerns About Conditions in Arizona Maximum Security Prisons." www.amnestyusa.org/research/reports/cruel-isolation-amnesty.

Angell, Marcia. 2004. *The Truth About Drug Companies: How They Deceive Us and What to Do About It*. New York: Random House.

Angell, Marcia. 2009. "Drug Companies and Doctors: A Story of Corruption." *The New York Review of Books*, January 15.

Arnstein, Paul, Margaret Caudill, Carolyn Mandle, Anne Norris, and Ralph Beasley. 1999. "Self-Efficacy as a Mediator of the Relationship Between Pain Intensity, Disability and Depression in Chronic Pain Patients." *Pain* 80 (3): 483–491.

Arrigo, Bruce A., and Jennifer L. Bullock. 2008. "The Psychological Effects of Solitary Confinement on Prisoners in Supermax Units: Reviewing What We Know and Recommending What Should Change." *International Journal of Offender Therapy and Comparative Criminology* 52 (6): 622–640.

Aveling, Emma-Louise, Michael Parker, and Mary Dixon-Woods. 2016. "What Is the Role of Individual Accountability in Patient Safety? A Multi-Site Ethnographic Study." *Sociology of Health and Illness* 38 (2): 216–232.

Averill, James R., Lawrence O'Brien, and Gary W. DeWitt. 1977. "The Influence of Response Effectiveness on the Preference for Warning and on Psychophysiological Stress Reactions." *Journal of Personality* 45 (3): 395–418.

Balko, Radley. 2011. "Private Crime Labs Could Prevent Errors, Analyst Bias: Report." *Huffington Post*, June 14. Huffingtonpost.com.

Ballantyne, Jane C., Daniel B. Carr, Thomas C. Chalmers, Keith B. Dear, Italo F. Angelillo, and Frederick Mosteller. 1993. "Post-Operative Patient-Controlled Analgesia: Meta-Analysis of Initial Randomized Control Trials." *Journal of Clinical Anesthesiology* 5 (3): 182–193.

Bandura, Albert. 1977. "Self-Efficacy: Toward a Unifying Theory of Behavioral Change." *Psychological Review* 84 (2): 191–215.

Bandura, Albert. 1982. "Self-Efficacy Mechanism in Human Agency." *American Psychologist* 37 (2): 122–147.

Bandura, Albert. 1997. *Self-Efficacy: The Exercise of Control.* New York: W. H. Freeman.

Bandura, Albert, and Daniel Cervone. 1983. "Self-Evaluative and Self-Efficacy Mechanisms Governing the Motivational Effects of Goal Systems." *Journal of Personality and Social Psychology* 45 (5): 1017–1028.

Bandura, Albert, Delia Cioffi, C. Bart Taylor, and Mary E. Brouillard. 1988. "Perceived Self-Efficacy in Coping with Cognitive Stressors and Opioid Activation." *Journal of Personality and Social Psychology* 55 (3): 479–488.

Barash, David P. 2005. "Redirected Aggression." CPS Working Papers No. 8:1–12.

Barash, David P., and Judith Eve Lipton. 2011. *Payback: Why We Retaliate, Redirect Aggression, and Take Revenge.* New York: Oxford University Press.

Barder, Louise, Lynda Slimmer, and Joan LeSage. 1994. "Depression and Issues of Control Among Elderly People in Health Care Settings." *Journal of Advanced Nursing* 20 (4): 597–604.

Barnett, Randy. 1977. "Restitution: A New Paradigm of Criminal Justice." In *Punishment and Rehabilitation*, second edition, edited by Jeffrie G. Murphy, 211–231. Belmont, CA: Wadsworth.

Barnett, Randy. 1980. "The Justice of Restitution." In *Moral Issues*, edited by Jan Narveson, 140–153. New York: Oxford University Press.

Baumard, Nicolas. 2010. "Has Punishment Played a Role in the Evolution of Cooperation? A Critical Review." *Mind and Society* 9 (2): 171–192.

Baumeister, Roy F., Ellen Bratslavasky, Mark Muraven, and Dianne M. Tice. 1998. "Ego Depletion: Is the Active Self a Limited Resource?" *Journal of Personality and Social Psychology* 74 (5): 1252–1265.

Beckett, Katherine. 1997. *Making Crime Pay: Law and Order in Contemporary American Politics.* New York: Oxford University Press.

Beckett, Katherine, and Bruce Western. 2001. "Governing Social Marginality: Welfare, Incarceration, and the Transformation of State Policy." *Punishment and Society* 3 (1): 43–59.

Bell, Sigali K., Tom Delbanco, Lisa Anderson-Shaw, Timothy B. McDonald, and Thomas H. Gallagher. 2011. "Accountability for Medical Error: Moving Beyond Blame to Advocacy." *CHEST* 140 (2): 519–526.

Benassi, Victor A., Paul D. Sweeney, and Charles L. Dufour. 1988. "Is There a Relationship Between Locus of Control Orientation and Depression?" *Journal of Abnormal Psychology* 97 (3): 357–366.

Bennett, Jonathan. 1980. "Accountability." In *Philosophical Subjects*, edited by Zak van Stratten, 14–47. Oxford: Clarendon Press.

Berman, Mitchell N. 2008. "Punishment and Justification." *Ethics* 118 (2): 258–290.

Bjork, James M. and Daniel W. Hommer. 2007. "Anticipating Instrumentally Obtained and Passively Received Rewards: A Factorial fMRI Investigation." *Behavioral and Brain Research* 177 (1): 165–170.

Bodek, Norman. 2011. "*Zenjidoka*, Solving Toyota's Quality Problems." *Quality Digest*, February 14.

Boonin, David. 2008. *The Problem of Punishment*. New York: Cambridge University Press.

Bowers, Kenneth S. 1968. "Pain, Anxiety, and Perceived Control." *Journal of Consulting and Clinical Psychology* 32 (5): 596–602.

Bown, Nicola J., Daniel Read, and Barbara Summers. 2003. "The Lure of Choice." *Journal of Behavioral Decision Making* 16 (4): 297–308.

Braithwaite, John. 1989. *Crime, Shame and Reintegration*. Cambridge: Cambridge University Press.

Braithwaite, John. 1999. "Restorative Justice: Assessing Optimistic and Pessimistic Accounts." *Crime and Justice: A Review of Research* 25 (1): 1–110.

Braithwaite, John. 2002. *Restorative Justice and Response Regulation*. Oxford: Oxford University Press.

Brembs, Björn. 2010. "Towards a Scientific Concept of Free Will as a Biological Trait: Spontaneous Actions and Decision-Making in Invertebrates." *Proceedings of the Royal Society B: Biological Sciences* 278 (1): 930–939.

Brembs, Björn. 2011. "Spontaneous Decisions and Operant Conditioning in Fruit Flies." *Behavioural Processes* 87 (1): 157–164.

Brewin, Chris R. 1985. "Depression and Causal Attributions: What Is Their Relation?" *Psychological Bulletin* 98 (2): 297–309.

Buchanan-Smith, Hannah M., and Inbal Badihi. 2012. "The Psychology of Control: Effects of Control Over Supplementary Light on Welfare of Marmosets." *Applied Animal Behaviour Science* 137 (3–4): 166–174.

Butler, Samuel. 1872. *Erewhon*. London: Trübner & Co.

Campbell, Charles. A. 1957. *On Selfhood and Godhood*. London: George Allen & Unwin, Ltd.

Cacioppo, John T. and Richard E. Petty. 1982. "The Need for Cognition." *Journal of Personality and Social Psychology* 42 (1): 116–131.

Caruso, Gregg D. 2016. "Free Will Skepticism and Criminal Behavior: A Public Health-Quarantine Model." *Southwest Philosophy Review* 32 (1): 25–48.

Casella, Jean, and James Ridgeway. 2016. "Introduction." In *Hell Is a Very Small Place: Voices from Solitary Confinement*, edited by Jean Casella, James Ridgeway, and Sarah Shourd, 16–24. New York: The New Press.

Castillo, Lisa. 2015. "No Child Left Alone: Why Iowa Should Ban Juvenile Solitary Confinement." *Iowa Law Review* 100 (3): 1259–1284.

Catania, A. Charles. 1975. "Freedom and Knowledge: An Experimental Analysis of Preference in Pigeons." *Journal of the Experimental Analysis of Behavior* 24 (1): 89–106.

Catania, A. Charles, and Terje Sagvolden. 1980. "Preference for Free Choice Over Forced Choice in Pigeons." *Journal of the Experimental Analysis of Behavior* 34 (1): 77–86.

Cavadino, Michael, and James Dignan. 2006a. "Penal Policy and Political Economy." *Criminology & Criminal Justice* 6 (4): 435–456.

Cavadino, Michael, and James Dignan. 2006b. *Penal Systems: A Comparative Approach*. London: Sage.

Center for Cognitive Liberty and Ethics. 2004. *Threats to Cognitive Liberty: Pharmacotherapy and the Future of the Drug War*. Davis, CA: CCLE.

Cerutti, Daniel, and Catania, Charles A. 1997. "Pigeons' Preference for Free Choice: Number of Keys Versus Key Area Over Forced Choice in Pigeons." *Journal of the Experimental Analysis of Behavior* 68 (3): 340–356.

Chiao, Vincent. 2013. "Punishment and Permissibility in the Criminal Law." *Law and Philosophy* 32 (6): 729–765.

Chipman, Nathaniel. 1793. *Sketches of the Principles of Government, 1793*; from Sketch V. "Of Equality, Section II. Of the Nature of Equality in Republics." J. Lyon Press: Rutland, Vermont.

Chisholm, Roderick M. 1982. "Human Freedom and the Self." In *Free Will*, edited by Gary Watson, 24–35. New York: Oxford University Press.

Christie, Nils. 1993. *Crime Control as Industry*. Abingdon, Oxon: Routledge.

Clark, Thomas W. 1999. "Fear of Mechanism: A Compatibilist Critique of 'The Volitional Brain.'" In *The Volitional Brain: Towards a Neuroscience of Free Will*, edited by Benjamin Libet, Anthony Freeman, and Keith Sutherland, 279–293. Thorverton, Exeter: Imprint Academic.

Clark, Thomas W., Daniel Dennett, and Bruce Waller. 2012. "Exchange on Waller's *Against Moral Responsibility*." Naturalism.org. http://naturalism.org/resources/book-reviews/exchange-on-wallers-aga . . .

Clarke, Randolph. 2002. "Libertarian Views: Critical Survey of Noncausal and Event-causal Accounts of Free Agency." In *The Oxford Handbook of Free Will*, edited by Robert Kane, 356–385. New York: Oxford University Press.

Clarke, Randolph. 2003. *Libertarian Accounts of Free Will*. New York: Oxford University Press.

Cockburn, Jeffrey, Anne G. E. Collins, and Michael J. Frank. 2014. "A Reinforcement Learning Mechanism Responsible for the Valuation of Free Choice." *Neuron* 83 (3): 551–557.

Corah, Norman L., and Joseph Boffa. 1970. "Perceived Control, Self-Observation, and Response to Aversive Stimulation." *Journal of Personality and Social Psychology* 16 (1): 1–4.

Corak, Miles. 2016. "Economic Mobility." Pathways, The Poverty and Inequality Report, 2016. The Stanford Center on Poverty and Inequality. inequality.stanford.edu.

Corrado, Michael Louis. 2001. "The Abolition of Punishment." *Suffolk University Law Review* 35 (2): 257–276.

Corrado, Michael Louis. 2013. "Why Do We Resist Hard Incompatibilism? Thoughts on Freedom and Punishment." In *The Future of Punishment*, edited by Thomas A. Nadelhoffer, 79–104. New York: Oxford University Press.

Corrado, Michael Louis. 2015. "Fichte and the Psychopath: Criminal Justice Turned Upside Down." http://dx.doi.org/10.2139/ssm.2585077.

Curry, Bill. 1979. "Convicted Murderer Executed in Florida." The Washington Post, May 26.

Dalbert, Claudia, and Lois Yamauchi. 1994. "Belief in a Just World and Attitudes Toward Immigrants and Foreign Workers: A Cultural Comparison

Between Hawaii and Germany." *Journal of Applied Social Psychology* 24 (18): 1612–1626.

Damasio, Antonio R. 1994. *Descartes' Error: Emotion, Reason, and the Human Brain.* New York: G. P. Putnam's Sons.

Darley, John M., and C. Daniel Batson. 1973. "From Jerusalem to Jericho: A Study of Situational and Dispositional Variables in Helping Behavior." *Journal of Personality and Social Psychology* 27 (1): 100–108.

Davis, Bruce. 2015. "Just Culture? Just Kidding." *Physician's Weekly*, May 26.

Davis, Michael. 2009. "Punishment Theory's Golden Half Century: A Survey of Developments From (About) 1957 to 2007." *Journal of Ethics* 13 (1): 73–100.

Dekker, Sidney W. A. 2009. "Just Culture: Who Gets to Draw the Line?" *Cognition, Technology, & Work* 11 (3): 177–185.

Dennett, Daniel C. 1984. *Elbow Room: The Varieties of Free Will Worth Wanting.* Cambridge, MA: MIT Press.

Dennett, Daniel C. 2003. *Freedom Evolves.* New York: Viking.

Dennett, Daniel C. 2008. "Some Observations on the Psychology of Thinking About Free Will." In *Are We Free? Psychology and Free Will*, edited by John Baer, James C. Kaufman, and Roy F. Baumeister, 248–259. New York: Oxford University Press.

Dennett, Daniel C. 2012. "Dennett Review of *Against Moral Responsibility*." Naturalism.org. http://naturalism.org/resources/book-reviews/dennett-review-of-again . . .

DeParle, Jason. 2012. "Harder for Americans to Rise from Lower Rungs." *New York Times*, January 4. Nytimes.com.

Devine, Patricia. 1989. "Stereotypes and Prejudice: Their Automatic and Controlled Components." *Journal of Personality and Social Psychology* 56 (1): 5–18.

Devins, Gerald M., Yitzchuk M. Binik, Patricia Gorman, Miriam Dattel, Betty McCloskey, Glenda Oscar, and Joan Briggs. 1982. "Perceived Self-efficacy, Outcome Expectancies, and Negative Mood States in End-stage Renal Disease." *Journal of Abnormal Psychology* 91 (4): 241–244.

Devins, Gerald M., Yitzchak M. Binik, David J. Hollomby, Paul E. Barre, and Ronald D. Guttmann. 1981. "Helplessness and Depression in End-Stage Renal Disease." *Journal of Abnormal Psychology* 90 (6): 531–545.

Devins, Gerald M., Yitzchak M. Binik, Tom A. Hutchinson, David J. Hollomby, Paul E. Barre, and Ronald D. Guttmann. 1984. "The Emotional Impact of End-Stage Renal Disease: Importance of Patients' Perceptions of Intrusiveness and Control." *International Journal of Psychiatry in Medicine*, 13 (4): 327–343.

De Waal, Frans. 1996. *Good Natured: The Origins of Right and Wrong in Humans and Other Animals.* Cambridge, MA: Harvard University Press.

Doob, Anthony N., and Julian V. Roberts. 1983. *Sentencing: An Analysis of the Public's View of Sentencing.* Ottawa: Department of Justice, Canada.

Doris, John M. 2002. *Lack of Character: Personality and Moral Behavior.* Cambridge: Cambridge University Press.

Dovidio, John F., Kerry Kawakami, and Samuel L. Gaertner. 2002. "Implicit and Explicit Prejudice and Interracial Interaction." *Journal of Personality and Social Psychology* 82 (1): 62–68.

Emmott, David. 2001. "Medical Errors in Surgery." *Bioethics Forum* 17 (2): 26–31.

Epp, Charles R., Steven Maynard-Moody, and Donald P. Haider-Markel. 2014. *Pulled Over: How Police Stops Define Race and Citizenship*. Chicago: University of Chicago Press.

Esping-Andersen, Gosta. 1990. *The Three Worlds of Welfare Capitalism*. Princeton, NJ: Princeton University Press.

Esping-Andersen, Gosta. 1999. *Social Foundations of Postindustrial Economies*. New York: Oxford University Press.

Fehr, Ernst, and Simon Gächter 2000."Cooperation and Punishment in Public Goods Experiments." The *American Economic Review* 90 (4): 980–994.

Fehr, Ernst, and Simon Gächter. 2002. "Altruistic Punishment in Humans." *Nature* 415 (6868): 137–140.

Feinberg, Joel. 2003. "Evil." In *Problems at the Roots of the Law: Essays in Legal and Political Theory*, 125–192. New York: Oxford University Press.

Fischer, John Martin. 1994. *The Metaphysics of Free Will: An Essay on Control*. Oxford: Blackwell.

Fischer, John Martin. 2007. "Compatibilism." In *Four Views on Free Will*, edited by John Martin Fischer, Robert Kane, Derk Pereboom, and Manuel Vargas, 44–84. Malden, MA: Blackwell Publishing.

Fischer, John Martin. 2012. *Deep Control: Essays on Free Will and Value*. New York: Oxford University Press.

Fishkin, James S. 1996. "Bringing Deliberation to Democracy." *The Public Perspective* 7 (1): 1–4.

Focquaert, Farah, Andrea Glenn, and Adrian Raine. 2013. "Free Will, Responsibility, and the Punishment of Criminals." In *The Future of Punishment*, edited by Thomas A. Nadelhoffer, 247–274. New York: Oxford University Press.

Focquaert, Farah, Andrea Glenn, and Adrian Raine. 2016. "Free Will Skepticism, Freedom, and Criminal Behavior." In *Neuroexistentialism: Meaning, Morals, and Purpose in the Age of Neuroscience*, edited by Gregg D. Caruso. New York: Oxford University Press.

Focquaert, Farah, and Adrian Raine. 2012. "Ethics of Community-Based Sanctions." In *Encyclopedia of Community Corrections*, edited by Shannon M. Barton-Bellessa, 144–148. Thousand Oaks, CA: Sage Reference Publications.

Fogarty, Gerard J., and Christine M. Mckeon. 2006. "Patient Safety During Medication Administration: The Influence of Organizational and Individual Variables on Unsafe Work Practices and Medication Errors." *Ergonomics* 49 (5–6): 444–456.

Francis, Nathan. 2014. "A Look at Life Inside Norway's Halden Prison, Where There Are No Bars and Inmates Have Flat-Screen TVs Inside Their Cells." *Inquisitr*. inquisitr.com.

Frankel, Mark. 1986. "The Healing of a Healer: A Doctor Decides That He Just Can't Play God." *Chicago Tribune*, October 5.

Frankfurt, Harry G. 1971. "Freedom of the Will and the Concept of a Person." *The Journal of Philosophy* 68 (1): 5–20.

Frankfurt, Harry G. 1973. "Coercion and Moral Responsibility." In *Essays on Freedom of Action*, edited by Ted Honderich, 63–86. London: Routledge & Kegan Paul.

Freedberg, Sydney P. 1999. "DNA Testing Denied to Inmates Seeking Justice." *St. Petersburg Times*, June 21.

French, Peter. 2001. *The Virtues of Vengeance*. Lawrence, KS: The University Press of Kansas.

Furnham, Adrian. 2003. "Belief in a Just World: Research Progress Over the Past Decade." *Personality and Individual Differences* 34 (5): 795–817.

Furnham, Adrian, and Barrie Gunter. 1984. "Just World Beliefs and Attitudes Towards the Poor." *British Journal of Social Psychology* 23 (3): 265–269.

Gächter, Simon, Benedikt Hermann, and Christian Thöni. 2010. "Culture and Cooperation." *Philosophical Transactions of the Royal Society B: Biological Sciences* 365 (1553): 2651–2661.

Galligan, Denis J. 1981. "The Return to Retribution in Penal Theory." In *Crime, Proof, and Punishment: Essays in Memory of Sir Rupert Cross*, edited by Colin F. H. Tapper, 144–171. London: Butterworths.

Garrett, Brandon L. 2011. *Convicting the Innocent: Where Criminal Prosecutions Go Wrong*. Cambridge, MA: Harvard University Press.

Gaylin, Willard. 1982. *The Killing of Bonnie Garland*. New York: Simon and Schuster.

Gershman, Bennett J. 2003. "Misuse of Scientific Evidence by Prosecutors." *Oklahoma City University Law Review* 28 (1): 17–41.

Gilligan, James. 2001. *Preventing Violence*. New York: Thames & Hudson.

Glannon, Walter. 1998. "Responsibility, Alcoholism, and Liver Transplantation." *Journal of Medicine and Philosophy* 23 (1): 31–49.

Goffman, Alice. 2014. *On the Run: Fugitive Life in an American City*. Chicago: University of Chicago Press.

Goldman, William. 1973. The Princess Bride. New York: Harcourt.

Goldmann, Donald. 2006. "System Failure Versus Personal Accountability—the Case for Clean Hands." *The New England Journal of Medicine* 355 (2): 121–123.

Golin, Sanford, Francis Terrell, and Barbara Johnson. 1977. "Depression and the Illusion of Control." *Journal of Abnormal Psychology* 86 (4): 440–442.

Grassian, Stuart. 2006. "Psychiatric Effects of Solitary Confinement." *Washington University Journal of Law & Policy* 22 (1): 325–383.

Hafer, Carolyn L., and Laurent Bègue. 2005. "Experimental Research on Just-World Theory: Problems, Developments, and Future Challenges." *Psychological Bulletin* 131 (1): 128–167.

Haidt, Jonathan. 2001. "The Emotional Dog and Its Rational Tail: A Social Intuitionist Approach to Moral Judgment." *Psychological Review* 108 (4): 814–834.

Haidt, Jonathan. 2012. *The Righteous Mind*. New York: Pantheon.

Haidt, Jonathan, and Judith Rodin. 1999. "Control and Efficacy as Interdisciplinary Bridges." *Review of General Psychology* 3 (4): 317–337.

Hanson, John D., Mark E. Larson, and Charles T. Snowdon. 1976. "The Effects of Control Over High Intensity Noise on Plasma Cortisol Levels in Rhesus Monkeys." *Behavioral Biology* 16 (3): 333–340.

Harcourt, Bernard. 2012. *The Illusion of Free Markets: Punishment and the Myth of Natural Order*. Cambridge, MA: Harvard University Press.

Harper, David, and Paul Manasse. 1992. "The Just World and the Third World: British Explanations for Poverty Abroad." *Journal of Social Psychology* 132 (6): 783–785.

Hart, H. L. A. 1968. *Punishment and Responsibility*. Oxford: Clarendon Press.

Heisenberg, Martin. 1994. "Voluntariness (willkürfähigkeit) and the General Organization of Behavior." In *Flexibility and Constraint in Behavioral Systems*, edited by Ralph. J. Greenspan and Charalambos P. Kyriacou, 147–156. Hoboken, NJ: Wiley.

Heisenberg, Martin, Reinhard Wolf, and Björn Brembs. 2001. "Flexibility in a Single Behavioral Variable of Drosophilia." *Learning and Memory* 8 (1): 1–10.

Hernu, Piers. 2011. "Norway's Controversial 'cushy prison' Experiment—Could It Catch on in the UK?" Updated July 25, 2011; MailOnline, www.dailymail.co.uk/home/moslive/article-1384308.

Herzog, William R. 1994. *Parables as Subversive Speech: Jesus as Pedagogue of the Oppressed*. Louisville, KY: Westminster John Knox Press.

Hieronymi, Pamela. 2004. "The Force and Fairness of Blame." *Philosophical Perspectives* 18 (1): 115–147.

Hilfiker, David. 1984. "Facing Our Mistakes." *New England Journal of Medicine* 310 (2): 118–122.

Hill, Harlan F., C. Richard Chapman, Judy A. Kornell, Keith M. Sullivan, Louis C. Saeger, and Constantino Benedetti. 1990. "Self-Administration of Morphine in Bone Marrow Transplant Patients Reduces Drug Requirement." *Pain* 40 (2): 121–129.

Hill, Harlan F., Adrian M. Mackie, Barbara A. Coda, Karen Iverson, and C. Richard Chapman. 1991. "Patient-Controlled Analgesic Administration: A Comparison of Steady-State Morphine Infusions with Bolus Doses." *Cancer* 67 (4): 873–882.

Holden, Richard J. 2009. "People or Systems? To Blame Is Human. The Fix Is to Engineer." *Professional Safety* 54 (12): 34–41.

Hollnagel, Erik, and David D. Woods. 2005. *Joint Cognitive Systems: Foundations of Cognitive Systems Engineering*. Boca Raton, FL: CRC Press.

Hospers, John. 1952. "Free Will and Psychoanalysis." In *Readings in Ethical Theory*, edited by Wilfrid Sellars and John Hospers, 560–575. New York: Appleton-Century-Crofts.

Hospers, John. 1958. "What Means This Freedom?" In *Determinism and Freedom in the Age of Modern Science*, edited by Sidney Hook, 126–142. New York: New York University Press.

Hsu, Spencer S. 2012. "D.C. Judge Exonerates Santae Tribble in 1978 Murder, Cites Hair Evidence DNA Test Rejected." *Washington Post*, December 14.

Hume, David. 1748/2000. *An Enquiry Concerning Human Understanding*. Oxford: Clarendon Press.

Husak, Douglas. 1992. "Why Punish the Deserving?" *Noûs* 26 (4): 447–464.

Husak, Douglas. 2000. "Retribution in Criminal Theory." *San Diego Law Review* 37 (4): 959–985.

Indermaur, David, Lynne Roberts, Caroline Spiranovic, Geraldine Mackenzie, and Karen Gelb. 2012. "A Matter of Judgment: The Effect of Information and Deliberation on Public Attitudes to Punishment." *Punishment & Society* 14 (2): 147–165.

Inesi, M. Ena, Simona Botti, David Dubois, Derek D. Rucker, and Adam D. Galinsky. 2011. "Power and Choice: Their Dynamic Interplay in Quenching the Thirst for Personal Control." *Psychological Science* 22 (8): 1042–1048.

Isaacs, Caroline. 2014. "Treatment Industrial Complex: How For-Profit Prison Corporations Are Undermining Efforts to Treat and Rehabilitate Prisoners for Corporate Gain." American Friends Service Committee. afsc.org.

Isen, A. M., and P. F. Levin. 1972. "Effect of Feeling Good on Helping: Cookies and Kindness." *Journal of Personality and Social Psychology* 21 (3): 384–388.

Iyengar, Sheena S., and Mark R. Lepper. 2000. "When Choice is Demotivating: Can One Desire Too Much of a Good Thing?" *Journal of Personality and Social Psychology* 79 (6): 995–1006.

Jacobson, Jessica, and Mike Hough. 2010. *Unjust Deserts: Imprisonment for Public Protection*. London: Prison Reform Trust.

James, William. 1907. *Pragmatism: A New Name for Some Old Ways of Thinking*. New York: Longmans, Green & Co.

Jäntti, Markus. 2008. "Mobility in the United States in Comparative Perspective." Institute for Research on Poverty, Discussion Paper No. 1359–08. irp.wisc.edu.

Jäntti, Markus, Knut Röed, Robin Naylor, Anders Björklund, Bernt Bratsberg, Odd-bjørn Raaum, Eva Österbacka, and Tor Erisson. 2006. "American Exceptionalism in a New Light: A Comparison of Intergenerational Earnings Mobility in the Nordic Countries, the United Kingdom and the United States." IZA Discussion paper No. 1938. ftp.iza.org.

Joekes, Katherine, Thérèse Van Elderen, and Karlein Schreurs. 2007. "Self-Efficacy and Overprotection Are Related to Quality of Life, Psychological Well-Being and Self-management in Cardiac Patients." *Journal of Health Psychology* 12 (1): 4–16.

Joffe, Justin M., Richard A. Rawson, James A. Mulick. 1973. "Control of Their Environment Reduces Emotionality in Rats." *Science* 180 (4093): 1383–1384.

Johnstone, Gerry, editor. 2003. *A Restorative Justice Reader*. Cullompton, Devon UK: Willan Publishing.

Kadish, Sanford H. 1987. *Blame and Punishment: Essays in Criminal Law*. New York: Collier Macmillan.

Kahan, Dan M. 1998. "Punishment Incommensurability." *Buffalo Criminal Law Review* 1 (2): 691–709.

Kahneman, Daniel. 2011. *Thinking, Fast and Slow*. New York: Farrar, Straus and Giroux.

Kamen-Siegel, Leslie, Judith Rodin, Martin E. P. Seligman, and John Dwyer. 1991. "Explanatory Style and Cell-Mediated Immunity in Elderly Men and Women." *Health Psychology* 10 (4): 229–235.

Kane, Robert. 1985. *Free Will and Values*. Albany: SUNY Press.

Kane, Robert. 1996. *The Significance of Free Will*. New York: Oxford University Press.

Kane, Robert. 2007. "Libertarianism." In *Four Views of Free Will*, edited by John Martin Fischer, Robert Kane, Derk Pereboom, and Manuel Vargas, 5–43. Malden, MA: Blackwell Publishing.

Kaplan, Martin F., and Gwen D. Kemmerick. 1974. "Juror Judgment as Information Integration: Combining Evidential and Nonevidential Information." *Journal of Personality and Social Psychology* 30 (4): 493–499.

Karpman, Benjamin. 1949. "Criminality, Insanity and the Law." *Journal of Criminal Law & Criminology* 39 (5): 584–605.

Kavanau, J. Lee. 1963. "Compulsory Regime and Control of Environment in Animal Behavior. 1. Wheel-Running." *Behaviour* 20 (3–4): 251–281.

Kavanau, J. Lee. 1967. "Behavior of Captive White-Footed Mice." *Science* 155 (3770): 1623–1639.

Kawamura, Syunzo. 1967. "Aggression as Studied in Troops of Japanese Monkeys." In *Aggression and Defense: Neural Mechanism and Social Patterns, Brain Function*, Volume V, edited by Carmine D. Clemente and Donald B. Lindsley, 195–224. Berkeley: University of California Press.

Keltner, Dacher, and Jonathan Haidt. 2001. "Social Functions of Emotions." In *Emotions: Current Issues and Future Directions*, edited by Tracy Mayne and George A. Bonanno, 192–213. New York: Guilford Press.

Kershnar, Stephen. 2012. "Does Necessity Justify Punishment? Assessing the Main Threat to David Boonin's Restitution Theory." *Public Affairs Quarterly* 26 (2): 71–79.

Khatri, Naresh, Gordon D. Brown, and Lanis L. Hicks. 2009. "From a Blame Culture to a Just Culture in Health Care." *Health Care Management Review* 34 (4): 312–322.

Krutch, Joseph Wood. 1954. *The Measure of Man*. Indianapolis: The Bobbs-Merrill Company Inc.

Kuhn, Thomas. 1962. *The Structure of Scientific Revolutions*. Chicago: University of Chicago Press.

Kunar, Milina A., Surani Ariyabandu, and Zaffran Jami. 2016. "The Downside of Choice: Having a Choice Benefits Enjoyment, but at a Cost to Efficiency and Time in Visual Search." *Attention, Perception, & Psychophysics* 78 (3): 736–741.

Kunzmann, Ute, Todd Little, and Jacqui Smith. 2002. "Perceiving Control: A Double-Edged Sword in Old Age." *The Journals of Gerontology Series B: Psychological Sciences and Social Sciences* 57 (6): 484–491.

Lachman, Margie E., and Suzanne L. Weaver. 1998. "The Sense of Control as a Moderator of Social Class Differences in Health and Well-Being." *Journal of Personality and Social Psychology* 74 (3): 763–773.

Lammers, Joris, Janka I. Stoker, Floor Rink, and Adam D. Galinsky. 2016. "To Have Control Over or to Be Free from Others? The Desire for Power Reflects a Need for Autonomy." *Personality and Social Psychology Bulletin* 42 (4): 498–512.

Landy, David, and Eliot Aronson. 1969. "The Influence of the Character of the Criminal and His Victim on the Decisions of Simulated Jurors." *Journal of Experimental Social Psychology* 5 (2): 141–152.

Lane, Kristin, Mahzarin Banaji, Brian Nosek, and Anthony Greenwald. 2007. "Understanding and Using the Implicit Association Test: IV." In *Implicit Measures of Attitude*, edited by Bernd Wittenbrink and Norbert Schwarz, 59–101. New York: The Guilford Press.

Lang, Frieder R., and Jutta Heckhausen. 2001. "Perceived Control Over Development and Subjective Well-Being: Differential Benefits Across Adulthood." *Journal of Personality and Social Psychology* 81 (3): 509–523.

Langer, Ellen J., Irving L. Janis, and John A. Wolfer. 1975. "Reduction of Psychological Stress in Surgical Patients." *Journal of Experimental Social Psychology* 11 (2): 155–165.

Langer, Ellen J., and Judith Rodin. 1976. "The Effects of Choice and Enhanced Personal Responsibilities for the Aged: A Field Experiment in an Institutional Setting." *Journal of Personality and Social Psychology* 34 (2): 191–198.

Lawton, Rebecca. 1998. "Not Working to Rule: Understanding Procedural Violations at Work." *Safety Science* 28 (2): 77–95.

Leape, Lucian L. 1994. "Error in Medicine." *JAMA* 272 (23): 1851–1857.

Lemos, John. 2015. "Self-Forming Acts and the Grounds of Responsibility." *Philosophia* 43 (1): 135–146.

Leotti, Lauren A., and Mauricio R. Delgado. 2011. "The Inherent Reward of Choice." *Psychological Science* 22 (10): 1310–1318.

Leotti, Lauren A., and Mauricio R. Delgado. 2014. "The Value of Exercising Control Over Monetary Gains and Losses." *Psychological Science* 25 (2): 596–604.

Leotti, Lauren A., Sheena S. Iyengar, and Kevin N. Ochsner. 2010. "Born to Choose: The Origins and Value of the Need for Control." *Trends in Cognitive Sciences* 14 (10): 457–463.

Lerner, Melvin J. 1980. *The Belief in a Just World: A Fundamental Delusion*. New York: Plenum Press.

Lerner, Melvin J., and Dale T. Miller. 1978. "Just World Research and the Attribution Process: Looking Ahead and Back." *Psychological Bulletin* 85 (5): 1030–1051.

Levy, Neil. 2011. *Hard Luck: How Luck Undermines Free Will and Moral Responsibility*. New York: Oxford University Press.

Lewis, Clive S. 1971. "The Humanitarian Theory of Punishment," In *Undeceptions*, edited by Walter Hooper, 318–333. London: Curtis Brown.

Locke, John. 1690. *An Essay Concerning Human Understanding*. London: Elizabeth Holt.

Luther, Martin. 1525/1823. *The Bondage of the Will*. Translated by Henry P. Cole. London: Simpkin and Marshall.

Mackie, Adam M., Barbara C. Coda, and Harlan F. Hill. 1991. "Adolescents Use Patient-Controlled Analgesia Effectively for Relief from Prolonged Oropharyngeal Mucositis Pain." *Pain* 46 (3): 265–269.

Major, John. 1993. Interview with the editor of the *Mail* (London), Jonathan Holbrow, February 21.

Martinson, Robert. 1974. "What Works? Questions and Answers About Prison Reform." *The Public Interest* 35 (1): 22–54.

Matthews, Roger. 2006. "Reintegrative Shaming and Restorative Justice: Reconciliation or Divorce?" In *Institutionalizing Restorative Justice*, edited by Ivo Aertson, Tom Daems, and Luc Robert, 237–260. Cullompton, Devon UK: Willan Publishing.

Mazzocco, Philip J., Mark D. Alicke, and Teresa L. Davis. 2004. "On the Robustness of Outcome Bias: No Constraint by Prior Culpability." *Basic and Applied Social Psychology* 26 (2–3): 131–146.

McCombs, Phil. 1985. "Eileen Gardner's Agenda for the Soul." *The Washington Post*, May 17.

McCormack, David. 2014. "How the Other Half Live." DailyMail.com, October 27.

McIntyre, Alison. 2001. "Doing Away with Double Effect." *Ethics* 111 (2): 219–255.

McNaughton, Mary Ellen, Lawrence W. Smith, Thomas L. Patterson, and Igor Grant. 1990. "Stress, Social Support, Coping Resources, and Immune Status in Elderly Women." *Journal of Nervous & Mental Disease* 178 (7): 460–461.

Meares, Tracey L., and Peter Neyroud. 2015. "Rightful Policing." In *New Perspectives in Policing Bulletin*. Washington, DC: U.S. Department of Justice, National Institute of Justice 2015. NCJ 248411.

Mele, Alfred R. 2006. *Free Will and Luck*. New York: Oxford University Press.

Menninger, Karl. 1959. "Verdict Guilty: Now What?" *Harper's Magazine*, August: 60–64.

Menninger, Karl. 1966/1968. *The Crime of Punishment*. New York: The Viking Press.

Milanovic, Nikola. 2010. "Norway's New Prisons: Could They Work Here?" *Stanford Progressive*, August. http://web.stanford.edu/group/progressive/cgi-bin/?p=653].

Milgram, Stanley. 1963. "Behavioral Study of Obedience." *Journal of Abnormal and Social Psychology* 67 (4): 371–378.

Mill, John Stuart. 1865/1979. "On Freedom of the Will." In *An Examination of Sir William Hamilton's Philosophy*. Volume 9 of *The Collected Works of John Stuart Mill*. Toronto: University of Toronto Press.

Mineka, Susan, Megan Gunnar, and Maribeth Chapoux. 1986. "Control and Early Socioemotional Development: Infant Rhesus Monkeys Reared in Controllable Versus Uncontrollable Environment." *Child Development* 57 (5): 1241–1256.

Mirowsky, John. 2013. "Depression and the Sense of Control: Aging Vectors, Trajectories, and Trends." *Journal of Health and Social Behavior* 54 (4): 407–425.

Mirowsky, John, and Catherine E. Ross. 1990. "Control or Defense? Depression and the Sense of Control Over Good and Bad Outcomes." *Journal of Health and Social Behavior* 31 (1): 71–86.

Mishel, Lawrence, Jared Bernstein, and John Schmitt. 2001. *The State of Working America 2000–2001*. Ithaca, NY: Economic Policy Institute Report.

Mischel, Walter, and Ebbe B. Ebbesen. 1970. "Attention in Delay of Gratification." *Journal of Personality and Social Psychology* 16 (2): 329–337.

Mischel, Walter, Yuichi Shoda, and Philip K. Peake. 1988. "The Nature of Adolescent Competencies Predicted by Preschool Delay of Gratification." *Journal of Personality and Social Psychology* 54 (4): 687–696.

Mitchell, Jeff, and Christopher Varley. 1990. "Isolation and Restraint in Juvenile Correctional Facilities." *Journal of the American Academy of Child and Adolescent Psychiatry* 29 (2): 251–255.

Momeni, Mona, Manuela Crucitti, and Mark De Kock. 2006. "Patient-Controlled Analgesia in the Management of Postoperative Pain." *Drugs* 66 (18): 2321–2337.

Montada, Leo. 1998. "Belief in a Just World: A Hybrid of Justice Motive and Self-interest." In *Responses to Victimizations and Belief in a Just World*, edited by Leo Montada and Melvin Lerner, 217–245. New York: Plenum.

Moore, Michael S. 1997. *Placing Blame: A General Theory of the Criminal Law*. Oxford: Oxford University Press.

Morris, Allison. 2001. "Revisiting Reintegrative Shaming." *Criminology Aotearoa/New Zealand* 16 (1): 10–12.

Morris, Allison. 2002. "Critiquing the Critics: A Brief Response to Critics of Restorative Justice." *British Journal of Criminology* 42 (3): 596–615.

Morris, Herbert. 1968. "Persons and Punishment." *The Monist* 52 (4): 475–501.

Morris, Jenny, and Graham. T. Royle. 1988. "Offering Patients a Choice of Surgery for Early Breast Cancer: A Reduction in Anxiety and Depression in Patients and Their Husbands." *Social Science & Medicine* 26 (6): 583–585.

Morse, Stephen J. 1984. "Undiminished Confusion in Diminished Capacity." *Journal of Criminal Law and Criminology* 75 (1): 1–55.

Murphy, Jeffrie G. 1973. "Marxism and Retribution." *Philosophy and Public Affairs* 2 (3): 217–243.

Murtagh, Kevin J. 2013. "Free Will Denial and Punishment." *Social Theory and Practice* 39 (2): 223–240.

Muscar, Jaime E. 2008. "Advocating the End of Juvenile Boot Camps: Why the Military Model Does Not Belong in the Juvenile Justice System." *UC Davis Journal of Juvenile Law & Policy* 12 (1): 1–50.

Nagel, Thomas. 1979. "Moral Luck," *Mortal Questions*, edited by Thomas Nagel, 24–38. Cambridge: Cambridge University Press.

National Academy of Sciences, the National Research Council. 2009. *Strengthening Forensic Science in the United States: A Path Forward*. Washington, DC: The National Academies Press.

New York City Bar Association, Committee on International Human Rights. 2011. *Supermax Confinement in U.S. Prisons*. New York: New York City Bar Association.

Nichols, Shaun. 2013. "Brute Retributivism." In *The Future of Punishment*, edited by Thomas Nadelhoffer, 25–46. New York: Oxford University Press.

Nichols, Shaun. 2015. *Bound: Essays on Free Will and Responsibility*. New York: Oxford University Press.

Nichols, Shaun, and Joshua Knobe. 2007. "Moral Responsibility and Determinism: The Cognitive Science of Folk Intuitions." *Noûs* 41 (4): 663–685.

O'Connor, Timothy. 2005. "Freedom with a Human Face." *Midwest Studies in Philosophy* 29 (1): 207–227.

O'Reilly, Gregory W. 1994. "England Limits the Right to Silence and Moves Towards an Inquisitorial System of Justice." *Journal of Criminal Law and Criminology* 85 (2): 402–452.

Paris, Margaret L. 1997. "Lying to Ourselves." *Oregon Law Review* 76: 817–832.

Payne, Daniel. 2014. "Bring Back the Welfare Stigma." *The Federalist*. http://thefederalist.com/2014/08/21/bring-back-the-welfare-stigma/.

Pellegrino, Edmund D. 2004. "Prevention of Medical Error: Where Professional and Organizational Ethics Meet." In *Accountability: Patient Safety and Policy Reform*, edited by Virginia A. Sharpe, 83–98. Washington, DC: Georgetown University Press.

Pennebaker, James W., M. Audrey Burnam, Mark A. Schaeffer, and David C. Harper. 1977. "Lack of Control as a Determinant of Perceived Physical Symptoms." *Journal of Personality and Social Psychology* 35 (3): 167–174.

Pereboom, Derk. 2001. *Living Without Free Will*. New York: Cambridge University Press.

Pereboom, Derk. 2014. *Free Will, Agency, and Meaning in Life*. New York: Oxford University Press.

Pereboom, Derk, and Gregg D. Caruso. forthcoming. "Hard-Incompatibilist Existentialism: Neuroscience, Punishment, and Meaning in Life." In *Neuroexistentialism: Meaning, Morals, and Purpose in the Age of Neuroscience*, edited by Gregg D. Caruso and Owen Flanagan. New York: Oxford University Press.

Pickard, Hanna. 2011. "Responsibility Without Blame: Empathy and the Effective Treatment of Personality Disorder." *Philosophy, Psychiatry, & Psychology* 18 (3): 209–223.

Pico della Mirandola, Giovanni. 1486/1948. "Oration on the Dignity of Man." Translated Elizabeth Livermore Forbes. In *The Renaissance Philosophy of Man*, edited by Ernst Cassirer, Paul O. Kristeller, and John H. Randall, 223–254. Chicago: University of Chicago Press.

Potegal, Michael. 1994. "Aggressive Arousal: The Amygdala Connection." In *The Dynamics of Aggression: Biological and Social Processes in Dyads and Groups*, edited by Michael Potegal and John F. Knutson, 73–112. Hillsdale, NJ: Lawrence Erlbaum Associates.

Quillian, Lincoln. 2006. "New Approaches to Understanding Racial Prejudice and Discrimination." *Annual Review of Sociology* 32 (1): 299–328.

Quillian, Lincoln. 2008. "Does Unconscious Racism Exist?" *Social Psychology Quarterly* 71 (1): 6–11.

Rabbitt, Patrick M., Lynn McInnes, Peter Diggle, Fiona Holland, Nuala Bent, Vicki Abson, Neil Pendleton, and Michael Horan. 2004. "The University of Manchester Longitudinal Study of Cognition in Normal Healthy Old-Age, 1983–2003." *Aging Neuropsychology and Cognition* 11 (2–3): 245–279.

Raeder, Myrna S. 2007. "See No Evil: Wrongful Convictions and the Prosecutorial Ethics of Offering Testimony by Jailhouse Informants and Dishonest Experts." *Fordham Law Review* 76 (3): 1413–1452.

Raine, Adrian. 2013. *The Anatomy of Violence: The Biological Roots of Crime.* New York: Pantheon.

Rawls, John. 1971. *A Theory of Justice.* Cambridge, MA: Harvard University Press.

Reason, James. 1997. *Managing the Risks of Organizational Accidents.* Aldershot, Hampshire: Ashgate.

Reason, James. 2000. "Human Error: Models and Management." *BMJ* 320 (7237): 768–770.

Reesor, Kenneth A., and Kenneth D. Craig. 1987. "Medically Incongruent Chronic Back Pain: Physical Limitations, Suffering, and Ineffective Coping." *Pain* 32 (1): 35–45.

Retzinger, Suzanne M., and Thomas J. Scheff. 1996. "Strategy for Community Conferences." In *Restorative Justice*, edited by B. Galaway and J. Ryan, 315–336. Monsey, NY: Criminal Justice Books.

Ripamonti, Carla, and Eduardo Bruera. 1997. "Current Status of Patient-Controlled Analgesia in Cancer Patients." *Oncology* 11 (3): 373–384.

Rodin, Judith. 1986. "Aging and Health: Effects of the Sense of Control." *Science* 233 (4770): 1271–1276.

Rodin, Judith, Karen Rennert, and Susan K. Solomon. 1980. "Intrinsic Motivation for Control: Fact or Fiction?" In *Advances in Environmental Psychology*, edited by Andrew Baum and Jerome E. Singer, 131–147. Hillsdale, NJ: Earlbaum.

Rodin, Judith, and Christine Timko. 1992. "Sense of Control, Aging, and Health." In *Aging, Health, and Behavior*, edited by Marcia G. Ory, Ronald P. Abeles, and Paula Darby Lipman, 174–206. Newbury Park, CA: Sage Publications.

Roskies, Adina. 2012. "Don't Panic: Self-Authorship Without Obscure Metaphysics." *Philosophical Perspectives* 26 (1): 323–342.

Roskies, Adina. 2014. "Can Neuroscience Resolve Issues About Free Will?" *Moral Psychology, Volume 4: Free Will and Moral Responsibility*, edited by Walter Sinnott-Armstrong, 103–126. Cambridge, MA: MIT Press.

Roskies, Adina, and Shaun Nichols. 2008. "Bringing Moral Responsibility Down to Earth." *Journal of Philosophy* 105 (7): 371–388.

Ross, Catherine E., and John Mirowsky. 1989. "Explaining the Social Patterns of Depression: Control and Problem Solving—or Support and Talking?" *Journal of Health and Social Behavior* 30 (2): 206–219.

Ross, Catherine E., and John Mirowsky. 2013. "The Sense of Personal Control: Social Structural Causes and Emotional Consequences." In *Handbook of the Sociology of Mental Health*, second edition, edited by Carol S. Aneshensel, Jo C. Phelan, and Alex Bierman, 379–402. Dordrecht: Springer Netherlands.

Ross, Lee. 1977. "The Intuitive Psychologist and His Shortcomings: Distortions in the Attribution Process." In *Advances in Experimental Social Psychology 10*, edited by Leonard Berkowitz, 173–220. New York: Academic Press.

Ryberg, Jesper. 2015. "Is Coercive Treatment of Offenders Morally Acceptable? On the Deficiency of the Debate." *Criminal Law and Philosophy* 9 (4): 619–631.

Salzberg, Sharon. 2010. "Buddhism: Between Desire and Emptiness." *Huffington Post*, May 3.

Sarkissian, Hasop, Anita Chatterjee, Felipe De Brigard, Joshua Knobe, Shaun Nichols, and Smita Kirker. 2010. "Is Belief in Free Will a Cultural Universal?" *Mind & Language* 25 (3): 346–358.

Sartre, J.-P. 1946/1989. "Existentialism Is a Humanism." Translated by Philip Mairet. In *Existentialism from Dostoyevsky to Sartre*, edited by Walter Kaufmann, 345–368. New York: Meridian.

Scalia, Antonin. 2002. "God's Justice and Ours." *First Things: The Journal of Religion and Public Life* 123 (1): 17–21.

Scanlon, Tim. 2008. *Moral Dimensions: Permissibility, Meaning, Blame.* Cambridge, MA: Harvard University Press.

Schlick, Moritz. 1939. "When Is a Man Responsible?" Translated by David Rynin. In *Problems of Ethics*, 141–158. New York: Prentice-Hall.

Schlosser, Eric. 1998. "The Prison-industrial Complex." *The Atlantic Monthly*, December.

Schorr, Dennis, and Judith Rodin. 1982. "The Role of Perceived Control in Practitioner-Patient Relationships." In *Basic Processes in Helping Relationships*, edited by Thomas A. Wills, 155–186. New York: Academic Press.

Schulz, Richard. 1976. "Effects of Control and Predictability on the Physical and Psychological Well-Being of the Institutionalized Aged." *Journal of Personality and Social Psychology* 33 (5): 563–573.

Schulz, Richard, and Barbara H. Hanusa. 1978. "Long-Term Effects of Control and Predictability-Enhancing Interventions: Findings and Ethical Issues." *Journal of Personality and Social Psychology* 36 (11): 1194–1201.

Schulz, Richard, Jutta Heckhausen, and Alison T. O'Brien. 1994. "Control and the Disablement Process in the Elderly." *Journal of Social Behavior and Personality* 9 (5): 139–152.

Schunk, Dale H. 1981. "Modeling and Attributional Effects on Children's Achievement: A Self-efficacy Analysis." *Journal of Educational Psychology* 73 (1): 93–105.

Seligman, Martin E. P. 1975. *Helplessness: On Depression, Development, and Death.* New York: W. H. Freeman.

Selman, Donna, and Paul Leighton. 2010. *Punishment for Sale: Private Prisons, Big Business, and the Incarceration Binge.* Lanham, MD: Rowman & Littlefield.

Sharma, Rakesh. 2015. "3 Reasons This "Perfect" Prison System Will Not Work in America." *The CheatSheet*, May 22. www.cheatsheet/business/3-reasons-why-norways-prison-system-should-not-be-replicated-in-america.html/?a=viewall.

Sharpe, Virginia. 2004. "Introduction: Accountability and Justice in Patient Safety Reform." In *Accountability: Patient Safety and Policy Reform*, edited by Virginia A. Sharpe, 1–26. Washington, DC: Georgetown University Press.

Sher, George. 1987. *Desert.* Princeton, NJ: Princeton University Press.

Sher, George. 2009. *Who Knew? Responsibility Without Awareness.* New York: Oxford University Press.

Shirley, Gayle. 1991. "Hospice Six: Nurses Pay Price for Easing Pain of Terminally Ill." *Chicago Tribune*, July 28. www.chicagotribune.com.

Siegel, Barry. 1991. "Reaching Out for the Dying: How Far Should Nurses Go to Help Those in Pain, Even If They Hasten Death? A Montana Hospice Case Ignites a Debate About the Risks of Compassion." *Los Angeles Times*, June 23.

Sigler, Mary. 2006. "By the Light of Virtue: Prison Rape and the Corruption of Character." *Iowa Law Review* 91 (2): 561–607.

Silver, Roxanne L., and Camille B. Wortman. 1980. "Coping with Undesirable Life Events." In *Human Helplessness: Theory and Applications*, edited by Judy Garber and Martin E. P. Seligman, 279–340. New York: Academic Press.

Simkins, Sandra, Marty Beyer, and Lisa M. Geis. 2012. "The Harmful Use of Isolation in Juvenile Facilities: The Need for Post Disposition Representation." *Journal of Law & Policy* 38 (24): 241–287.

Singh, Devendra. 1970. "Preference for Bar Pressing to Obtain Reward Over Free-loading in Rats and Children." *Journal of Comparative and Physiological Psychology* 73 (2): 320–327.

Skevington, Suzanne M. 1983. "Chronic Pain and Depression: Universal or Personal Helplessness?" *Pain* 15 (3): 309–317.

Smart, John J. C. 1961. "Free Will, Praise, and Blame." *Mind* 70 (279): 291–306.

Smilansky, Saul. 2000. *Free Will and Illusion*. Oxford: Clarendon Press.

Smilansky, Saul. 2011. "Hard Determinism and Punishment: A Practical *Reductio*." *Law and Philosophy* 30 (3): 353–367.

Smilansky, Saul. 2016a. "Parfit on Free Will, Desert, and the Fairness of Punishment." *Journal of Ethics* 20 (1–3): 139–148.

Smilansky, Saul. 2016b. "Pereboom on Punishment: Punishment, Innocence, Motivation, and Other Difficulties." *Criminal Law and Philosophy* 10 (1): 1–13.

Smith, Angela M. 2008. "Control, Responsibility, and Moral Assessment." *Philosophical Studies* 138 (3): 367–392.

Solanki, Narendra, Reinhard Wolf, and Martin Heisenberg. 2015. "Central Complex and Mushroom Bodies Mediate Novelty Choice Behavior in *Drosophilia*." *Journal of Neurogenetics* 29 (1): 30–37.

Solomon, Robert C. 2004. *In Defense of Sentimentality*. New York: Oxford University Press.

Staub, Ervin, Bernard Tursky, and Gary E. Schwartz. 1971. "Self-control and Predictability: Their Effects on Reactions to Aversive Stimulation." *Journal of Personality and Social Psychology* 18 (2): 157–162.

Strawson, Galen. 2008. "The Impossibility of Ultimate Moral Responsibility." In *Real Materialism and Other Essays*, 319–336. Oxford: Oxford University Press.

Strawson, Peter F. 1962. "Freedom and Resentment." *Proceedings of the British Academy* 36. Page references as reprinted in *Free Will*, edited by Gary Watson, 59–80. New York: Oxford University Press, 1982.

Stuntz, William J. 2011. *The Collapse of American Justice*. Cambridge, MA: Harvard University Press.

Suzuki, Shuji. 1997. "Effects of Number of Alternatives on Choice in Humans." *Behavioural Processes* 39 (2): 205–214.

Suzuki, Shuji. 1999. "Selection of Forced- and Free-Choice by Monkeys (*Macaca Fasicularis*)." *Perceptual and Motor Skills* 88 (1): 242–250.

Suzuki, Shuji. 2000. "Choice Between Single-Response and Multichoice Tasks in Humans." *The Psychological Record* 50 (1): 105–115.

Tancredi, Lawrence R. 2007. "The Neuroscience of 'Free Will.'" *Behavioral Sciences & the Law* 25 (2): 295–308.

Tasioulas, John. 2006. "Punishment and Repentance." *Philosophy* 81 (2): 279–322.

Taylor, Polyanna E., Nancy C. A. Coerse, and Marie Haskell. 2001. "The Effects of Operant Control Over Food and Light on the Behaviour of Domestic Hens." *Applied Animal Behavioral Science* 71 (4): 319–333.

Taylor, Shelley E. 1983. "Adjustment to Threatening Events: A Theory of Cognitive Adaptation." *American Psychologist* 38 (11): 1161–1173.

Taylor, Shelley E., Margaret E. Kemeny, Geoffrey M. Reed, Julienne E. Bower, and Tara L. Grunewald. 2000. "Psychological Resources, Positive Illusions, and Health." *American Psychologist* 55 (1): 99–109.

Thompson, Suzanne, C., Alexandria Sobolew-Shubin, Michael E. Galbraith, Lenore Schwankovsky, and Dana Cruzen. 1993. "Maintaining Perceptions of Control: Finding Perceived Control in Low-control Circumstances." *Journal of Personality and Social Psychology* 64 (2): 293–304.

Thompson, Suzanne C., and Shirlynn Spacapan. 1991. "Perceptions of Control in Vulnerable Populations." *Journal of Social Issues* 47 (4): 1–21.

Tuomala, Jeffrey C. 1995. "The Value of Punishment: A Response to Judge Richard L. Nygaard." *Regent University Law Review* 5 (1): 13–30.

Turk, Dennis C., and Ephrem Fernandez. 1990. "On the Putative Uniqueness of Cancer Pain: Do Psychological Principles Apply?" *Behavioral Research Therapy* 28 (1): 1–13.

Valla, Lorenzo. 1443/1948. "Dialogue on Free Will." Translated by Charles Edward Trinkaus, Jr. In *The Renaissance Philosophy of Man*, edited by Ernst Cassirer, Paul O. Kristeller, and John H. Randall, 155–182. Chicago: University of Chicago Press.

Van den Haag, Ernest. 1985. "The Death Penalty Once More." *University of California Davis Law Review* 18 (4): 957–972.

Van Inwagen, Peter. 1983. *An Essay on Free Will.* Oxford: Clarendon Press.

Vargas, Manuel. 2007. "Revisionism." In *Four Views on Free Will*, edited by John Martin Fischer, Robert Kane, Derk Pereboom, and Manuel Vargas, 126–165. Malden, MA: Blackwell Publishing.

Vilhauer, Benjamin. 2013. "Persons, Punishment, and Free Will Skepticism." *Philosophical Studies* 162 (2): 143–163.

Virgin, C. E. and Robert Sapolsky. 1997. "Styles of Male Social Behavior and Their Endocrine Correlates Among Low-ranking Baboons." *American Journal of Primatology* 42 (1): 25–39.

Voss, Stephen C., and Marvin. J. Homzie. 1970. "Choice as a Value." *Psychological Report* 26 (3): 912–914.

Wachter, Robert M. 2012. "Personal Accountability in Healthcare: Searching for the Right Balance." *BMJ Quality and Safety* 22 (2): 176–180.

Wagstaff, Graham F. 1983. "Correlates of the Just World in Britain." *Journal of Social Psychology* 121 (1): 145–146.

Waller, Bruce N. 1989. "Denying Responsibility: The Difference it Makes." *Analysis* 49 (1): 44–47.

Waller, Bruce N. 1990. *Freedom Without Responsibility.* Philadelphia, PA: Temple University Press.

Waller, Bruce N. 1998. *The Natural Selection of Autonomy.* Albany: State University of New York Press.

Waller, Bruce N. 2007. "Sincere Apology Without Moral Responsibility." *Social Theory and Practice* 33 (3): 441–465.

Waller, Bruce N. 2011. *Against Moral Responsibility.* Cambridge, MA: MIT Press.

Waller, Bruce N. 2015a. *The Stubborn System of Moral Responsibility.* Cambridge, MA: MIT Press.

Waller, Bruce N. 2015b. *Restorative Free Will: Back to the Biological Base.* Lanham, MD: Lexington Books.

Wallhagen, Margaret I. and Meryl Brod. 1997. "Perceived Control and Well-Being in Parkinson's Disease." *Western Journal of Nursing Research* 19 (1): 467–483.

Watson, Gary. 1987. "Responsibility and the Limits of Evil." In *Responsibility, Character, and the Emotions*, edited by Ferdinand Schoeman, 256–286. Cambridge: Cambridge University Press.

Weber, Monica M. 2008. "Using Managing Toward Daily Compliance Methodology to Improve Hand Hygiene on an Oncology Nursing Unit." Presented at Society for Healthcare Epidemiology in America meeting, Orlando, FL, April 2008.

Weller, Ken. 1974. *The Lordstown Struggle and the Real Crisis in Production*. London: Solidarity.

White, Rob. 1994. "Shame and Reintegration Strategies: Individuals, State Power and Social Interests." In *Family Conferencing and Juvenile Justice: The Way Forward or Misplaced Optimism?* edited by Christine Alder and Joy Wundersitz, 181–196. Australian Institute of Criminology: Canberra ACT.

Whitman, James Q. 1998. "What Is Wrong with Inflicting Shame Sanctions?" *Yale Law Journal* 107 (5): 1055–1092.

Wiedenfeld, Sue A., Albert Bandura, Seymour Levine, Ann O'Leary, Shirley Brown, and Karel Raska. 1990. "Impact of Perceived Self-Efficacy in Coping with Stressors on Components of the Immune System." *Journal of Personality and Social Psychology* 59 (5): 1082–1094.

Williams, Bernard. 1993. *Shame and Necessity*. Berkeley: University of California Press.

Wittgenstein, Ludwig. 1969. *On Certainty*. Edited by G. Elizabeth M. Anscombe and Georg H. von Wright. Oxford: Basil Blackwell.

Wolf, Susan. 1981. "The Importance of Free Will." *Mind* 90 (359): 386–405.

Wolf, Susan. 1990. *Freedom Within Reason*. Oxford: Oxford University Press.

Wolfe, Sidney M. 2003. "Bad Doctors Get a Free Ride." *The New York Times*, March 4.

Wolson, Richard J. and Aaron M. London. 2004. "The Structure, Operation, and Impact of Wrongful Conviction Inquiries: The Sophonow Inquiry as an Example of the Canadian Experience." *Drake Law Review* 52 (4): 677–693.

Yancey, Philip, and Paul Brand. 1997. *The Gift of Pain: Why We Hurt and What We Can Do About It*. Grand Rapids, MI: Zondervan Publishing House.

Yang, Zhenghong, Franco Bertolucci, Reinhard Wolf, and Martin Heisenberg. 2013. "Flies Cope with Uncontrollable Stress by Learned Helplessness." *Current Biology* 23 (9): 799–803.

Young, Kathryne M., and Joan Petersilia. 2016. "Keeping Track: Surveillance, Control, and the Expansion of the Carceral State." *Harvard Law Review* 129 (5): 1318–1360.

Zimbardo, Philip. 1974. "On 'Obedience to Authority.'" *American Psychologist* 29 (7): 566–567.

Zimmerman, Michael J. 2011. *The Immorality of Punishment*. Peterborough, ON: Broadview Press.

# Index